Foundations French 1

Dounia Bissar
French Co-ordinator on the Open Language Programme
at the London Metropolitan University

Helen Phillips
Deputy Director of Applied Foreign Languages
at the University of Bristol

Cécile Tschirhart
Independent Learning Co-ordinator on the Open Language Programme
at the London Metropolitan University

Series Editor
Tom Carty
Formerly IWLP Programme Leader at Staffordshire University
and the University of Wolverhampton

First published 2001 by
PALGRAVE
Houndmills, Basingstoke, Hampshire RG21 6XS and
175 Fifth Avenue, New York, N.Y. 10010
Companies and representatives throughout the world

PALGRAVE is the new global academic imprint of
St. Martin's Press LLC Scholarly and Reference Division and
Palgrave Publishers Ltd (formerly Macmillan Press Ltd).

ISBN 0–333–91992–0 book
ISBN 0–333–91993–9 cassettes

This book is printed on paper suitable for recycling and made from fully managed and sustained forest sources.

A catalogue record for this book is available from the British Library.

Audio production: University of Brighton Media Centre
Produced by Brian Hill

Voices: Hubert Liagre, Marie-Stéphanie Labattu, Jean-Louis Ropers, Micheline Maupoint, Dominique Le Duc

Original design by Wendi Watson
Formatted by
The Ascenders Partnership, Basingstoke

10   9   8   7   6   5
10 09 08 07 06 05 04

Printed and bound in Great Britain by
J.W. Arrowsmith Ltd, Bristol

CONTENTS

Acknowledgements

The following illustration sources are acknowledged:

Helen Bugler pp. 51, 53; Ann Carlisle pp. 16, 18, 28, 37, 39, 71, 80, 98, 111, 133, 136, 140; Tim Eaton p. 23; Emer McNicholl p. 13; Helen Phillips pp. 1, 2, 4, 35, 36, 37, 48, 68, 77, 92, 103, 113; Alison Self pp. 37, 122, 144; Ben Thackeray p. 34; Cécile Tschirhart pp. 12, 21, 22, 33, 37, 62, 75, 76.

The authors would like to thank everyone who helped by posing for photographs.

Every effort has been made to trace all copyright holders, but if any have inadvertently been overlooked the publishers will be pleased to make the necessary arrangements at the first opportunity.

INTRODUCTION

Mainly for the tutor

Foundations French 1 is a French language course for beginners aimed at students taking a language option or similar module on an Institution-Wide Languages Programme (IWLP).

Many of the textbooks used on beginners' and intermediate language courses in higher education were not designed for that purpose and it shows. Tutors and students particularly complain of inappropriate topics (too much on food and drink or shopping, for example) and excessive length (with units and sections having to be skipped or the book not completed). Tutors often also find they have to supplement the textbook to make up for deficiencies in the coverage of skills, tasks or grammatical topics required by university or college module descriptors.

The Foundations languages series is specifically designed for Institution-Wide Language Programmes (IWLPs) and similar provision in HE. Its structure and content are informed by market research and consultation within the sector. All the authors are experienced tutors on IWLP-style university courses.

This textbook is designed to fit the typical 24-week teaching year and assumes two or three hours of class contact per week. There are ten units (five per semester if your academic year is organised that way), each structured in the same way. For more details on the book's structure and suggestions on using it, see the "Mainly for the student" section of this Introduction. Encourage your students to read the tips on learning a language which follow it.

Mainly for the student

What follows is a guide to the textbook. Take time to read it so you get maximum benefit from your course. You should also read the section *Learning a language* which follows this introduction.

There are ten units. These have the same clear, consistent structure, which you will soon get used to. Each unit is focused on one or more topics or situations in which the language is used. The short **summary** at the start of the unit tells you what the topics are and describes what you will be able to do with the language once you have completed the unit. That's a key word ('do'): while language-learning requires and develops knowledge and understanding, it above all means developing the capability of using the language in given circumstances.

The half a dozen pages that follow are **the core** of the unit. The core contains the 'input' (new language) for the unit and various tasks designed to help you master it and make it your own. For ease of reference, each unit is divided into numbered items or sections, each with an icon and a French keyword to indicate the language skill or skills you will be using (listening, reading, speaking, writing). A sub-heading in French indicates a group of related items.

Dialogues and other listening items are on the cassette which accompanies the book. There are boxes highlighting and explaining grammatical points as they occur. Answers to the various tasks and exercises set can be found on pages 171–184.

The key inputs are carefully designed to introduce new vocabulary and/or structures. They take various forms. Sometimes they are 'Read and listen' exercises in the form of dialogues or monologues on the audio cassette which accompanies this book. You read the script, then listen to the recording. 'Listen' inputs might, for instance, involve filling in gaps in the transcript of a dialogue. Sometimes the input will be a 'Read and observe' exercise, where you will be asked to look out for some feature of the language, or a 'Read' exercise involving matching up French phrases with their English equivalents. Whatever form the input takes, it is absolutely vital to spend time and effort on this material. Be guided by your tutor. He or she will introduce it in class or ask you to prepare it in advance. If there's a word or phrase you're unsure of, turn to the vocabulary page for the unit and check.

The material introduced in an input exercise flows into exercises in the section(s) immediately following, enabling you to practise and master this language. These exercises are varied, ranging from listening carefully to a dialogue in order to put a scrambled script in the right order to answering questions on a short text. After you have done these exercises in class (or gone over them there, having prepared them in advance), make sure you revise the input material and key structures in your private study time.

When you have practised and mastered material on a given topic, you will want to produce your own French (especially in speech but also, where appropriate, in writing). There are exercises to enable you to do this, simple role-plays, for example.

The various 'Listen' sections on tape also provide you with a model for practising and improving your French pronunciation.

The unit core is followed by a page headed **Extra!** As the heading implies, this material makes extra demands, is that bit more challenging. It gives you the opportunity of further developing your understanding of French, taking listening and reading skills beyond the confines of the core input material while staying on related topics.

Two pages are then devoted to the **grammatical structures** you have encountered in the unit. The first gives you a clear overview of the grammar, the second provides a set of short exercises so you can test yourself (answers at the back of the book). Don't skip these pages: they simply clarify and check off grammatical structures you have met with and used in the course of the unit. This is how you become aware of the French language as a system.

The **vocabulary** page gives the new words occurring in the unit. Learn and revise them. Note that you can use a noun in French properly only if you know whether it is masculine or feminine.

Each unit has two **partner work pages** giving prompts for each partner in a structured dialogue. This material can be used in or out of the classroom to develop communication skills. The scenarios are always based on the material in the unit core, so you are securely in a known context. The challenge is to use the language you have learnt to communicate information your partner needs and to respond to what he or she says.

The **supplementary exercises** beginning on page 125 give further practice on a unit-by-unit basis and are designed to be used in private study. Answers are given at the back of the book. As the section 'Learning a Language' stresses, work outside the classroom, both that set by the tutor and that done on your own initiative to meet your own priorities, is an essential part of a taught language course.

For reference, as well as the **answers to exercises**, there is an overall **grammar summary** and a **glossary** (word-list).

LEARNING A LANGUAGE

The introduction above outlines the structure of this book and indicates how it is designed to be used: make sure you read it. The aim here is to give more general guidance on language learning. You should read it before you begin your course and refer to it regularly.

The advice which follows takes into account that you are beginning a taught course rather than a course of self-tuition. The good news is you will probably find it refreshingly different from the rest of your studies. The language learning programme revolves round sessions in an active language classroom rather than an anonymous lecture theatre. These regular classroom sessions will involve you in a range of social interactions, small-group activities such as pair-work and simple role-play, for example, as well as in answering questions and working through exercises individually. Feeding into these classroom sessions and flowing from them is what is called directed study, set by your tutor but allowing you a lot of scope for organising your work in ways that suit you. Beyond that is private study, where you decide the priorities.

Increasing attention is being paid in higher education to what are called transferable skills. These are skills acquired in one context which can be used in another. Successful language learning is recognised as particularly rich in transferable skills valued by employers, such as communication skills and self-management.

So your language course will be both a stimulatingly different learning experience giving you CV-enhancing competence in a language *and* a vehicle for developing useful transferable skills. What should you do to get maximum benefit from the course? …

1. Know in advance exactly what's expected of you. Check the course or module guide and/or **syllabus** and, in particular, find out how it is assessed. Is it a semester-based or a year-long course? Is there an exam? What assessed coursework is there? When are the assessments? The course guide and assessment information will probably be expressed in terms of the four language skills of listening, speaking, reading and writing. The relative importance of these skills can vary between institutions.

2. Remember you're not on your own. You are on a taught course and **your tutor** is there to guide you through it. You benefit from his or her experience and knowledge. Using the material in the book, he or she will introduce new structures, ensure you practise them in class and then enable you to produce similar language as you develop the capacity to use French autonomously. The tutor will also answer your questions on language and language-learning. The first rule of a taught language course, then, is to follow your guide.

3. Of course a guide can't travel for you. While your tutor will show you the way, **only you can do the learning**, both in the classroom and outside the timetabled hours.

4. **Regular attendance** at the language class is vital. Don't miss out on it. A language class is a workshop, not a lecture. The classroom is a place of performance: you *do* things that can't easily be done elsewhere. Or to put it more formally, you take part in structured activities designed to develop your linguistic competence.

5. It follows that you benefit from the language class by being active, by **participating**. This means listening carefully, working through the exercises, answering questions, taking part in simple dialogues, contributing to group work, taking the risk of speaking without the certainty of being right. It also means preparing before classes and following up afterwards …

6. … because what you do **outside the classroom** is vital, too. While new topics will normally be introduced in class, your tutor will also set tasks which feed in to what you will be doing in the next session. Classroom contact time is precious, normally no more than two or three hours a week, and it's essential to use it to the best effect, so make sure you get the most from each session by doing the preparation. Similarly, the tutor will ask you to follow up work in class with tasks designed to consolidate or develop what you have done.

7. You should take time to **review** and reflect on your language-learning, regularly going over what you have done in class, checking back, testing yourself. This will also enable you to decide your priorities for private study, working on aspects which are particular priorities for you (see point nine below).

8. This assumes that you are **organised**: keep a file or notebook, in which you jot down what you have done and what you plan to do. Take charge of your learning. It's a good idea to work for several shortish bursts a week rather than for a long time once a week.

9. While a lot of out-of-class work will be done at home, your university or college will probably have a Learning Centre, **Language Centre** or similar facilities in the library. Check this out and use what is on offer to reinforce and supplement what you are doing in class and from this textbook. Make sure any material you use is suitable for your level: it will probably be classified or labelled using categories such as 'Beginners', 'Intermediate' and 'Advanced'.

    Possible resources are: audio cassettes, videos, satellite TV, computer-based material, the internet, books (language courses, grammar guides, dictionaries, simple readers), magazines and newspapers, worksheets. Possible activities include: listening comprehension, pronunciation practice, reading comprehension, grammar exercises, vocabulary exercises. Worksheets and computer-based materials will usually have keys with answers.

    It's possible your tutor will set specific work to be done in the Language Centre or that you will be expected to spend a certain amount of time there, otherwise you should find times during your week when you can drop in.

    You can use private study to work on areas which need improvement (such as a point of grammar), to develop increased competence at a specific language skill (such as reading) or to find out more about a topic which interests you in a country where the language is spoken (such as cinema, sport or fashion). You decide the priorities.

10. Point nine referred to **grammar**. Don't be afraid of it! It is simply the term for how we talk about the way a language works. Learn the grammar and revise it as you go along. There are boxes with grammar points throughout each of the units in this book, a grammar summary for each unit and a grammar overview for the whole book. You probably feel hesitant about grammatical terms such as 'direct object' or 'definite article' but they are useful labels and easily learned. If in doubt, refer to the Guide to grammatical terms.

11. In addition to listening-based work in class, you should regularly work in your own time on the accompanying audio cassette material. In particular, try to reproduce the **pronunciation and intonation** (the 'music' of the language) of the native speakers on the tape. It's easier if you work at this from the start and establish good habits than if you approximate to the sounds of the language and have to correct them later. It is important that you repeat and speak out loud rather than in your head. Why not work with a friend?

12. Always bear in mind that, in learning a foreign language, you can normally understand (listening and reading) more than you can express (speaking and writing). And understanding is essential for communication. Above all, relax

when listening or reading: remember **you don't have to be sure of every word** to get the message. Above all, you don't need to translate into your native language as you go along.

13. To develop your ability to produce the language, work regularly with a partner on some of the exercises you have already done in class. Regular **practice** is the key. Remember fluency means speaking 'flowingly', not necessarily getting everything perfectly right. It is also a good idea to dip back into earlier units in the book to check you can still do your stuff.

14. To learn a language is to acquire something that can be used. Universities and colleges are increasingly international and you will almost certainly be able to make contact with **native speakers**. Try out your language, even at a basic level. Get them to correct your pronunciation, find out about their country and culture. And enjoy yourself!

15. In fact that's the way to approach your language-learning, as something special and **enjoyable**.

Tom Carty, *Series Editor*

Toi et moi

When you have completed this unit you will be able to greet someone, introduce yourself, talk about yourself, and ask/answer questions about yourself and others.

Bonjour!

1 Lire et écouter

a Listen to the following dialogues and notice the different ways of greeting someone. Then listen again to the recording, taking particular notice of the pronunciation.

Juliette	Salut Bernard!	Bernard	Bonjour Madame!
Bernard	Salut! Ça va?	Shopkeeper	Bonjour Monsieur!
Juliette	Oui, ça va?		
		Juliette	Bonsoir Monsieur!
		Neighbour	Bonsoir!

b Listen to three other exchanges and decide which conversation matches with which picture.

> Salut!   Bonsoir!   Salut Bernard!   Bonsoir Monsieur!   Ça va?   Au revoir!
> Bonjour!   Au revoir Monsieur!   Bonjour Madame!   Bonne nuit!

2 Jeu de rôle

With your partner, take on the role of different characters, at different times of the day, and greet each other, paying particular attention to your pronunciation and intonation.

Je suis...

3 Lire et écouter

a Listen to two dialogues, the first one at a seminar, the second at a party, and underline in the transcripts below three different expressions to introduce oneself.

– Bonjour, je suis Hélène Dupuis. Et vous?
– Moi, je m'appelle Anne Petit.
– Je m'appelle Antoine Lebœuf.
– Moi, je m'appelle Jean-Marc Latour.

– Salut! Je m'appelle Alain, et toi?
– Moi, c'est Sabine.

Je m'appelle... / Je suis... / Moi, c'est...	Et vous?/Et toi?

 ## 4 Lire

With a partner, try to guess the meaning of the following nationalities and occupations.

espagnol(e)   secrétaire
français(e)   infirmier(ière)
irlandais(e)   médecin
africain(e)   professeur
italien(ne)   directeur (directrice)
indien(ne)   étudiant(e)
sénégalais(e)   avocat(e)
écossais(e)   journaliste
grec(que)   serveur (serveuse)
allemand(e)   réceptionniste
anglais(e)   technicien(ne)
gallois(e)   vendeur (vendeuse)

grammaire	masculine	feminine	masculine or feminine
	français	française	belge
	italien	italie**nne**	suisse
	étudiant	étudiant**e**	journaliste
	infirmier	infirmi**ère**	secrétaire

5 Ecouter

Listen to six people each introducing themselves. Using the list above, tick the nationalities and occupations that you hear.

 ## 6 Jeu de rôle

Work with a partner introducing yourself. State your name and nationality.

7 Ecouter

Listen to a list of nationalities and occupations and tick which form is given.

	masculine	feminine	masculine or feminine
a			
b			
c			
d			
e			
f			
g			
h			
i			
j			

 8 Lire et écouter

Listen to Muriel's short monologue reprinted below, then listen to six other people introducing themselves and fill in the box below.

Muriel: Bonjour. Je m'appelle Muriel. Je suis française. Je suis vendeuse. Je suis de Bordeaux mais j'habite à Paris.

		nationality	occupation	town of origin	town of residence
a	Electra				
b	Ravi				
c	Mesenge				
d	Matthias				
e	Silva				
f	Steve				

9 Jeu de rôle

Introduce yourself to a few members of your group stating your name, nationality, occupation, where you are from and where you live.

Vous êtes …?

10 Ecouter

Listen to a dialogue at an international conference and fill in the gaps in the following text:

– Bonjour, je m'**a**_____ David Brown. Et vous (*looking at her badge*), vous êtes Stéphania Gardon?
– Oui, c'est **b**_____. Bonjour. Vous êtes anglais?
– Oui, et vous, vous êtes française?
– Non, je **c**_____ sénégalaise. J'habite **d**_____ Paris mais je **e**_____ de Dakar. Et vous, vous êtes d'où?
– Je suis **f**_____ Manchester. Je suis **g**_____ de Funn Holly. Et vous, qu'est-ce que vous faites?
– Moi, je suis **h**_____ .

grammaire		
Je <u>suis</u> Stéphania.	Tu <u>es</u> Malika?	Vous <u>êtes</u> français?
Je m'appell<u>e</u> David.	Tu t'appell<u>es</u> Stéphane.	Vous vous appel<u>ez</u> Hélène?
Je travaille dans un magasin.	Tu travaill<u>es</u>?	Vous travaill<u>ez</u> dans un magasin?
Je <u>fais</u>…	Qu'est-ce que tu <u>fais</u>?	Qu'est-ce que vous <u>faites</u>?

11 Ecrire

Imagine that you are Stéphania (in the dialogue above). Take turns with a partner to answer the following questions orally and then write down the answers.

a Vous êtes Stéphania Gardon? _____
b Vous êtes de quelle nationalité? _____
c Vous êtes d'où? _____
d Qu'est-ce que vous faites? _____

12 Exercice

You hear your friend Joseph answering questions on the phone. Can you guess what questions are being asked?

a Oui, je m'appelle Joseph Toure.

b Non, je suis africain.

c Je suis de Dakar.

d Je suis infirmier.

13 Lire et écouter

In pairs, read the following dialogue and re-order the sentences so that it makes sense. Then, listen to the recording to check your answers.

Une soirée

a Je suis technicienne en informatique… Tu es algérien?
b Non, j'habite à Angers. Et toi, tu habites où?
c A Paris. Je suis étudiant à la Sorbonne. Et toi, qu'est-ce que tu fais?
d Mehdi. Tu habites ici?
e Non, je ne suis pas algérien, je suis marocain.
f Salut. Moi c'est Juliette. Comment tu t'appelles?
g Oui, je suis serveur dans un café.
h Et … tu travailles?

grammaire

Tu es algérien?	Non, je <u>ne</u> suis <u>pas</u> algérien.
Tu habites à Paris?	Non, je <u>n'</u>habite <u>pas</u> à Paris.

14 Ecrire

Write the appropriate questions to the following sentences. (Note: this is an informal context, you should therefore use **tu**.)

Rencontre à l'université

a Salut, moi c'est Janet. **b** Je suis étudiante en maths, et toi?
c Oui, je suis anglaise. **d** Je suis de Liverpool.
e J'habite à Newcastle. **f** Non, je ne travaille pas.

15 Jeu de rôle

Find out from three people in your group the following information by asking them the relevant questions. Choose whether you are going to use **tu** or **vous** and keep to it for the whole conversation.

	Person 1	Person 2	Person 3
Name			
Occupation			
Nationality			
Where they live			
Where they are from			

Il est.../Elle est...

 16 Lire et écrire

Look at these registration forms from an international student conference.

> **nom:** Jacques Vandevelde
> **nationalité:** belge
> **domicile:** Liège
> **études:** informatique

> **nom:** Isabelle Chamfraud
> **nationalité:** canadienne
> **domicile:** Montréal
> **études:** chimie

Using the above, fill in the missing information.

a Il s'appelle _____ .

b Il est _____ .

c Il habite _____ .

d Il est _____ en informatique.

e Elle s'appelle _____ .

f Elle est _____ .

g Elle habite _____ .

h Elle est _____ en chimie.

17 Jeu de rôle

With a partner, practise introducing other people. Use the registration cards below as prompts.

nom: **Boris Neumann**
nationalité: **allemand**
domicile: **Berlin**
études: **histoire de l'art**

nom: **Nicos Micaleas**
nationalité: **grec**
domicile: **Athènes**
études: **philosophie**

nom: **Rosa Fernandez**
nationalité: **espagnole**
domicile: **Alicante**
études: **géographie**

nom: **Pritti Patel**
nationalité: **indienne**
domicile: **Calcutta**
études: **droit**

18 Ecouter

Listen to four people talking about themselves. Take notes and then in pairs practise talking about them. (E.g. **Elle s'appelle …, elle est …**, etc.)

Extra!

1 Ecouter

Six students are enrolling at a student housing agency. An administrator is asking for a number of details. Fill in the grid below with the information they provide. (N.B. **Vous étudiez quoi?** = What do you study?)

	Name	Nationality	Town of residence	Subject of study	Job
a					
b					
c					
d					
e					
f					

2 Lire

Salut Rebecca,

Comment ça va? Moi, ça va. Pour le moment, j'habite à Paris avec Bertrand, Lucille et leur bébé. Je suis étudiante en droit à la Sorbonne, c'est super! Je travaille aussi à mi-temps dans un bar comme serveuse. C'est un travail fatigant, mais c'est bien payé. Bertrand travaille à plein temps comme ingénieur. Il travaille à Versailles. Lucille ne travaille pas, elle s'occupe du bébé. Voilà. Ecris-moi!

A bientôt,

Stéphanie

a Where does Stéphanie live?

b What does she study?

c What type of job does she do?

d What does Bertrand do for a living?

e Where does he work?

Grammaire/GRAMMAR

- ## Gender
  Each noun in French has a gender, either masculine (m) or feminine (f).
  E.g. **le droit** (m)   **la chimie** (f)

  Most words used to refer to people have a masculine and a feminine form.
  E.g. **un étudiant** (m)   **une étudiante** (f)

  The most common endings for nationalities and occupations are as follows:
  ais (m) – aise (f)   (e.g. angl<u>ais</u>, angl<u>aise</u>)
  ain (m) – aine (f)   (e.g. améric<u>ain</u>, améric<u>aine</u>)
  ien (m) – ienne (f)   (e.g. ital<u>ien</u>, ital<u>ienne</u>)
  ier (m) – ière (f)   (e.g. infirm<u>ier</u>, infirm<u>ière</u>)
  eur (m) – euse (f)   (e.g. vend<u>eur</u>, vend<u>euse</u>)
  teur (m) – trice (f)   (e.g. ac<u>teur</u>, ac<u>trice</u>)

- ## Verbs
  So far you have seen the verbs **être** (to be), **faire** (to do) and the **-er** verbs **habit<u>er</u>** (to live), **travaill<u>er</u>** (to work) and **s'appel<u>er</u>** (to be called). You have been using the pronouns **je** (I), **tu** (you, informal), **il/elle** (he/she) and **vous** (you, formal). Notice the regular pattern of endings in verbs ending in **-er**:

je <u>suis</u>	je <u>fais</u>	j'habit<u>e</u>	je travaill<u>e</u>	je m'appell<u>e</u>
tu <u>es</u>	tu <u>fais</u>	tu habit<u>es</u>	tu travaill<u>es</u>	tu t'appell<u>es</u>
vous <u>êtes</u>	vous <u>faites</u>	vous habit<u>ez</u>	vous travaill<u>ez</u>	vous vous appel<u>ez</u>
il/elle <u>est</u>	il/elle <u>fait</u>	il/elle habit<u>e</u>	il/elle travaill<u>e</u>	il/elle s'appell<u>e</u>

- ## Negatives
  In order to make a sentence negative you need to add two words: **ne** before the verb and **pas** after the verb: e.g. **Je <u>ne</u> suis <u>pas</u> serveuse.** (Note: **ne** in front of a vowel or an '**h**' becomes **n'**.) When people speak fast, they tend to omit the **ne**: e.g. **je suis <u>pas</u> française.**

- ## Asking questions
  There are three ways of asking questions in French:
  – in informal speech, just rising the intonation at the end of the sentence:
  e.g. **Ça va? / Tu es anglais? / Vous êtes de Paris? / Il travaille dans un magasin?**
  – in all situations, informal or formal, using **est-ce que** to signal that a question is being asked:
  e.g. **<u>Est-ce que</u> tu es espagnole? / <u>Est-ce que</u> vous êtes vendeur? / <u>Est-ce qu</u>'elle habite à Londres?**
  – in formal speech and in writing, inverting the verb and the subject pronoun:
  e.g. **Etes-vous de Bruxelles?**
  Note the position of the question word in the following sentences:

Tu habites <u>où</u>?	**<u>Où</u> habitez-vous?**
Tu es <u>d'où</u>?	**<u>D'où</u> êtes-vous?**
Tu t'appelles <u>comment</u>?	**<u>Comment</u> vous appelez-vous?**
<u>Qu'est-ce que</u> tu fais / vous faites?	

Exercices de grammaire

Gender

1   Look at the following list of nationalities and occupations. Fill in the masculine and feminine alternatives as appropriate.

Masculine (m)	Feminine (f)	Masculine (m)	Feminine (f)
a _____	espagnole	h infirmier	_____
b irlandais	_____	i _____	réceptionniste
c _____	sénégalaise	j secrétaire	_____
d gallois	_____	k _____	directrice
e _____	suisse	l vendeur	_____
f belge	_____	m _____	professeur
g _____	grecque	n étudiant	_____

Negatives

2   Use the information below to write a paragraph about each person described.

(–) false   (+) true

E.g. (–) Jean (+) français = Il ne s'appelle pas Jean. Il est français.

a (–) Mary (+) étudiante (–) américaine (+) Rome (–) bureau
b (+) Laurent (–) infirmier (+) français (–) Toulouse (+) café

Asking questions

3   Find the appropriate question(s) for the following answers, then, with a partner, imagine the possible context(s).

a Non, moi c'est Michèle.
b Je viens de Lyon. Et toi?
c Elle est avocate.
d Non, il ne travaille pas.

e J'habite à Edimbourg.
f Oui, je suis américaine.

4   The words in the following sentences have been jumbled up: put them back in the right order to make questions.

a à / habite / elle / Marseille?
b il / qu' / fait / est-ce qu'?
c Londres / es / étudiant / tu / à?
d Rome / est-ce que / de / êtes / vous?

e t' / tu / comment / appelles?
f un / travaille / il / café / dans?

Vocabulaire

Salutations/Greetings

Salut!	Hi!/Goodbye! (informal)
Bonjour!	Hello!
Bonsoir!	Good evening!
Bonne nuit!	Goodnight!
Au revoir!	Goodbye!
Ça va?/Ça va.	How are you?/I am fine.
Madame	Madam
Monsieur	Sir

Nationalités/Nationalities

français(e)	French
anglais(e)	English
écossais(e)	Scottish
irlandais(e)	Irish
sénégalais(e)	Senegalese
gallois(e)	Welsh
américain(e)	American
marocain(e)	Moroccan
italien(ne)	Italian
indien(ne)	Indian
algérien(ne)	Algerian
canadien(ne)	Canadian
espagnol(e)	Spanish
allemand(e)	German
grec(que)	Greek
belge	Belgian
suisse	Swiss

Professions/Occupations

vendeur(euse)	sales assistant
serveur(euse)	waiter/tress
directeur(trice)	director
acteur(trice)	actor/tress
infirmier(ière)	nurse
technicien(ne)	technician
étudiant(e)	student
avocat(e)	lawyer
secrétaire	secretary
réceptionniste	receptionist
journaliste	journalist
médecin	doctor
chauffeur	driver
professeur	teacher
ingénieur	engineer

Etudes/Studies

l'informatique (f)	Computing
la physique	Physics
les mathématiques	Maths
la chimie	Chemistry
la géographie	Geography
la philosophie	Philosophy
le droit	Law
l'histoire (f) de l'art (m)	History of Art

Lieux de travail/Work places

le magasin	shop
le bureau	office
le café	pub/café
le supermarché	supermarket
à mi-temps	part-time
à plein temps	full-time
les études (f)	studies
le domicile	residence

Pronoms/Pronouns

je	I
tu	you (informal)
vous	you (formal)
il	he
elle	she
moi	me
tu	you (informal)
vous	you (formal)
ce	it

Questions/Questions

Où?	Where?
Comment?	How?
Qu'est-ce que...?	What...?
oui / non	yes / no

Verbes/Verbs

être	to be
s'appeler	to be called
habiter	to live
travailler	to work
s'occuper (de)	to look after
faire	to do/to make
lire	to read
écrire	to write
à/dans	in/at/to
de	from
avec	with
mais	but

Travail en paires

1 Introduce yourself to your partner. After greeting him/her, tell him/her:

your name
the town or city you are from
your nationality
where you live
that you are a student…
…and what you are studying
that you work (if you do)…
…and what your job is

When you have got all the information across, your partner will check it back with you.

Then swap roles.

2 You meet someone in a bar. Introduce yourself to him/her and then introduce your friend who has just left the bar, using the information below.

You are Alex Andrews. You are English and you come from Liverpool, but you live and work in New York as an engineer.

Your friend is Carmen Bradley, She is a manager and she works in Ireland. She has dual nationality (Irish and Spanish). She comes from Bilbao and lives in Dublin.

Your partner will then introduce himself/herself and his/her friend who has gone to the bathroom! In order to make sure that you have understood what your partner has said, fill in the following grid. Ask for repetition if necessary.

	your partner	**his/her friend**
Nom:		
Nationalité:		
Travail:		
Lieu de travail:		
Ville d'origine:		

Travail en paires

B

1 Greet your partner in French, then listen carefully to what s/he tells you, jotting down key words when it helps. You can ask for any items of information that you want again but you must request it in French.

Check with your partner that you have understood everything by repeating some of the information, i.e. **Tu es français**, **Tu ne travailles pas**, etc.

Then swap roles.

2 You meet someone in a bar. S/he is introducing him/herself and his/her friend who has just left the bar. In order to make sure that you have understood what your partner has said, fill in the following grid. Ask for repetition if necessary.

	your partner	**his/her friend**
Nom:		
Nationalité:		
Travail:		
Lieu de travail:		
Ville d'origine:		

Now introduce yourself and your friend who has gone to the bathroom!

Your name is Bernie Lyons. You are a taxi driver in Glasgow. You work part-time. You live in Paisley and originally come from Motherwell.
Your friend is Christos Panalopoulou. He is Greek. He is a teacher. He comes from Athens and he lives in Edinburgh. He is also studying literature.

2 Les autres

When you have completed this unit, you will be able to give and understand information about your friends and your family, ask and answer questions about age, count up to sixty, order drinks and snacks.

Quel âge as-tu?

 1 Lire et écouter

Read the dialogue between three people outside a nightclub and note how people talk about their age, then listen to the recording for pronunciation.

Maria	Tu as quel âge?
Pierre	J'ai 19 ans. Et toi?
Maria	Moi, j'ai 18 ans.

(*The bouncer checking age at the entrance*)

Bouncer	Quel âge avez-vous, mademoiselle?
Maria	J'ai 18 ans. Et il a 19 ans.

> Tu <u>as</u> quel âge?/ Quel âge <u>avez</u>-vous?   J'<u>ai</u> 18 ans.   Elle/il <u>a</u> 19ans.

 2 Ecouter

So you can talk about age, listen to and read the following numbers. Learn them!

1 un	6 six	11 onze	16 seize	21 vingt et un
2 deux	7 sept	12 douze	17 dix-sept	22 vingt-deux
3 trois	8 huit	13 treize	18 dix-huit	23 vingt-trois
4 quatre	9 neuf	14 quatorze	19 dix-neuf	24 vingt-quatre
5 cinq	10 dix	15 quinze	20 vingt	25 vingt-cinq

30 trente   40 quarante   50 cinquante   60 soixante

 3 Ecouter

Tick the numbers your hear on the cassette:

☐ 1	☐ 2	☐ 3	☐ 4	☐ 6	☐ 7	☐ 8	☐ 9
☐ 10	☐ 12	☐ 13	☐ 14	☐ 15	☐ 18	☐ 22	☐ 25
☐ 27	☐ 30	☐ 31	☐ 40	☐ 42	☐ 44	☐ 55	☐ 60

4 Jeu de rôle

In pairs, find out each other's age, then swap around and find out about other students.

J'ai un copain ...

5 Ecouter

Here is a dialogue in the university bar. Tick the words that your hear in the conversation.

salut!	bonjour!	tu travailles	j'ai un copain	congolais	j'ai vingt ans
français	tu as quel âge?	une copine			

Tu as des amis?   J'ai un copain/ une copine.   Je n'ai pas de copain.

6 Ecouter

Listen to a conversation between two students (note that because they do not know each other very well they use **vous** rather than **tu**). With a partner, work out what the following words mean:

marié	divorcé	un copain	un fils
une fille	femme	mari	enfants

7 Ecouter

Listen to Nadia showing some holiday pictures to her friend Marc and answer the following questions:

a Who is next to her friend Anne in the first picture?

b Who are the other two people in the picture with Nadia?

c What job does Nadia's boyfriend do?

d How old is his daughter?

C'est <u>ma</u> copine, avec <u>son</u> fils.   C'est <u>mon</u> copain, avec <u>sa</u> fille.   C'est <u>ton</u> copain?

grammaire	JE	TU	IL/ELLE	VOUS
	<u>mon</u> fils	<u>ton</u> fils	<u>son</u> fils	<u>votre</u> fils
	<u>ma</u> fille	<u>ta</u> fille	<u>sa</u> fille	<u>votre</u> fille

8 Lire, écrire et écouter

Read the following dialogue, in which a student is asking his friend lots of questions about his girlfriend. Fill in the gaps with the appropriate word and then listen to check your answers.

– Elle s'appelle comment, **a**_____ copine?

– Elodie.

– Elle a **b**_____ âge?

– Dix-neuf **c**_____.

– Et, **d**_____ est-ce qu'elle habite?

– Ici, **e**_____ Paris, mais elle **f**_____ de Marseille.

– Elle est **g**_____?

– Oui, en biologie. Et elle **h**_____ le soir dans un supermarché.

9 Jeu de rôle et écrire

With a partner, find out as much as you can about each other's boyfriend, girlfriend, husband or wife (or just a friend). Then write down a short piece about that person and give it to your partner to check (both the content and the language).

10 Lire

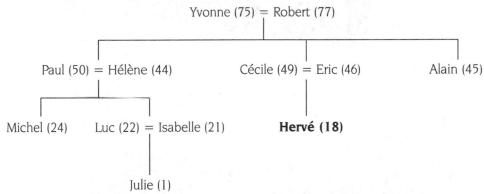

Look at Hervé's family tree and indicate whether the statements below are true (vrai) or false (faux). (You should be able to guess the meaning of the new words). Then, check your answers with a partner.

a Il a deux cousins.

b Sa grand-mère a 77 ans.

c Il a une nièce et un neveu.

d Son grand-père s'appelle Eric.

e La femme de son oncle s'appelle Hélène.

f La copine de son cousin a 20 ans.

g Le frère de Luc s'appelle Alain.

h La mère d'Hervé est la sœur de Paul et d'Alain.

i Il n'a pas de cousine.

j Sa tante a 49 ans.

le père <u>de</u> Michel = <u>son</u> père   la mère <u>de</u> Michel = <u>sa</u> mère

Mes copines et mes cousines ...

11 Ecouter

Re-order the jumbled text below and then listen to the conversation between two students in a bar.

a Non, ce sont mes copines!

b Hélène, Rachel et Corinne.

c Elles habitent avec Didier?

d Ce sont tes cousines?

e Oui, ce sont ses sœurs!

f Comment s'appellent les trois filles, au bar?

Singular	Plural
C'est ma/ta/sa copine	Ce sont mes/tes/ses copines
C'est mon/ton/son copain	Ce sont mes/tes/ses copains
elle/il s'appelle/habite	elles/ils s'appell**ent**/habit**ent**
elle/il a	elles/ils ont

12 Ecrire

Transform the following sentences in the singular into plural sentences.

e.g. C'est mon frère. ⇨ Ce sont mes frères.

a C'est ma copine.

b Il travaille à Londres.

c Il habite à Paris.

d C'est ton copain?

e Il a treize ans.

f Mon amie est étudiante.

Nos enfants ...

13 Ecouter

Listen to Nadia who is still describing her holiday pictures to her friend Marc and indicate whether the following statements are true or false. (Beware: there are two people called Michel.)

a Her daughter is three years old.

b Michel is a cousin of hers.

c Michel's children are not in the picture.

d The two couples' children are friends.

e The cousins have jobs.

f They live in Paris.

> C'est votre fille, à Michel et à toi?   Oui, c'est notre fille.
> Nous habitons dans la même rue.   Ce sont mes cousins et leurs amis.

 # Tu veux un café?

14 Lire et écouter

Read the following dialogues, match them with the drawings and listen to the recording for pronunciation.

1    2    3

a – Bonjour monsieur, vous voulez une bière?
   – Oui, merci.
   – Vous voulez un croque-monsieur ou un sandwich peut-être?
   – Non merci, juste une bière.

b – Salut Béatrice, ça va?
   – Oui, ça va bien merci.
   – Tu veux un café?
   – Ah, oui, merci.
   – Et un croissant?
   – Non, merci.

c – Salut Josette, ça va?
   – Bien, merci.
   – C'est ta fille?
   – Oui, c'est ma fille Manon.
   – Manon, tu veux une glace?
   – Oui, merci.

> Tu veux un thé?   Tu veux une limonade?
> Vous voulez un sandwich?   Vous voulez une bière?
> Tu veux quelque chose à boire?   Oui, merci.
> Vous voulez quelque chose à manger?   Non, merci.

15 Ecrire et écouter

Read the following conversation between three friends, Marie, Juliette and Bettina and fill in the gaps. Once you have done this, listen to the conversation and check your answers.

Marie	Salut Bettina, **a**_____ va?
Bettina	Oui, très bien merci.
Marie	Bettina, je te présente Juliette, **b**_____ sœur.
Bettina	Bonjour Juliette.
Juliette	Bonjour Bettina.
Marie	Tu **c**_____ un café ou un thé peut-être?
Bettina	Oui, **d**_____ café s'il te plaît.
Marie	Et toi Juliette?
Juliette	**e**_____ chocolat chaud pour moi
Marie	Bettina, tu veux **f**_____ à manger aussi?
Bettina	Ah non, pas pour moi **g**_____.
Marie	Et toi, Juliette?
Juliette	Oui, **h**_____ croissant, s'il te plaît

un café	un coca	un sandwich	une glace
un thé	une limonade	un croque-monsieur	une pâtisserie
un chocolat chaud	un citron pressé	un croissant	un gâteau

16 Jeu de rôle

Now take turns with a partner offering each other snacks and drinks.

Extra!

 1 Ecouter

Listen to three students who are talking about their friends and their family. Make some notes in the grid below before writing a short summary in English.

	Family	Friends	Places mentioned
François			
Anne-Marie			
Gabriella			

 **2 Lire**

Jane, who is learning French, writes a letter to her new penfriend in France, Monique. (NB: **curieuse** = nosy.)

Chère Monique,

C'est moi, Jane, ta correspondante anglaise. J'ai vingt et un ans. Je suis de Southport, mais j'habite à Liverpool parce que je suis étudiante en histoire à l'université. J'habite dans un appartement avec deux amies et leurs copains. Moi, je n'ai pas de copain, mais j'ai beaucoup d'amis. Je travaille à mi-temps dans un cinéma. Le reste de ma famille habite à Southport: mes parents et mes quatre sœurs! Une sœur est mariée (j'ai un petit neveu qui a deux ans!) et les trois autres sont toujours à la maison. Et toi? Quel âge as-tu? Est-ce que tu as un copain?   Ecris-moi vite, s'il te plaît, parce que je suis très curieuse!

A bientôt,

Jane

a How old is Jane?
b Why does she live in Liverpool?
c With how many people does she live?
d Does she have a boyfriend?
e How many brothers and sisters does she have?
f Where do they live?
g Why does she want Monique to write to her soon?

2 Les autres

Grammaire

- **Verbs**

  You will notice that a number of the verbs that you have used so far end in **er**.

  E.g.   travaill**er** = to work   habit**er** = to live

  Here are the plural endings for **-er** verbs (used when talking about more than one person)

vous travaill**ez**	vous habit**ez**	you
nous travaill**ons**	nous habit**ons**	we
ils/elles travaill**ent**	ils/elles habit**ent**	they

  Vous is used formally for one or more people, informally only for more than one.

  Avoir means 'to have'. Note that in French **avoir** is used to talk about age.
  E.g.   Tu as quel âge?   J'ai 20 ans.
  This verb does not follow a regular pattern.

J'**ai** un ami	Nous **avons** une copine.
Tu **as** une amie?	Vous **avez** un ami.
Il/elle **a** un copain.	Ils/elles **ont** un ami.

- **Possessive adjectives** (my, your, his/her, our, their)

JE	TU	IL/ELLE	NOUS	VOUS	ILS/ELLES
mon père	ton père	son père	notre père	votre père	leur père
ma mère	ta mère	sa mère	notre mère	votre mère	leur mère
mes parents	tes parents	ses parents	nos parents	vos parents	leurs parents

  Possessive adjectives agree in gender (masculine or feminine) and number (singular or plural) with the thing or person that is 'possessed'. So, depending on what follows, 'my' will be translated by either **mon**, **ma** or **mes**. Similarly, 'his' or 'her' (no matter which one) will be translated by **son**, **sa** or **ses**, etc.

- **Un, le or mon?**

  So far, you have seen three types of words which can go before a noun: (i) **un/une/des**, (ii) **le** (or **l'**)/**la** (or **l'**)/**les** and (iii) the possessive adjectives (see above).

  (i) **un,** etc. is used when the person or thing referred to is not specified (e.g. **Il travaille dans un magasin.**): we don't know which shop.

  (ii) **le,** etc. is used to refer to a specific person or thing, which can be identified by the person you are talking to (e.g. **C'est la copine de Paul.**): not any friend of Paul but his girlfriend.

  (iii) possessives are used when the person or thing referred to is specified as 'belonging' to someone (e.g. **Il est dans mon groupe.** : my group / **C'est ma copine.** : my girlfriend).

Exercices de grammaire

Verbs

1 Read the following text and replace the infinitive verbs in italics with the appropriate form.

E.g. Elle *travailler* à Lyon > Elle travaille à Lyon.

La famille Lemire **a** *habiter* à Paris. Luc et Marie-Claude Lemire **b** *avoir* un fils et un chien. Leur fils **c** *s'appeler* Marcel et il **d** *avoir* vingt-deux ans. Il **e** *être* étudiant en histoire de l'art. Marcel **f** *travailler* aussi dans un supermarché. Son chien **g** *s'appeler* Toby. Marcel **h** *avoir* une copine, Gabriella. Elle **i** *être* italienne. Elle **j** *être* de Rome mais elle **k** *habiter* à Paris. Elle **l** *travailler* comme vendeuse dans un magasin. Elle **m** *avoir* dix-neuf ans.

Possessive adjectives

2 Read the following dialogue and fill in the blanks with an appropriate possessive adjective.

Isabelle, who lives with her sister, tells her new friend Josée about the rest of the family:

Isabelle: **a**_____ sœur et moi, nous habitons à Paris, mais **b**_____ parents habitent en Normandie. **c**_____ père est agriculteur. Nous avons un frère qui est marié. **d**_____ femme s'appelle Raymonde, elle est présentatrice de télévision. Ils habitent aussi à Paris, avec **e**_____ deux enfants.

Josée: Et **f**_____ copain, il habite avec vous?

Isabelle: Non, il habite avec **g**_____ cousin qui est aussi étudiant.

Un, le or *mon?*

3 Read the following sentences and select the appropriate form(s). (There may be more than one).

a Comment s'appelle une/la/ta copine?
b Nous habitons avec une/la/notre sœur.
c Tu as des/les/tes enfants?
d Elle travaille dans un/le/son supermarché.
e Un/Le/Mon professeur est de Genève.
f Un/Le/Son copain est étudiant en chimie.
g C'est un/le/son frère de Jacqueline.
h J'habite avec un/le/mon ami.
i C'est un/le/votre mari?
j Tu veux un/le/ton café?

Vocabulaire

L'âge/Age

quel âge...?	how old...?
sept ans	seven years old
mademoiselle	miss

La famille/The family

le mari	husband
la femme	wife
le copain, l'ami	boyfriend, friend (m)
la copine, l'amie	girlfriend, friend (f)
les parents	parents
le père	father
la mère	mother
les enfants	children
le fils	son
la fille	daughter
le frère	brother
la sœur	sister
les grands-parents	grandparents
le grand-père	grandfather
la grand-mère	grandmother
l'oncle	uncle
la tante	aunt
le cousin	cousin(m)
la cousine	cousin(f)
le neveu	nephew
la nièce	niece

Au café/At the snack bar

le café	coffee
le thé	tea
le chocolat chaud	hot chocolate
la bière	beer
la limonade	lemonade
le coca	coke
le citron pressé	fresh lemon juice
le croque-monsieur	toasted ham and cheese sandwich
le gâteau	cake
le biscuit	biscuit
la pâtisserie	pastry
le croissant	croissant
le sandwich	sandwich
la glace	ice cream
l'orange pressée(f)	fresh orange juice
merci	thank you
s'il te plaît	please
boire	drink
manger	eat
vouloir	want
quelque chose	something

Le travail et la maison/Home and work

le soir	in the evening
le supermarché	supermarket
l'appartement	flat
la maison	house
à mi-temps	part-time
curieuse(f)	nosy

Travail en paires

1 Your friend is asking you questions about your brother. Answer them using the following information.

He is 27 years old.
He is a student of biology.
He lives in Manchester.
He works in a café.
He is divorced.
He has two children, a five year old daughter and a three year old son.
The children live in Bolton with their mother.
He has a girlfriend. She is a teacher.

2 You are meeting a friend that you have not seen for a long time in a café.
Use the following prompts in English. You start the conversation.

– Say 'Hello.'
– Say 'How are you'?'
– Say 'Do you want something to drink?'
– Say 'Where do you live?'
– Say 'I live in Limoges too.'
– Say 'No, I work in an office … Are you married?'
– Say 'How old is your son?'
– Say 'Do you want something to eat?'

Travail en paires

B

1 You are asking your friend questions about her/his brother. Find out the following information. Your partner will start the conversation.

How old is he?
What does he do?
Where does he live?
Is he working?
Is he married?
Has he got children?
Where do the children live?
Does he have a girlfriend?

You can use the questions below to guide you if you wish:

Est-ce qu'il a une copine?   Où habitent les enfants?   Est-ce qu'il travaille?
Quel âge a-t-il?   Qu'est-ce qu'il fait?   Où habite-t-il?
Est-ce qu'il a des enfants?   Est-ce qu'il est marié?

2 You are meeting a friend that you have not seen for a long time in a café.
Use the following prompts in English. Your partner will start the conversation.

– Say 'Hello.'
– Say 'I am very well.'
– Say 'I would like a coke.'
– Say 'I live in Limoges.'
– Say 'Are you a student?'
– Say 'No, I am not married but I have a son.'
– Say 'He is two years old.'
– Say 'I would like a sandwich.'

3 La routine

When you have completed this unit, you will be able to talk about everyday activities; ask for/give the time; explain when you do things; say what you like/dislike doing and what you have to do.

Qu'est-ce que tu fais?

 1 Lire et observer

Look at the pictures below and note the French expression used to describe them.

Ils regardent la télévision.

Elles écoutent un CD.

Il mange un sandwich.

Elle fait des courses.

Il lit un livre.

Elle écrit une lettre.

 2 Ecouter

Listen to six conversations on the telephone between friends explaining what they are doing, and note down each activity. (Note: **une dissertation** = an essay.)

> Qu'est-ce que tu fais/vous faites? Je regarde la télé.
> Je lis un livre.
> Je fais une dissertation.
> Rien de spécial.

<table>
<tr><td rowspan="7">grammaire</td><td>regard<u>er</u> (to watch)</td><td>li<u>re</u> (to read)</td><td>écri<u>re</u> (to write)</td><td>fai<u>re</u> (to do/to make)</td></tr>
<tr><td>je regard<u>e</u></td><td>je li<u>s</u></td><td>j'écri<u>s</u></td><td>je fai<u>s</u></td></tr>
<tr><td>tu regard<u>es</u></td><td>tu li<u>s</u></td><td>tu écri<u>s</u></td><td>tu fai<u>s</u></td></tr>
<tr><td>il/elle regard<u>e</u></td><td>il/elle li<u>t</u></td><td>il/elle écri<u>t</u></td><td>il/elle fai<u>t</u></td></tr>
<tr><td>nous regard<u>ons</u></td><td>nous li<u>sons</u></td><td>nous écri<u>vons</u></td><td>nous fai<u>sons</u></td></tr>
<tr><td>vous regard<u>ez</u></td><td>vous li<u>sez</u></td><td>vous écri<u>vez</u></td><td>vous fai<u>tes</u></td></tr>
<tr><td>ils/elles regard<u>ent</u></td><td>ils/elles li<u>sent</u></td><td>ils/elles écri<u>vent</u></td><td>ils/elles f<u>ont</u></td></tr>
</table>

3 Parler

To practise the new verbs, take it in turns to mime a few activities and ask your partner to guess what you are doing. E.g. **Qu'est-ce que je fais?**   **Tu écris une lettre.**

4 Lire

To find out more vocabulary, match the following verbs/expressions with their English equivalent. Do what you can by guesswork and a process of elimination and then check the vocabulary page or use a dictionary.

1	faire le ménage	**a**	to go sailing
2	faire une promenade	**b**	to play the piano
3	faire du sport	**c**	to go swimming/to go to the swimming pool
4	faire du vélo	**d**	to play sport
5	faire de la voile	**e**	to do the housework
6	jouer au football	**f**	to go to the cinema
7	jouer du piano	**g**	to go for a walk
8	aller au cinéma	**h**	to go cycling
9	aller à la piscine	**i**	to go out to a nightclub/to go clubbing
10	aller en boîte	**j**	to play football

5 Ecouter

It is Saturday morning: two flatmates, Gabrielle and Bertrand, are having breakfast and discuss their plans for the weekend. Listen to their conversation and answer the following questions (Note: **aujourd'hui** = today; **demain** = tomorrow).

a Whose turn is it to do the housework?
b Where is Bertrand going with his friend Michel?
c What is he doing afterwards?
d What is Gabrielle doing tonight?
e Who is going with her?
f What is she doing tomorrow after her piano lesson?

grammaire

Je vais <u>à la</u> piscine.   Je vais <u>au</u> cinéma.   Je joue <u>à la</u> balle.   Je joue <u>au</u> football.
Je joue <u>de la</u> guitare.   Je joue <u>du</u> piano.

6 Jeu de rôle

Working with a partner, find out from each other what you are doing tonight (**ce soir**) and at the weekend (**ce week-end**).

Il est quelle heure?

7 Lire et observer

Look at the drawings below and note how to tell the time in French.

a Il est midi.

b Il est quatre heures.

c Il est onze heures dix.

d Il est neuf heures moins vingt.

e Il est une heure et demie.

f Il est minuit et quart.

Il est	une heure	cinq/dix/vingt/ …
	deux heures	et quart
	trois heures	et demie
	…	moins cinq/dix/vingt/ …
	midi/minuit	moins le quart

8 Ecouter

a Listen to various people asking for and giving the time, and write down what time it is.

a _____	b _____	c _____
d _____	e _____	f _____

b Listen to the conversations again and note down the different ways of asking for the time.

9 Parler

Draw six blank clock faces. Working with a partner, each of you should write down six different times. Take it in turns to ask each other what time it is and use the answers to fill in the times on your clocks. Check to see if your answers are correct.

10 Ecouter

Listen to the days of the week in French and put them in the correct order.

Les jours de la semaine: mercredi – lundi – dimanche – mardi – jeudi – samedi – vendredi

11 Lire

Read the following opening and closing times and work out what they mean in English.

a Ouvert de 9h à 13h, du lundi au vendredi.

b Fermé le week-end.

c Ouvert de midi à 16h, le mardi et le jeudi.

d Fermé le dimanche après-midi de 13h à 15h.

e Ouvert le soir de 18h à 21h.

Heures d'ouverture
de votre boutique SNCF
du **lundi** au **vendredi**
de **9h00** à **19h45**
le **samedi**
de **9h00** à **18h15**
Ventes et informations SNCF
Grandes Lignes

SNCF

| ouvert | fermé | le matin | l'après-midi |
| le soir | le week-end | le lundi | de midi à 2 heures |

12 Ecouter

a Listen to Nicolas describing a typical day at university. Tick the verbs that you hear.

je mange   je prends   je travaille   j'habite
j'étudie   je pars   je termine   j'ai
j'arrive   je finis   je vais   je suis
je regarde   je commence

b Listen to Nicolas a second time and indicate whether the statements below are true or false. (Note: **petit déjeuner** = breakfast; **déjeuner** = lunch.)

i Il prend son petit déjeuner à 8h.   **v** Il travaille à la bibliothèque jusqu'à 16h.
ii Les cours commencent à midi.   **vi** Il va à la piscine entre 16h30 et 18h.
iii Il termine à 14h.   **vii** Le soir il prend le train.
iv Il prend son déjeuner à 13h.   **viii** Il arrive à la maison à 19h.

grammaire

Je <u>prends</u> mon petit déjeuner.   je pren<u>ds</u>
Je <u>prends</u> le bus.   tu pren<u>ds</u>
Je <u>commence</u> les cours à dix heures et je <u>termine</u> à 2 heures.   il/elle pren<u>d</u>
Je <u>finis</u> mon travail.   nous pren<u>ons</u>
J'<u>arrive</u> à la maison à 7 heures. Je <u>pars</u> à 6 heures.   vous pren<u>ez</u>
       ils/elles pren<u>nent</u>

13 Parler

With a partner, practise asking and answering the following questions:

A quelle heure …

a … est-ce que tu prends ton petit déjeuner?

b … est-ce que tu commences tes cours?

c … est-ce que tu finis?

d … est-ce que tu vas à la bibliothèque?

e … est-ce que tu arrives à la maison?

Qu'est-ce que tu aimes faire?

14 Ecouter

Listen to four people stating their likes and dislikes and underline the deliberate mistakes and omissions in the statements below.

a J'aime le sport. J'aime l'athlétisme.

b J'aime le ski et je n'aime pas la planche à voile.

c J'aime beaucoup le football et je déteste le rugby.

d J'aime bien le cinéma mais je n'aime pas le théâtre.

J'aime bien (+)	J'aime (++)	J'aime beaucoup (+++)
Je n'aime pas beaucoup (–)	Je n'aime pas (– –)	Je déteste (– – –)

 15 Ecouter et écrire

Now listen to Marco talking about the types of things he likes to do. Fill in the gaps.

J'aime bien le sport. J'aime **a**_____ à la piscine et j'aime **b**_____ au tennis. J'aime aussi **c**_____ au ping-pong et au volley-ball. J'aime beaucoup **d**_____ de l'athlétisme, surtout de la course. Je n'aime pas beaucoup **e**_____ du ski et je déteste **f**_____ aux fléchettes.

16 Ecouter

Listen to four dialogues and put a tick by the things that the speakers like doing and a cross by the ones that they dislike doing.

a Archie
- going swimming ☐
- playing football ☐
- playing rugby ☐
- going to the cinema ☐

c Electra
- doing aerobics ☐
- going shopping ☐
- listening to music ☐
- going to the theatre ☐

b Thomas
- going dancing ☐
- playing sport ☐
- going cycling ☐
- going windsurfing ☐

d Claudia
- watching television ☐
- playing cards ☐
- doing yoga ☐
- cooking ☐

grammaire

J'aime <u>jouer</u> au tennis.   J'aime beaucoup <u>faire</u> du sport.   Je n'aime pas <u>lire</u>.
Je dois <u>finir</u>.

Tu dois finir

17 Ecouter et lire

Catherine has a problem and is asking her friend Pierre what to do. Read their conversation and then listen to the recording for pronunciation.

Catherine	Pierre, qu'est-ce que je dois faire?
Pierre	Tu as un problème?
Catherine	Oui, c'est dimanche soir et je n'ai pas fini ma dissertation et je dois finir ce soir.
Pierre	Il est huit heures, tu as le temps!
Catherine	Mais je voudrais regarder la télé!
Pierre	Ecoute Catherine, tu dois travailler!

Qu'est-ce que je <u>dois</u> faire?   Tu <u>dois</u> travailler.   Vous <u>devez</u> travailler.

18 Parler

With a partner and using the verb 'devoir', practise finding solutions to the following problems E.g. **Je suis très fatigué.   >   Tu dois aller au lit.**

a Je n'ai pas d'argent.

d Oh la la! Il est 3 heures.

b Nous n'avons pas de lait.

e Je n'ai pas fini ma dissertation.

c Zut! La bibliothèque est fermée.

f Le bus n'arrive pas.

Extra!

 1 Ecouter

Listen to three people describing their weekend and list three activities below.

Ricardo _____

_____

_____

_____

Anne _____

_____

_____

_____

Daniela _____

_____

_____

_____

 2 Lire et écrire

Read through a description of Madeleine's weekend and answer the questions below.

Le week end je suis toujours très occupée. Le samedi j'aime beaucoup faire des courses avec mes amis. D'habitude nous prenons le petit déjeuner ensemble à neuf heures et puis nous allons au centre ville. Nous faisons le tour des magasins et puis nous déjeunons ensemble vers une heure. Le samedi après-midi je vais à la gym ou à la piscine avec ma copine Hélène. Le samedi soir j'aime sortir avec mes amis aussi. Souvent, nous allons au restaurant et puis nous regardons un film ou bien nous allons dans un bar ou en boîte. Le dimanche, par contre, j'aime faire la grasse matinée, j'aime rester au lit jusqu'à midi.

a What does Madeleine like doing on Saturday mornings?

b At what time does she have breakfast?

c What does she often do at about one o'clock?

d Name two things she might do on a Saturday afternoon.

e Describe a typical Saturday evening.

f What time does Madeleine get up on Sundays?

Grammaire

- **à and *de* followed by *le* or *les***

  Some verbs can be constructed with a preposition (**à** or **de**), for example **aller à**, **jouer à** (+ musical instrument), **jouer de** (+ game). If **à** or **de** are followed by the articles **le** and **les**, they always merge as follows:

à + le > **au**	de + le > **du**	e.g. **Je vais <u>au</u> parc. / Nous allons <u>à la</u>**
à + la = à la	de + la = de la	**piscine.**
à + l' = à l'	de + l' = de l'	**Ils jouent <u>au</u> football. / Elle joue <u>de la</u>**
à + les > **aux**	de + les > **des**	**guitare.**

- ***aller***

  The very useful verb **aller** (to go) is the only **-er** verb which does not follow the regular pattern: je **vais**, tu **vas**, il/elle **va**, nous all<u>ons</u>, vous all<u>ez</u>, ils/elles **vont**

- **Verbs ending in *-ir* and *-re***

  Most verbs ending in **-ir** and **-re** follow a regular pattern when conjugated.
  There are two types of verbs ending in **-ir**, the **partir** and **sortir** type and the **finir** type.

part<u>ir</u> (to leave)	**sort<u>ir</u>** (to go out)	**fin<u>ir</u>** (to finish)
je par<u>s</u>	je sor<u>s</u>	je fini<u>s</u>
tu par<u>s</u>	tu sor<u>s</u>	tu fini<u>s</u>
il/elle par<u>t</u>	il/elle sor<u>t</u>	il/elle fini<u>t</u>
nous part<u>ons</u>	nous sort<u>ons</u>	nous finiss<u>ons</u>
vous part<u>ez</u>	vous sort<u>ez</u>	vous fini<u>ssez</u>
ils/elles part<u>ent</u>	ils/elles sort<u>ent</u>	ils/elles fini<u>ssent</u>

  Note that the present tense in French can be used to express both something that you do and something that you are doing. E.g. **Je vais au parc.** = I go to the park or I am going to the park.

- **Verbs followed by the infinitive**

  If you want to say that you or someone likes something, you need to use the <u>article</u> **le/la/les/l'**. E.g. **J'aime le football. / Elles aiment la danse. / Il aime les fléchettes.**

  If you want to say that you like doing something, e.g. 'I like playing golf' you need to use the infinitive after the verb. E.g. **Il aime regarder la télévision. / Nous aimons jouer au tennis. / Elles aiment faire de la natation**.

  The verb **devoir** is used in order to indicate the fact that you must do something. Note again that the infinitive is used after the verb. E.g.

Je dois aller à la banque.	**Il/elle doit rester au lit.**
Vous dev<u>ez</u> arrêter de fumer.	**Nous dev<u>ons</u> faire du sport.**

Exercices de grammaire

à and *de* followed by *le* or *les*

1 Complete the following sentences with the correct pronoun (**je**, **tu**, **il**, **elle**, **nous, vous, ils, elles**) and the appropriate preposition (**à** or **de**) combined with the article (e.g. **au**, **à la**, **à l'**, **aux**, **du**, **de la**, **de l'**, **des**). E.g. **Je joue au football**.

a _____ jouons _____ piano.

b _____ joues _____ tennis.

c _____ vais _____ cinéma.

d _____ allez _____ université?

e _____ jouent _____ cartes.

f _____ vas _____ piscine?

Verbs followed by the infinitive.

2 Read the following text and put the verb in italics in the appropriate form.

Je suis très active et je **a** *aimer* faire du sport. Deux fois par semaine je **b** *aller* à la piscine et j'aime aussi **c** *faire* du yoga. Je **d** *n'aimer pas* lire. Le weekend je **e** *sortir* avec mes amis. Nous **f** *aller* au cinéma ou au théâtre et après nous **g** *aimer* aller au café ou au bar ensemble. Mon copain **h** *n'être* pas très sportif. Il **i** *préférer* faire des choses plus tranquilles, par exemple il **j** *aimer* aller à la pêche et surtout il **k** *adorer* regarder la télévision.

How would you say the following in French?

3 a Do you (*formal*) like playing sport?

b She does not like swimming.

c We really like playing cards.

d He does not like going to the cinema.

e I like watching television.

4 Re-order the following jumbled sentences.

a à/dimanche/l'église/matin/il/aller/le/doit

b soir/ce/je/sortir/dois

c lit/au/doivent/ils/aller

d quelque/tu/boire/chose/dois

e après-midi/devons/cet/travailler/nous

f faire/vous/du/sport/devez

Vocabulaire

Les jours de la semaine/Days of the week

lundi	Monday
mardi	Tuesday
mercredi	Wednesday
jeudi	Thursday
vendredi	Friday
samedi	Saturday
dimanche	Sunday
fermé	shut
ouvert	open

Les repas/meals

le petit déjeuner	breakfast
le déjeuner	lunch
le dîner	evening meal
prendre	to take
manger	to eat

Quand?/When?

avant	before
après	after
quand?	when?
à quelle heure?	what time?
à 1 heure	at 1 o'clock
de 3 heures à 5 heures	from 3 o'clock to 5 o'clock
les cours (m)	lectures, lessons
toujours	always
le matin	in the morning
l'après-midi (m) or (f)	in the afternoon
le soir	in the evening
le week-end	at the weekend
aujourd'hui	today
demain	tomorrow
à la maison	at home
devoir	to have to

Les loisirs/Leisure activities

regarder la télévision	to watch television
écouter de la musique	to listen to music
lire un livre	to read a book
aller à la gym/piscine	to go to the gym/ swimming pool
aller au cinéma/ théâtre	to go to the cinema/ theatre
aller en boîte	to go to a nightclub/ to go clubbing
écrire une lettre	to write a letter
écouter un CD	to listen to a CD
jouer du piano/violon	to play the piano/violin
jouer de la guitare	to play the guitar
jouer au tennis/ fléchettes/football	to play tennis/darts/ football
jouer à la balle/ pétanque	to play ball/boules
faire une dissertation	to write an essay
faire le ménage	to do the housework
ne rien faire de spécial	to do nothing special
faire de l'aérobic/ l'athlétisme	to do aerobics/to do athletics
faire du sport	to do sport
faire du vélo/yoga/ footing	to cycle/to do yoga/ to go jogging
faire du rugby/volleyball	to play rugby/volleyball
faire du ping-pong	to play table tennis
faire de la marche/ danse/photographie	to go walking/to do dancing/to do photography
faire de la planche à voile/la voile/la cuisine	to go windsurfing/to go sailing/to cook
faire des courses	to do the shopping
aimer bien/beaucoup	to like/like a lot
préférer/détester	to prefer/detest

Travail en paires

1 Working with a partner, use the prompts below to ask about the different types of things s/he likes and dislikes doing. You start.

Do you like to play sport?

What different types of sport do you like doing?

What different types of sport do you not like doing?

What do you like to do at the weekend?

2 Prendre rendez-vous/Arranging a meeting

You are trying to organise a meeting with your partner. Look at your diary below and ask your partner whether he or she is free at the times of the day you are available. S/he will try to find out when you are available. E.g. **Tu es libre mardi matin? Non, je ne suis pas libre, je …**

lundi	10h00 – 12h00 anglais / 2h00 – 5h00 séminaire
mardi	rendez-vous chez le dentiste 10h15
mercredi	9h00 – 10h30 chimie / 6h00 match de foot
jeudi	2h00 bibliothèque / 7h00 piscine
vendredi	9h30 – 12h30 maths / 2h00 – 4h00 biologie
samedi	2h30 rendez-vous avec Richard / 8h00 cinéma
dimanche	12h00 déjeuner chez grand-mère

Travail en paires

1 Tu aimes…/Do you like…

Working with a partner, use the prompts below to answer questions about the different types of things you like and dislike doing.

You like playing sport, in particular swimming, jogging and cycling. You also like watching football.

You do not like watching or playing rugby. You hate golf!

At the weekend you like to go shopping on Saturdays and in the evenings you often go out with friends to the cinema or to a bar. On Sundays you go swimming or you go to the gym.

2 Prendre rendez-vous/Arranging a meeting

You are trying to organise a meeting with your partner. Look at your diary below and ask your partner whether he or she is free at the times of the day you are available. She will try to find out when you are available. E.g. **Tu es libre mardi matin? Non, je ne suis pas libre, je…**

lundi	0h30 – 11h00 linguistique / 6h00 supermarché
mardi	10h00 – 12h30 espagnol / 2h00 – 4h00 littérature / 6h00 supermarché
mercredi	2h00 – 4h30 séminaire / 6h00 supermarché
jeudi	3h00 – 5h00 poésie / 6h00 supermarché
vendredi	10h00 – 12h30 espagnol / 6h00 supermarché
samedi	8h30 anniversaire Jacqueline
dimanche	2h00 tennis

4 En ville

When you have completed this unit, you will be able to understand street signs, ask for and give directions, describe locations, shop for clothes and express preferences.

Où est la gare?

 1 Lire et observer

Look at the pictures below and indicate which sign you would need to follow if:

a you wanted to send a postcard;
e you wanted to travel to another town;

b you needed to buy medication;
f you wanted information about the town;

c you wanted to use the underground;
g you needed to get an official document;

d you had badly hurt yourself;
h you were looking for the name of a street.

1 Hôtel de Ville

2 Rue de la Monnaie

3 Pharmacie

4 Station de Métro

5 Hôpital

6 Poste

7 Gare SNCF

8 Office du Tourisme

2 Lire et écouter

Listen to four people asking for directions and fill in the gap in the transcript below with the place they are looking for.

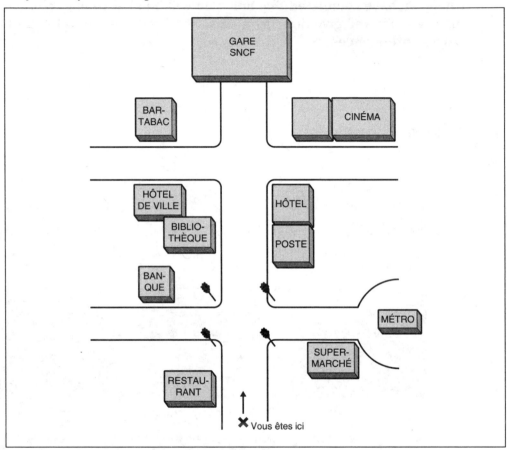

a – Pardon monsieur, où est _____, s'il vous plaît?
– C'est là, tout droit.
– Ah! Merci.

b – Pardon madame, vous savez où est _____, s'il vous plaît?
– Alors, vous allez tout droit, et c'est … la deuxième à gauche.
– Merci beaucoup.
– Je vous en prie.

c – Pardon, il y a _____ près d'ici?
– Oui. Prenez la première rue à droite, et c'est sur la place.
– Merci.
– De rien.

d – Pardon, où est _____, s'il vous plaît?
– C'est là, tout droit, à droite, après les feux.
– Merci!

Pardon monsieur/madame,	(vous savez) où est l'Hôtel de ville, s'il vous plaît?	
	il y a une station de métro près d'ici?	

C'est tout droit.	(Vous) prenez la première (rue)	à gauche.
(Vous) allez …	la deuxième (rue)	à droite.
(Vous) continuez …	la troisième (rue)	
C'est ici / là / là-bas.	(Vous) tournez	à gauche / à droite.
	(Vous) traversez	la rue / la place / le carrefour.

3 Lire, écrire et parler

a Read the following instructions and, looking at the map in exercise 2, find out which two places they lead to.
  – C'est là, tout droit, à gauche après les feux.
  – Alors, vous prenez la première rue à droite, et c'est là, à droite.

b Still looking at the map, write down directions to go to the cinema and the bank. Then practise this with a partner.

4 Ecouter

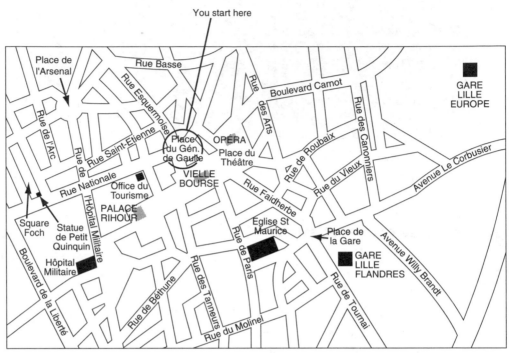

Listen to four people giving directions, *each time starting* from Place du Général de Gaulle in Lille. Using the map above, follow the directions and find out which four places of interest they lead to.

C'est	à	gauche / droite.	– C'est près / loin d'ici?
	sur la		– Non, c'est à 200 m / 1 km (d'ici).
	sur votre		5 min. / $^1/_2$ h
Prenez la Rue Nationale, puis la deuxième à gauche.			

5 Jeu de rôle

You are in Lille, in Place du Général de Gaulle. With a partner, practise asking for and giving directions to go to the following places: the opera, the train station Lille-Flandres, the tourist information office, Place de l'Arsenal (near Square Foch).

La boulangerie est en face

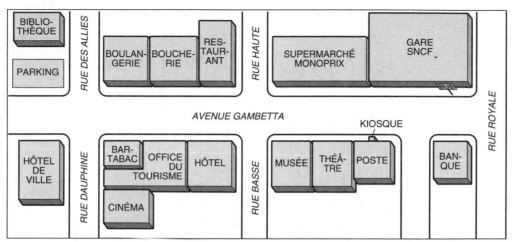

 6 Ecouter et traduire

Listen to a conversation in a tourist information office. Using the map above, work out what the following prepositions mean in English.

a à côté de   **d** devant

b entre   **e** au coin de

c en face de   **f** derrière

 7 Lire

Still looking at the map, decide which of the following sentences are true or false and then correct the false statements.

a Le restaurant est derrière la boucherie.

b La bibliothèque est dans l'Avenue Gambetta.

c Entre la poste et le musée, il y a une pharmacie.

d Le supermarché est à côté de la gare SNCF.

e L'office du tourisme est au coin de la Rue Dauphine et de l'Avenue Gambetta.

f La boucherie est à côté du restaurant.

g La boulangerie est en face du bar-tabac.

h Il y a un arrêt d'autobus devant la poste.

 8 Jeu de rôle

Working with a partner: each of you describes a couple of locations on the map and the other finds out which building it is. E.g. **C'est au coin de la Rue Haute et de l'Avenue Gambetta, à côté de la boucherie. > C'est le restaurant.**

Au magasin

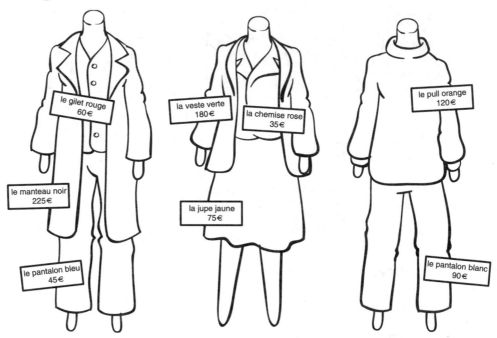

le gilet rouge
60€

la veste verte
180€

la chemise rose
35€

le pull orange
120€

le manteau noir
225€

la jupe jaune
75€

le pantalon bleu
45€

le pantalon blanc
90€

 9 Ecouter

Listen to the conversation between David and a sales assistant and answer the following questions. (Note: **essayer** = to try, **Je peux vous aider?** = Can I help you?, **Il y a d'autres couleurs?** = Are there other colours?)

a What does David want to try on?

b What else does he want?

c What is wrong with the item he has tried on?

d What colours are available?

e What does he eventually buy?

grammaire

Vous prenez le manteau? Oui, je le prends.
Vous prenez la chemise? Oui, je la prends.
Vous prenez les chemises? Oui, je les prends.

le manteau noir   la chemise noire
les pulls noirs   les jupes noires

Elle coûte combien? Elle coûte 40 €.

70 soixante-dix	80 quatre-vingts
71 soixante-et-onze	81, 82, 83 quatre-vingt-un, -deux, -trois, etc.
72 soixante-douze	
73 soixante-treize	90 quatre-vingt-dix
74 soixante-quatorze	91, 92, 93 quatre-vingt-onze, -douze, -treize, etc.
75 soixante-quinze	
76 soixante-seize	100 cent
77 soixante-dix-sept	101, 102 cent un, cent deux, etc.
78 soixante-dix-huit	200 deux cents
79 soixante-dix-neuf	1000 mille, 10 000 dix mille, 100 000 cent mille
	1 000 000 un million

10 Ecouter

Listen to a shop assistant in a clothes shop dealing with two customers who are making purchases. For both transactions you will hear prices being listed for each item of clothing. Fill in the missing items and prices in the grid.

Item	Price
jupe	a
b	60 €
gilet vert	c
d	100 €
veste	e
f	55 €
g	55 €
pantalon	h

11 Ecouter

Two friends are looking at a shop window. Read their conversation, then listen to the recording and correct the deliberate mistakes in the transcript (there are ten of them).

– Je voudrais ce pull rose.
– Il coûte combien?
– 80 euros.
– Moi, je voudrais cette veste bleue et ces deux tee-shirts jaunes.
– Et ce pantalon?
– (Jokingly) Non merci, il est rose!

– Et tu n'aimes pas la jupe verte là?
– Non, je n'aime pas beaucoup les jupes.
– Oh là là!, elle coûte 220 euros!
– Regarde ce pull! Quelle couleur!
– Ah oui, il est bleu-rose.
– Non, il est bleu-rouge.
– Ah bon! Je dois aller chez l'opticien!

grammaire

un/le pull > **ce** pull   une/la veste > **cette** veste   des/les tee-shirts > **ces** tee-shirts

43

12 Ecrire et lire

Choose somebody in your class and write a description of their clothing. (E.g. **Il/Elle porte un pantalon noir et un tee-shirt blanc, etc.**). In groups of three or four, swap pieces of paper and work out who is being described.

Tu préfères le rouge?

13 Ecouter

a Listen to a conversation between two friends who are on a shopping spree and answer the following questions. (Note: **des chaussures** = shoes; **les deux** = both.)
   i What does Jacques need to buy?
   ii What does he finally purchase? Give all the details.

b Listen to the dialogue again and work out how to say the following in French.
   i   Do you like these trousers?
   ii Me too.
   iii I like both of them.
   iv I prefer the black ones.
   v   Do you want to try them on?

Tu aimes ce pull marron?	Non, je ne l'aime pas, je préfère le bleu.
Tu aimes cette jupe verte?	Non, je ne l'aime pas, je préfère la rouge.
Tu aimes ces chaussures noires?	Non, je ne les aime pas, je préfère les grises.

14 Ecouter

Listen to another conversation in a shop and fill in the gaps in the text below. (Note: **une robe** = a dress; **un imperméable** = a raincoat.)

– Qu'est-ce que tu dois acheter, Julie?
– Euh… Une **a**_____, une robe et un imperméable.
– Regarde là, cette petite robe **b**_____ elle est jolie, non?
– Oui, mais je n'**c**_____ pas le noir.
– Et cette **d**_____, tu l'aimes?
– Ah oui! Je **e**_____ prends! Je prends aussi cette jupe bleue pour essayer.

– Bon. Un imperméable …
– Tu aimes **f**_____ blanc, ou tu préfères le beige?
– Oh, j'aime les **g**_____.
– Tu **h**_____ essaies?
– D'accord.
– Bon. Je prends la jupe **i**_____ et l'imperméable blanc. Où est la caisse?
– Là-bas, à **j**_____.

15 Jeu de rôle

Working with a partner, write a dialogue practising the above scenario. This time you are looking to buy a jacket, a jumper and shoes.

Extra!

 1 Lire

Alain is going to visit his English friend Dennis in London for the first time. He has just received a letter from him, with directions on how to get to his place. Read the letter and indicate whether the following statements are true or false.

a Alain loves London.

b Dennis's brother will be staying with them as well.

c When Alain comes out of the station, he has to turn right.

d Dennis lives in the second street on the right after the supermarket.

e The house is opposite a library.

f It is a long walk from the tube station.

> Cher Alain,
>
> Comment ça va? Je suis impatient de te voir ici, à Londres. J'adore cette ville! Il y a beaucoup de choses à faire: promenades, musées, shopping, cinéma, sorties en boîte, etc., etc.! Mon frère est là aussi en ce moment, ce sera sympa!
>
> Alors, pour aller à l'appartement de la station de métro de Holloway Road (sur la ligne Piccadilly), tu tournes à gauche et tu continues tout droit dans Holloway Road. Au carrefour, tu tournes à droite, puis tu prends la première rue à gauche (derrière un supermarché) et puis la deuxième à droite. C'est là, au numéro 25a. C'est à côté d'une petite bibliothèque.
>
> Voilà. Ce n'est pas très loin, à dix minutes environ. Bon voyage!
>
> A très bientôt,
>
> Dennis

 2 Ecouter

Listen to a conversation between Sarah and Alex in a clothes shop and answer the questions below in English.

a What item of clothing does Alex try on?

b What items of clothing does Sarah try on?

c How much is the skirt?

d What does Alex eventually buy?

Grammaire

- **Verbs: imperative form**
When giving instructions or telling someone to do something, the imperative form can be used: e.g. **Attendez!** (= Wait!) / **Faites attention!** (= Be careful!). It is generally constructed like the present indicative (the form you have been using up until now, e.g. **vous faites…**), but without the pronoun **vous**. Similarly, in informal style the pronoun **tu** is left out.
E.g. **Tournez à droite. / Prenez la deuxième à gauche.
Prends la Rue Dauphine. / Continue tout droit.** (Note that with **-er** verbs, the final **-s** is dropped.)
However, because the imperative form is very direct, the **vous/tu** of the present indicative form is generally preferred, especially when giving instructions (e.g. **Vous tournez à droite. / Tu prends la Rue Basse.**).

- **Prepositions of location**
When you are describing where something is in relation to something else, you need to use a preposition. Some prepositions of location are constructed with **de** (e.g. **en face de la banque**), others not (e.g. **la boulangerie est derrière le parking**). Remember that when **de** is followed by **le** or **les** it merges to become **du/des**.
E.g. **La banque est près du bar-tabac. / Il y a un téléphone près des toilettes.**

- *le/la/l'/les*
The direct object pronouns **le/la/les** are used to avoid repetition of the object in a sentence.
E.g. – **Vous prenez la jupe bleue? – Oui, je la prends.**
When the object is masculine it is replaced with **le** (or **l'**), when it is feminine with **la** (or **l'**), and when it is plural with **les**. Note that these pronouns come before the verb.

- *ce/cet/cette/ces*
The demonstrative adjectives **ce/cet/cette** ('this' or 'that') and **ces** ('these' or 'those') are used when referring to an object or a person by pointing at them. Eg. **Ce manteau, dans le magasin.** When the noun that follows is masculine, **ce** and **cet** (+vowel) are used. If it is feminine **cette** is used and if it is plural **ces** is used. E.g. **Je prends cette jupe, cet imperméable, ce pull et ces chemises.**

- **Adjectives**
Adjectives are usually placed directly after the noun and agree in gender (**la chemise grise**) and number (**les chemises grises**). With a masculine noun, the adjective does not change. With a feminine noun, an **-e** is added to the ending: e.g. **la veste verte.** However, there are some exceptions: e.g. **le pull blanc/la veste blanche.** Adjectives which already end with an **-e** do not change with a feminine noun: e.g. **le pull rouge/la veste rouge.** With a plural noun, an **-s** is added to the ending: e.g. **les jupes bleues**, unless the adjective already ends in **-s**.

Exercices de grammaire

Verbs: imperative form

1 Fill in the gaps in the text below with the imperative form of the verb in brackets:

Vous voulez aller au Musée d'Art Ancien? Eh bien, (*prendre*) **a**_____ cette rue, (*aller*) **b**_____ tout droit et (*tourner*) **c**_____ à gauche aux feux. Vous arrivez à une place; (*traverser*) **d**_____ la place et (*prendre*) **e**_____ la rue entre la poste et le cinéma. (*Continuer*) **f**_____ toujours tout droit et c'est là, en face de vous.

Prepositions of location

2 Fill in the gaps in the following sentences.

La bibliothèque est dans **a**_____ Rue de Nancy au coin **b**_____ Rue de Guise et **c**_____ Avenue Charles de Gaulle. C'est en face **d**_____ théâtre et à côté **e**_____ hôtel de ville.

La gare SNCF n'est pas loin. C'est près **f**_____ supermarché Océan. Il y a une pharmacie juste en face.

L'office du tourisme est sur **g**_____ Place Gambetta. C'est entre **h**_____ boucherie et **i**_____ bar-tabac.

le/ la/ l'/ les

3 Read the following sentences and fill in the gap with the appropriate object pronoun.

– Je voudrais le manteau blanc. – Vous voulez **a**_____ essayer?
– J'aime bien la jupe rouge. – Tu **b**_____ prends? – Oui je **c**_____ prends.
– Vous prenez les deux pantalons verts? – Oui, je **d**_____ prends.
– Elle aime la chemise rose? – Oui, elle **e**_____ aime beaucoup.

ce/ cet/ cette/ ces

4 Replace the underlined article with the appropriate demonstrative adjective.

E.g.: **Prenez <u>la</u> rue à droite, ici > Prenez <u>cette</u> rue à droite, ici**.

a <u>La</u> boulangerie est excellente.
b Tournez à gauche après <u>les</u> feux.
c C'est tout droit après <u>le</u> carrefour.
d <u>La</u> jupe rouge est magnifique!
e Vous prenez <u>les</u> pantalons?
f Je voudrais essayer <u>l'</u>imperméable.

Adjectives

5 Change the following sentences to the plural form.

E.g.: **le pull vert > les pulls verts**

a la chemise rose >
b le tee-shirt blanc >
c le pantalon rouge >
d la jupe bleue >
e le gilet gris >
f la robe jaune >

4 En ville

Vocabulaire

Trouver le chemin/Finding the way

aller	to go
continuer	to carry on / continue
prendre	to go
tourner	to turn
traverser	to cross
savoir	to know
la rue	street
l'avenue (f)	avenue
le boulevard	boulevard
la place	square
le carrefour	crossroads
les feux (m)	traffic lights
puis	then
avant	before
là-bas	over there
après	after
tout droit	straight on
à gauche	on the left
à droite	on the right
près (de)	near
loin (de)	far (from)
entre	between
devant	in front (of)
derrière	behind
à côté (de)	beside
en face (de)	opposite
au coin (de)	on the corner of
ici	here
là	there

Les vêtements/Clothing

la veste	jacket
l'imperméable	rain coat
le manteau	coat
la robe	dress
la jupe	skirt
le pantalon	trousers
le pull	jumper
le gilet	cardigan
la chemise	shirt
le tee-shirt	tee-shirt
les chaussures (f)	shoes
la cabine d'essayage	changing room
aider	to help
essayer	to try
la caisse	cash desk

Les couleurs/Colours

blanc(he)	white
bleu(e)	blue
marron	brown
noir(e)	black
rouge	red
orange	orange
jaune	yellow
vert(e)	green
rose	pink
beige	beige
gris(e)	grey

Les bâtiments et magasins/Buildings and shops

l'hôtel (m) de ville	town hall
la biblothèque	library
l'office (m) du tourisme	tourist office
le musée	museum
la gare	train station
la station de métro	underground station
l'arrêt (m) d'autobus	bus stop
l'épicerie (f)	grocer's
l'hôtel (m)	hotel
le restaurant	restaurant
la poste	post office
l'hôpital (m)	hospital
le théâtre	theatre
la boulangerie	baker's
la boucherie	butcher's
la pharmacie	chemist's
le tabac	tobacconist's
le parking	car park
le plan	map

Travail en paires

1 Demander son chemin/Asking the way

a Find out from your partner where the following places are on the map and mark them on: the nearest underground station, the 'Hôtel du Centre', the restaurant 'Chez Marcel' and the library.

b Answer your partner's questions about where certain buildings are.

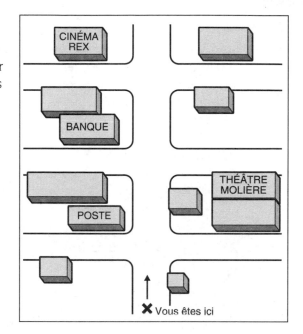

2 Au magasin de vêtements/In a clothes shop

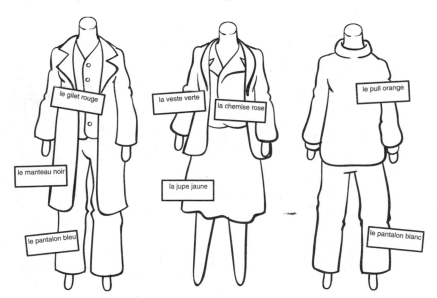

You are shopping for clothes and you have a budget of 350 €.
Ask the shop assistant for the price of each item you are interested in and work out what you are going to buy.

Travail en paires

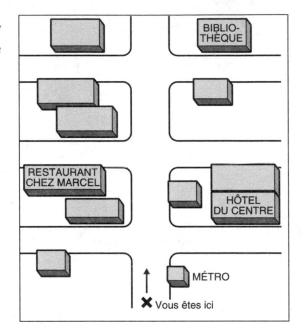

1 Demander son chemin/Asking the way

    a Find out from your partner where the following places are on the map and mark them on: the Rex Cinema, the nearest bank, the Molière Theatre and the post office.

    b Answer your partner's questions about where certain buildings are.

2 Au magasin de vêtements / In a clothes shop

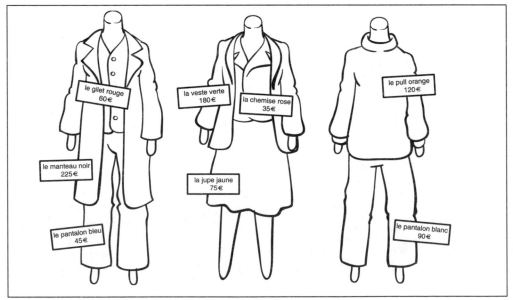

A customer who has a specific amount of money to spend is enquiring about the price of different items of clothing. Tell him/her the prices and ask if they would like to try and/or buy the said items.

5 En train

When you have completed this unit, you will be able to locate places on a map and state what you are going to do; request and give information about travelling by train and other means of transport; deal with timetables.

Je vais partir en France!

1 Ecouter

Three students are discussing where they are going to go on holiday in the summer. Listen to their conversation and on the map over the page tick the places (cities and countries) which are mentioned.

> la France > aller en France   l'Angleterre > aller en Angleterre
> le Portugal > aller au Portugal   les Pays-Bas > aller aux Pays-Bas
> Rome > aller à Rome   Paris > aller à Paris

2 Lire

Here is a summary of the previous conversation. Find the missing prepositions.

Je vais aller **a**_____ Porto **b**_____ Portugal.
Je vais commencer par aller **c**_____ Suisse puis **d**_____ Italie.
Tu vas aller **e**_____ Grèce?
Non, je vais partir **f**_____ Pays-Bas.
Mon copain va travailler **g**_____ Madrid **h**_____ Espagne.

La Seine, Paris

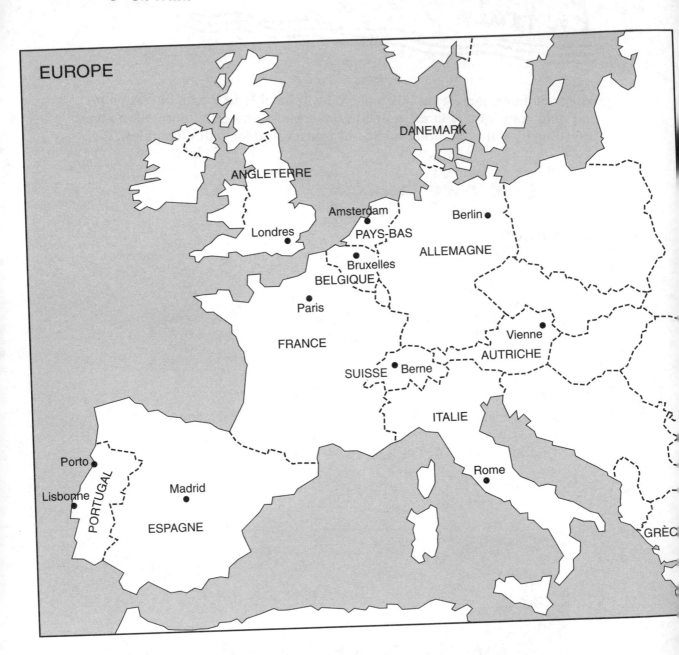

EUROPE

DANEMARK

ANGLETERRE

Amsterdam

Berlin

Londres

PAYS-BAS

ALLEMAGNE

Bruxelles

BELGIQUE

Paris

Vienne

FRANCE

AUTRICHE

SUISSE Berne

ITALIE

Porto

Rome

Madrid

Lisbonne

PORTUGAL

ESPAGNE

GRÈC

grammaire

Qu'est-ce que vous <u>allez faire</u> pendant les vacances?   Je <u>vais aller</u> à Madrid.
Où est-ce que tu <u>vas aller</u>?   Elle <u>va partir</u> aux Pays-Bas.

3 Jeu de rôle

Think about what you are planning to do during the next holiday and discuss it with your partner, using **aller** + infinitive. Here are some verbs you could use: **partir, travailler, faire, aller etc**. E.g. **Je vais travailler en Italie**. Find out what your partner's plans are.

L'Arc de Triomphe

Montmartre

Un aller-retour...

4 Ecouter et lire

Marie is at the ticket office in Lille train station. Listen to and read the dialogue in order to answer the questions below.

– A quelle heure part le prochain train pour Arras?
– Euh, attendez … à dix heures onze.
– Bien. Trois aller-retour, s'il vous plaît.
– Seconde classe?
– Oui, oui.
– Voilà. Ça fait vingt-quatre euros.
– Voilà. Le train arrive à quelle heure à Arras?
– Alors, il arrive à Arras à … dix heures cinquante-deux.
– Merci. C'est quel quai?
– Quai deux, mademoiselle.
– Bon. Merci beaucoup!

A quelle heure part le prochain train pour Arras?	Un (billet)	aller-retour, SVP.
premier		aller simple
dernier		
Il arrive à quelle heure?		première / seconde classe
C'est quel quai?		

a What time does the next train for Arras leave?
b How many tickets does Marie need? First or second class?
c What time does the train arrive in Arras?
d Which platform does Marie have to go to?

grammaire

un quai > *quel* quai?	des quais > *quels* quais?
une heure > *quelle* heure?	des heures > *quelles* heures?

5 Jeu de rôle

How would you ask the following in French:
– What time does the next train for Calais leave?
– What time does the last train for Paris leave and what time does it arrive in Paris?
– Two single tickets to Paris, please.
– One return ticket to Arras, second class, please.
– What platform is it?
Work this out with a partner, then practise asking the questions and improvising answers.

6 Ecouter

Listen to another conversation, this time in Lille Europe, the station for Eurostar and high speed trains (**TGV – train à grande vitesse**), and fill in the gaps in the French summary below.

La cliente veut une **a**_____ pour **b**_____ personnes.
La cliente veut aller **c**_____ Bruges en Belgique.
La cliente veut **d**_____ le matin, vers **e**_____.
Il faut changer à Bruxelles. Il y a une **f**_____ à 10h36.
Le train **g**_____ à Bruges à 11h26.
Les billets coûtent **h**_____ euros.
La cliente réserve des places **i**_____-_____.
Il n'y a pas de **j**_____ pour le train de Bruxelles à Bruges.
Il ne faut pas **k**_____ les billets Eurostar.

> Je peux faire une réservation?
> Je voudrais partir/arriver le matin/l'après-midi/le soir/vers 9h.
> Départ de Lille Europe à 9h47, arrivée à Bruxelles Midi à 10h25.
> Une place côté couloir/fenêtre, en voiture fumeurs/non-fumeurs.
> Vous avez un horaire, SVP?
> Il faut changer à Bruxelles. Il y a une correspondance à 21h02.
> Il faut composter les billets?

grammaire

Je <u>peux réserver</u>? / Vous <u>voulez aller</u> à Bruges? / <u>Il faut changer</u> à Bruxelles.

 7 Parler et écouter

With a partner, practise saying the following times, using the 24 hour clock. E.g. 07:15 = **sept heures quinze**; 20:32 = **vingt heures trente-deux**, then listen to the recording for pronunciation.

a 01:45   **b** 19:51   **c** 12:24   **d** 15:30   **e** 23:16   **f** 10:05

8 Jeu de rôle

With a partner, act out the following situation:

– One of you wants to travel with two friends from Paris (Gare de Lyon station) to Lyon (Perrache station) by TGV. You want to leave on Friday afternoon, travel second class, non-smoking. You want to return on Sunday evening and be in Paris before 22:00.
– One of you works at the ticket desk and has to supply the relevant information for the journey (approx. journey time from Paris to Lyon is two hours and ten minutes).

Billets, s'il vous plaît?

numéro de train		7207	7007	73291	73293	73295	73301	7211	7015	7021	73311	7229	73313	7033	73333	7235	7043	73353
notes à consulter		3	4	5	6	7	8	9	10		8					9		
		TGV ♿	TGV ♿		🚲	🚲		TGV ♿	TGV ♿	TGV ♿		TGV ♿		TGV ♿	🚲	TGV ♿	TGV ♿	
Paris-Nord.	Dep	07.28	07.28					07.58	08.28	08.58		09.58		10.58		11.58	12.58	
Lille Flandres	Arr			07.35	08.00	08.09	08.29	08.59	09.29	09.59	09.35		10.09	11.59	12.08	12.59	13.59	14.08
Lille Europe	Arr	08.27	08.27									10.56						
Croix Wasquehal	Arr			07.43	08.07	08.17	08.37	09.17			09.43		10.16		12.15	13.17		14.15
Roubaix	Arr			07.48	08.10	08.20	08.42	09.22			09.47		10.20		12.20	13.22		14.20
Tourcoing	Arr			07.52	08.14	08.23	08.47	09.28			09.52		10.23		12.23	13.28		14.23

JOURS DE CIRCULATION ET SERVICES DISPONIBLES

3. tous les jours sauf les sam, dim et fêtes ; circule le 1er nov.
4. Les 30 mai et 2 juin ; du 6 juin au 11 juil et à partir du 29 août : les mar, mer et jeu sauf les 13 juin et 1 er nov.
5. jusqú'au 30 juin et à partir du 28 août: tous les jours sauf les dim et fêtes.
6. tous les jours sauf les sam, dim et fêtes.
7. les sam sauf le 11 nov.
8. jusqú au 30 juin et à partir du 28 août : tous les jours sauf les sam, dim et fêtes.
9. tous les jours sauf les 11 et 12 juin.
10. jusqu'au 15 juil et à partir du 28 août : tous les jours sauf les dim et sauf le 12 juin.

🚲 Vélo : transport gratuit

♿ Place(s) handicapés

TGV Réservation obligatoire

9 Lire

Match the French expressions or abbreviations in this timetable with their equivalent in English.

1 les mar, mer et jeu
2 TGV
3 tous les jours
4 sauf
5 fêtes
6 les sam, dim
7 jusqu'au

a until
b every day
c bank holidays
d on Tuesdays, Wednesdays and Thursdays
e high speed train
f on Saturdays and Sundays
g except

10 Lire

On the timetable, find a train (or trains) which will suit each of the following travellers.

a Anne et son mari veulent un train qui arrive à Lille Flandres, le lundi, vers neuf heures du matin. Ils préfèrent prendre un train rapide.

b Lorraine habite à Lille. Elle a un vélo et elle ne veut pas prendre le TGV (c'est plus cher) pour aller à Tourcoing. Elle voudrait partir avant 9 heures.

c C'est samedi matin, et Pierre et son ami veulent aller à Lille pour le congrès des personnes handicapées qui commence à dix heures. Pierre voyage en chaise roulante et désire prendre un train rapide.

11 Ecouter

Listen to three conversations at the station and match the conversation number with each of the three situations described above in exercise 10.

Je vais y aller à pied

12 Ecouter

Listen to the dialogue and fill in the gaps. (Note: **circulation** = traffic, **moins cher** = cheaper, **aéroport** = airport.)

– Georges, tu **a** _____ aller en Ecosse la semaine prochaine?
– Oui, je vais **b** _____ vendredi soir.
– Tu y vas en **c**_____?
– Non, pas cette fois, c'est trop **d** _____. Je vais y aller en avion.
– En avion?
– Oui, c'est beaucoup moins cher le **e**_____ soir. Un aller-retour Londres-Edimbourg coûte **f** _____ euros. En plus le trajet ne dure qu'une heure. Pas mal, hein?
– Oui, c'est super. Tu vas à l'**g** _____ en voiture?
– Non, en train, c'est plus simple. Il y a toujours **h** _____ de circulation le vendredi soir.

en bus	en voiture	en taxi	en moto
en vélo	en avion	en bateau	à pied

grammaire	
Est-ce tu vas <u>à</u> Paris ce week-end?	Oui, j'<u>y</u> vais.
Est-ce qu'elle va aller <u>à</u> Londres la semaine prochaine?	Oui, elle va <u>y</u> aller.
Comment est-ce qu'elle va <u>à</u> l'université?	Elle <u>y</u> va à pied.
Comment vont-ils aller <u>au</u> cinéma?	Ils vont <u>y</u> aller à pied.

13 Parler

Working in pairs, think about the different types of transport you use and then answer the following questions.

a Comment allez-vous à l'université tous les jours?
b Après une soirée au café, comment est-ce que vous rentrez chez vous?
c Comment est-ce que vous allez d'Angleterre en Irlande?
d Vous voulez aller en France. Comment est-ce que vous y allez?

14 Ecrire

Now write a short summary about what you are going to do during the holidays. Start with **Pendant les vacances**… and make sure you include the following information:

a Where you are going to go, with whom.
b Details of how you are going to get there.
c A few things that you are going to do.

Il y a une grève

15 Lire

Here are some problems that you might encounter when travelling. With a partner match the French sentences with the appropriate English phrases below.

La voiture est en panne. ⇨ **The car has broken down.**

a Il y a une grève.

b Je n'ai plus d'essence.

c Mon vélo a un pneu crevé.

d Le train est annulé.

e Je suis en retard.

1 The train is cancelled.

2 I am late.

3 There is a strike.

4 My bicycle has a flat tyre.

5 I have run out of petrol.

> être en avance / être à l'heure / être en retard

16 Lire et écouter

Re-order the sentences in the dialogue below and listen to the recording to check your answers.

a Ce n'est pas possible!

b Il est à la gare. Je vais le chercher demain.

c Ah! Bonjour Yelena! Tu es en retard …

d Il est où ton vélo?

e Parce qu'il y a une grève demain!

f Pourquoi?

g Oui, je suis désolée – mon vélo a un pneu crevé.

17 Ecouter

Listen to four short dialogues. In each case someone is experiencing a problem connected with travel. Note down each problem.

a …

b …

c …

d …

Extra!

1 Ecouter

Listen to some announcements that you might hear in a train station in France, and fill in the grid below with the relevant information (you will notice that not all the boxes need to be filled in!). (Note: **Le train 917 <u>en provenance de</u> Paris, <u>à destination de</u> Lyon** = Train 917 <u>from</u> Paris <u>to</u> Lyon; **la voie** = track.)

	Train number	From	To	Platform	Track	Delay
a						
b						
c						
d						
e						
f						
g						

2 Lire

Read the travel information about the Paris métro below and answer the following questions in English.

> **Quatre kiosques d'information sont à votre disposition. Vous pouvez obtenir tous les documents d'information sur les lignes de bus et de métro. Vous pouvez également y acheter vos cartes d'abonnements et vos billets de transport.**
>
> **Renseignements:** Du lundi au vendredi: 8h30 à 12h.   Le samedi: 9h à 17h.
> **Horaires Métro:** Du lundi au samedi:
> Ligne 1   Premier métro:5h12   Dernier métro:0h12
> Ligne 2   Premier métro:6h24   Dernier métro:0h30
>
> *Notez bien!*
> *Un métro passe environ chaque minute aux heures d'affluence et toutes les 4 à 6 minutes aux heures creuses. La station est fermée le dimanche.*

a How many information desks are there?

b What different types of information can you get from these desks?

c What time are the desks open at the weekend?

d At what time does the last train leave on Line 1?

e How frequent are the trains during the rush hour?

Grammaire

- **Prepositions before countries and towns**
  Names of countries can be either feminine, masculine or plural. When talking about where you are or where you are going to go, the following prepositions are used:
  Before feminine countries (the majority) and countries starting with a vowel: **en** (e.g. **Je vais en France. J'habite en Irak.**)
  Before singular masculine countries: **au** (e.g. **Je pars au Portugal.**)
  Before plural countries: **aux** (e.g. **Je vais aux Pays-Bas.**)
  Remember before cities the preposition **à** is used. (e.g. **J'habite à Paris.**)

- *aller* + **infinitive verb**
  One way to talk about the near future is to use the verb **aller** and to add the infinitive form of the verb describing what you are going to do. E.g. **Je vais prendre le train./Tu vas aller où? /Nous allons partir en Afrique./Vous allez faire des courses?**
  Note: You can also use the present tense to talk about the near future. (E.g. **Demain, je prends le train**.)

- *Pouvoir, vouloir* **and il** *faut*

pouvoir + infinitive	**vouloir** + infinitive	**il faut** + infinitive
(can/be able)	(want/wish)	(have to)
je peux	je veux	'impersonal' verb
tu peux	tu veux	(only **il** form)
il/elle peut	il/elle veut	
nous pouvons	nous voulons	
vous pouvez	vous voulez	
ils/elles peuvent	ils/elles veulent	

- **The pronoun** *y*
  The basic meaning of the pronoun **y** is 'there'. It replaces a word or an idea introduced by **à** e.g.

  Est-ce que tu vas à Montpellier?   **Oui, j'y vais.**
  Are you going to Montpellier?   Yes, I'm going there.

  Note: When using the immediate future, **y** changes place and comes before the infinitive verb **aller**.

  Est-ce qu'elles vont aller à Lyon?   **Oui, elles vont y aller.**
  Are they going to go to Lyon?   Yes, they are going to go there.

Exercices de grammaire

Prepositions before countries and towns

1 Indicate which preposition you would use in front of the following countries and continents (using **aller** or **habiter**). E.g.: l'Allemagne. > Je vais aller en Allemagne.

   a le Portugal   **e** le Royaume-Uni   **i** l'Irak   **m** l'Irlande
   b les Antilles   **f** la Suède   **j** l'Afrique   **n** l'Ouganda
   c la Belgique   **g** le Danemark   **k** l'Egypte
   d l'Ecosse   **h** les Etats-Unis   **l** le Liban

Aller + infinitive verb

2 Make up complete sentences out of the information below using **aller** + infinitive verb.

   E.g. **je/aller/vacances/Italie = Je vais aller en vacances en Italie**.

   a Je/prendre/train/Milan   **d** Elle/prendre le bateau/Corse

   b Nous/prendre l'avion/Rome   **e** Tu/visiter la ville/acheter souvenirs?

   c Ils/partir/Naples   **f** Nous/aller Corse/faire de la randonnée

Pouvoir, vouloir and il faut

3 Complete the following sentences with **faut** or the appropriate form of **pouvoir** or **vouloir**.

   Ils **a** _____ voyager en 1ère classe: c'est plus confortable.
   Elle ne **b** _____ pas prendre l'avion: il y a une grève!
   Dans les gares françaises, il **c** _____ composter son billet.
   Vous **d**_____ le plein d'essence?
   Il **e**_____ aller en France pour voir sa copine.
   Nous ne **f**_____ pas partir à 23h00: le dernier train est à 22h35!
   Il **g** _____ changer à Paris; il y a une correspondance à 11h34.
   Elles **h** _____ réserver leur billet ici?

The pronoun y

4 Translate the following questions and answers. Be careful - the word "there" is not always needed in English but the French **y** is always included. It replaces a word introduced by **à**.

   a How are you getting to Bordeaux? / I am going there by car.
   b Are they going to France on Tuesday? / No, they are going on Monday.
   c Does she go to the supermarket every day? / Yes, she goes there every day.
   d How do you get to work? / We get there on foot.
   e Are you going to Paris by plane? / No, I'm going by Eurostar.

Vocabulaire

Voyager en train/Travelling by train

le train	train
le TGV	high speed train
réserver	to book
la réservation	booking
prochain(e)	next
dernier(ière)	last
vers 1h	at around 1.00
le billet	ticket
l'aller simple (m)	single ticket
l'aller-retour (m)	return ticket
en première classe	first class
en seconde classe	second class
circuler	to run (trains)
tous les jours	everyday
sauf	except
les fêtes (f)	bank holidays
la place	seat
le côté fenêtre	window seat
le côté couloir	aisle seat
la voiture	carriage
(non-)fumeurs	(non) smoking
changer	to change
la correspondance	connection
le quai	platform
composter	to validate
l'arrivée (f)	arrival
le départ	departure
l'horaire (m)	timetable
cher	expensive
jusqu'au	until
une chaise roulante	wheelchair
personnes handicapées	disabled people

Pays et régions/Countries and regions

l'Afrique du sud (f)	South Africa
l'Allemagne (f)	Germany
l'Angleterre (f)	England
les Antilles (f)	West Indies
la Belgique	Belgium
la Corse	Corsica
le Danemark	Denmark
l'Espagne (f)	Spain
l'Irak (m)	Irak
l'Ouganda (m)	Uganda
dans le sud/nord/ est/ouest	in the south/north/ east/west
les Etats-Unis (m)	United States
la France	France
la Grèce	Greece
l'Italie (f)	Italy
les Pays-Bas (m)	Netherlands
le Portugal	Portugal
la Suède	Sweden
la Suisse	Switzerland

Autres moyens de transport/Other means of transport

la voiture	car
le taxi	taxi
le vélo	bike
la moto	motorbike
le bus	bus
l'essence (f)	petrol
la station-service	petrol station
la grève	strike
fermé	closed
annulé	cancelled
être en avance	to be early
être à l'heure	to be on time
le car	coach
le bateau/ferry	boat/ferry
l'avion (m)	airplane
à pied	on foot
le garage	garage
l'aéroport (m)	airport
la gare routière	coach station
en panne	broken down/out of order
le pneu crevé	a flat tyre
être en retard	to be late

Travail en paires

1 Arrivées et départs

Find out from your partner the missing information about arrivals in and departures from the 'Gare Montparnasse' in Paris, and complete the grid below.

Arrivées				Départs			
Provenance	Train	Heure	Quai	Destination	Train	Heure	Quai
Rennes		08:05	5	Quimper	763		
Brest	644			Rennes		10:40	
Le Mans		12:46	3	Le Mans		11:15	6
Nantes	595		1	Brest	770		
Saint-Nazaire	904			Nantes		13:55	2
Poitiers		21:28		Saint-Nazaire	814		8
Tours			7	Bordeaux		17:12	
Limoges	319	23:05		Toulouse	558		2

2 Réservations

You are in Paris and would like to go to Nancy for the weekend. You intend to travel by train and need to make the necessary travel arrangements. Create a dialogue with a partner (the ticket assistant) using the information below.

Two return tickets to Nancy.
Second class.
Non-smoking carriage.
You would like to leave on Friday morning at around 11:00 and return on Sunday evening, leaving Paris at around 19:00. You would prefer a direct train.

Find out:

a From which station the train leaves.

b The train times – you may be given a choice of trains.

c Whether you need to reserve.

d The price.

Travail en paires

1 Arrivées et départs

Find out from your partner the missing information about arrivals in and departures from the 'Gare Montparnasse' in Paris, and complete the grid below.

Arrivées				Départs			
Provenance	Train	Heure	Quai	Destination	Train	Heure	Quai
Rennes	259		7	Quimper		07:38	8
Brest		09:15	5	Rennes	438		4
Le Mans	622			Le Mans	251		
Nantes		13:32		Brest		13:30	4
Saint-Nazaire		16:50	3	Nantes	486		
Poitiers	230		9	Saint-Nazaire		14:12	
Tours	546	21:47		Bordeaux	671		6
Limoges			5	Toulouse		20:42	

2 Réservations

You work for SNCF behind the ticket desk. A customer would like to make some travel arrangements. Create a dialogue with a partner (the customer) using the information below.

The customer will tell you what s/he requires. Remember to find out the destination, the type of ticket and the class.

Les trains pour Nancy partent de Paris Gare de l'Est.

Vendredi
Paris Est 10:50   Nancy Ville 12:49 (direct)   Réservation obligatoire
Paris Est 12:49   Nancy Ville 15:50 (direct)   Réservation obligatoire

Dimanche
Nancy Ville 18:53   Paris Est 22:07 (direct)   Réservation obligatoire
Nancy Ville 19:25   Paris Est 22:20 (direct)   Réservation recommandée

Aller-simple 16 euros
Aller-retour 33 euros

6 A l'hôtel

When you have completed this unit, you will be able to make a hotel booking, make complaints, understand holiday brochures and describe accommodation.

Je voudrais une chambre ...

Je voudrais une chambre…

pour deux personnes…

pour deux nuits.

 1 Ecouter

Listen to Nadia booking a hotel room and fill in the gaps with the missing words.

– Bonsoir, je **a**_____ une chambre, s'il **b**_____ plaît.
– Oui, pour **c**_____ de personnes?
– Pour **d**_____ personnes. Pour **e**_____ nuit seulement.
– Bon, ça **f**_____ 110 €.

 2 Ecouter

Listen to three conversations at a hotel reception and fill in the grid below.

	chambres?	personnes?	nuits?	prix?
Conversation 1				
Conversation 2				
Conversation 3				

3 Jeu de rôle

With a partner, practise booking rooms in a hotel using the dialogue in exercise 1 as a model.

4 Ecouter et écrire

First listen to the alphabet in French and then write down the names of three people who have made a booking at a hotel reception.

5 Ecouter

Work out the meaning of the expressions below and match them with their English equivalent. Then listen to a conversation at the hotel reception and note in which order the expressions come in the dialogue.

1	au premier étage	a	in the name of…
2	à quel nom?	b	lift
3	au nom de…	c	satellite television
4	télévision par satellite	d	bathroom
5	salle de bains	e	under what name?
6	ascenseur	f	on the first floor

6 Lire et écouter

The ends of each of the following sentences have been cut off and jumbled up. Work out where they best fit in in order to reconstruct the dialogue. Then listen to the recording to check your answers.

a	Bonjour, je voudrais	1	chambre avec salle de bains.
b	Pour combien	2	cinquième étage.
c	Pour deux nuits,	3	la prends.
d	Je voudrais une	4	une chambre pour trois personnes.
e	Voilà, ça fait	5	s'il vous plaît.
f	C'est très bien. Je	6	de nuits?
g	Voilà, une chambre avec un lit	7	98 €.
h	C'est la chambre numéro 526 au	8	double et un lit simple.

> Une chambre avec un lit <u>double/simple</u>. Une chambre avec <u>douche</u> au premier <u>étage</u>.

Excusez-moi, monsieur, le téléphone ne marche pas dans ma chambre.

La télévision ne fonctionne pas et la fenêtre est cassée.

Il y a un problème avec la douche dans notre chambre. Il n'y a pas d'eau chaude.

Il n'y a pas d'oreillers dans la chambre.

Il y a un problème

 7 Écouter

Listen to two people who are having a few difficulties with their hotel room. Write down in English the nature of the problems and the solutions proposed. (Note: **interrupteur/bouton** = switch, **appuyer** = press, **armoire** = wardrobe.)

 8 Traduire et parler

With a partner, translate and practise saying the following sentences in French:
The shower is broken. / There is no hot water. / The heating (**le chauffage**) does not work.

Il se réveille…   Il se lève…   Il se rase…   Il ne se douche pas!

grammaire

Reflexive verbs have an extra pronoun in front of them.

E.g.   se réveiller (to wake up)   se plaindre (to complain)
       je me réveille   nous nous réveillons
       je me plains   nous nous plaignons
       tu te réveilles   vous vous réveillez
       tu te plains   vous vous plaignez
       il se réveille   ils se réveillent
       elle se plaint   elles se plaignent

 9 Écrire

Suzanne is visiting Paris for the first time. Describe her day using the following outlines.
(Note: **se promener** = to go for a walk,   **s'amuser** = to have fun,
rentrer = to come back,   **se coucher** = to go to bed,   **parce que** = because.)

E.g.: se réveiller tard/téléphone/hôtel/cassé
= **Elle se réveille tard parce que le téléphone de l'hôtel est cassé**.

a se lever/se laver/problème douche

b aller réception/se plaindre

c se promener/Tour Eiffel/Notre Dame

d s'amuser beaucoup

e rentrer/hôtel/se coucher tard

Petit déjeuner en chambre ...

10 Ecouter et écrire

Listen to a customer asking about breakfast in a hotel and answer the questions in French.

Note: **La veille** = the day before

a A quelle heure est-ce qu'il peut prendre le petit déjeuner?

b Où peut-il le prendre?

c Quel est le prix du petit déjeuner?

> Dans la salle de restaurant, c'est une formule buffet à volonté.
> Il faut commander la veille.

11 Lire et traduire en paires

Read the following information about the hotel *Les Mimosas* and with a partner work out the meaning of the expressions underlined. You may use a dictionary.

Hôtel Les Mimosas

a <u>Un réveil automatique est à votre disposition</u> dans toutes les chambres.

b <u>La piscine est ouverte</u> de 8 heures à 21 heures et le sauna de 10 heures à 20 heures.

c L'hôtel accepte <u>les cartes suivantes</u>: Carte bleue, Master card, American Express..

d Les <u>chèques de voyages et les devises</u> peuvent être changés à la réception.

e Le parking est ouvert <u>24h/24</u>.

f Le petit déjeuner <u>est servi</u> entre 7 heures et 9 heures.

g <u>La télévision par satellite est disponible</u> dans toutes les chambres et dans le bar.

h <u>La direction n'est pas responsable</u> des objets de valeur placés dans les chambres.

C'est ouvert ...

le printemps   l'été   l'automne   l'hiver

janvier–février–mars–avril–mai–juin–juillet–août–septembre–octobre–novembre–décembre

 12 Lire

Read the information below which explains how hotel prices vary throughout the year. Work out whether the statements in English are true or false.

Hôtel Catalan

Haute saison: *Du 4 juillet au 29 août.*
Demi saison: *Vacances d'hiver et vacances de printemps.*
Vacances de noël: *du 19 décembre au 2 janvier.*
Basse saison: *Autres périodes.*

a Spring holidays are in the low season.
b The high season starts on 4th July.
c Christmas holidays end in January, which is the mid-season.

Haute/demi/basse saison   du 19 décembre au 2 janvier

 13 Ecouter

Listen to the hotel answerphone message and fill in the gaps in the text.

Bonjour, l'Hôtel de la Ruche est **a**_____ toute l'année sauf le 25 **b**_____ et le premier **c**_____ . Notre restaurant est ouvert **d**_____ mardi **e**_____ dimanche midi et soir, sauf en **f**_____ saison du 25 **g**_____ au 30 **h**_____ .

 14 Jeu de rôle

With a partner, take it in turns to practise dealing with the following situations in a hotel.

1 Book two bedrooms with bathroom, one with single bed, one with double bed for two nights from 12 June until 14 June.
2 Complain at reception that your television set does not work and that you have not got any towels (**serviettes**) for the bathroom.
3 Ask for information about facilities in the hotel, e.g. car park, swimming pool, etc.

Une maison à la campagne...

15 Ecouter

Listen to Jean-Marc and Stéphanie who are comparing two holiday houses (**gîtes**) in a brochure and check that the transcript of the dialogue is correct.

Jean-Marc	Il y a deux gîtes dans le livre, ils sont très bien tous les deux.
Stéphanie	Quelle est la différence entre les deux?
Jean-Marc	Tu vois, le premier est plus petit, il fait 80 m².
Stéphanie	Oui, mais celui-ci est plus beau, il est à la campagne.
Jean-Marc	Le deuxième est moins intéressant que celui-ci mais il est moins cher.
Stéphanie	Lequel est-ce que tu préfères? Celui-ci ou celui-là?
Jean-Marc	Celui-ci est aussi beau mais je préfère celui-là.

> Il est <u>plus petit</u>.   Il est <u>moins cher que</u> le deuxième.   Il est <u>aussi</u> beau.
> <u>Lequel</u> est-ce que tu préfères? <u>Celui-ci</u> ou <u>celui-là</u>?

16 Lire, écouter et parler

Read the description of a holiday house in France and using the plan, work out what the description means. Then listen to the owner describing the house and make a list of the changes made to the property. Then, working with a partner compare this house with your ideal holiday home.

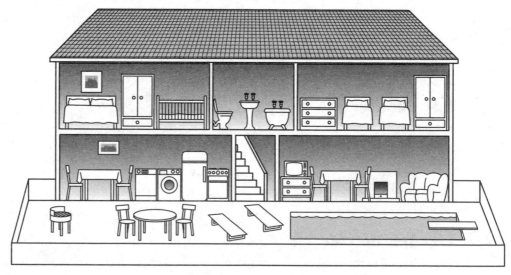

Maison indépendante rénovée en 1998, située en campagne.
Rez-de-chaussée: salle de séjour avec canapé-lit, cheminée, meuble et télévision couleur.
Cuisine avec lave-linge et lave-vaisselle, cuisinière, réfrigérateur.
Première chambre: lit double, armoire et lit d'enfant.
Deuxième chambre: deux lits, commode et armoire.
Salle de bains: baignoire, lavabo et toilettes.
Extérieur: piscine dans jardin clos, salon de jardin, relax, barbecue.

Extra!

1 Lire

Read the descriptions of facilities in three hotels and decide which hotel would best suit your needs.

1 You want a quiet hotel by the sea.
2 You are looking for a peaceful holiday and walks in the country.
3 You are interested in wines and enjoy good food.
4 Your priority is being able to play tennis every day and go for a swim.
5 You want a small hotel, in the country. You do not mind being in the country as long as you can park your car safely.
6 You want to go between 6th November and 8th November.

Hôtel beau site

Fermeture annuelle: du 5 novembre au 30 novembre
75 chambres de 65 € à 102 €
Petit déjeuner 9,50 €   Menus: 42 €, 52 €
Dans un cadre de verdure, vous allez découvrir la nature environnante, promenade, étangs et centre équestre. Vous pouvez utiliser les équipements de l'hôtel quand vous voulez: piscine, sauna, ping-pong, jardin etc. Le restaurant vous propose des spécialités régionales et une carte des vins exceptionnelle.

Hôtel Saint Denis

Fermeture annuelle: du 3 janvier au 31 janvier
15 chambres de 70 € à 115 €   Petit déjeuner 8,30 €
Situé dans un site exceptionnel, l'hôtel Saint Denis propose ses chambres tout confort avec douche ou bain, téléphone, wc, vue sur la mer. Merveilleusement situé près de la rivière et de la forêt. Vue panoramique sur le golfe, entouré de montagnes. Le confort et le calme ensoleillé, des véritables vacances, piscine, tennis.

Hôtel-restaurant les Pinsons

Ouvert toute l'année   20 chambres de 60 € à 160 €
Petit déjeuner 7,30 €   Menus 30 €, 35 € et 50 €
Près des volcans d'Auvergne, l'hôtel-restaurant les Pinsons propose dans un cadre calme des chambres confortables et ensoleillées, en face d'un bois. Son restaurant vous propose une cuisine diététique gourmande et régionale. Nos équipements sont nombreux: piscine, mini-golf, grand jardin, parking privé.

2 Ecouter

Listen to two people at a hotel reception and note down in English their requirements and/or problems.

Grammaire

- **Reflexive verbs**

  Reflexive verbs are used with an extra pronoun, e.g. **se laver**, **se promener**, etc. The pronoun changes with each person.

se laver	se promener
(to get washed/to wash oneself)	(to go for a walk)
je **me** lave	je **me** promène
tu **te** laves	tu **te** promènes
il **se** lave	il **se** promène
nous **nous** lavons	nous **nous** promenons
vous **vous** lavez	vous **vous** promenez
ils **se** lavent	ils **se** promènent

- **Reflexive verbs in a negative sentence**

  In a negative sentence, the reflexive pronouns (**me**, **te**, **se**, etc.) are placed immediately in front of the verb Eg. **Je ne <u>me</u> lave pas**.

- **Reflexive verbs with the near future**

  In the case of the near future (**aller** + infinitive Eg. **Je vais manger** = I am going to eat), the reflexive pronoun is always placed in front of the verb in the infinitive. Eg. **Je vais <u>me</u> réveiller à 2 heures**. Note that in this case, the pronoun changes depending on the person, Eg. **Tu vas te réveiller à 2 heures**.

  Note the negative form : **Je ne vais pas <u>me</u> laver**. The reflexive pronoun is placed before the the verb and after the negation **ne…pas**.

- **Comparatives (adjectives)**

  To make a comparaison, you can use **plus** (more), **moins** (less) or **aussi** (as) before the adjective in a sentence. Eg. **Cet hôtel est plus beau, il est moins grand et il est aussi cher que l'autre hôtel.**
  When you want to compare two things you use **que** to introduce the second element. Eg. **Mon appartement est <u>plus</u> beau <u>que</u> ta maison.**

- *Il n'y a pas de …*

  When using **il y a** (there is/there are) Eg. **Il y a <u>une</u> piscine dans l'hôtel** in a negative sentence, **un/une/des** becomes **de**. Eg. **Il n'y a pas <u>de</u> piscine dans l'hôtel**.

Exercices de grammaire

Reflexive verbs

1 Fill in the gaps in the text with the appropriate pronoun. (Note: **se baigner** = to swim/bathe, **se fatiguer** = to get tired, **se coucher** = to go to bed.)

En vacances, je **a**_____ lève à dix heures du matin. Je **b**_____ lave avant de prendre mon petit déjeuner. Je vais à la piscine avec mon frère et nous **c**_____ baignons pendant une heure. Ensuite nous **d**_____ promenons près de la plage. En général, nous **e**_____ amusons bien. Ici le soleil **f**_____couche tard et les gens **g**_____ promènent jusqu'à minuit! Mon frère **h**_____ fatigue rapidement alors nous rentrons tôt à l'hôtel et nous **i**_____ couchons tout de suite.

2 Put the words in the following sentences in the appropriate order.

a nous/réveillons/ne/pas/avant/nous/dix heures.
b aujourd'hui/lèves/tôt/tu/te!
c ne/vous/habillez/pas/vous?
d promènent/se/elles/dans/le jardin.
e ne/elle/se/pas/douche/tous/les/matins.
f tôt/je/vais/réveiller/me/demain.

Comparatives

3 You have been looking at two houses in a holiday brochure and have made a few notes. Using the grid below, compare the two houses and write your answer in a full sentence. Note: + indicates **plus**, – indicates **moins**, = indicates **aussi**.

	maison 1	maison 2
E.g. petit salon	=	=

Dans la première maison, le salon est aussi petit que dans la deuxième maison.

		maison 1	maison 2
a	agréable		+
b	cuisine spacieuse	–	
c	salle de bains moderne	=	=
d	jardin pratique	+	
e	tranquille		–
f	grandes chambres		+

Il n'y a pas de ...

4 Fill in the gaps.

Dans ma maison, il y a **a**_____ petite chambre mais il n'y a pas **b**_____ salon. Dans la cuisine il y a **c**_____ grande table. Dans le bureau de mon frère il n'y a pas **d**_____ table. A l'extérieur, il n'y a pas **e**_____ jardin mais il y a **f**_____ piscine.

73

Vocabulaire

L'hôtel/Hotels

l'armoire (f)	wardrobe
l'ascenseur (m)	lift
à votre disposition	available
la carte	card
cassé	broken
la chambre	bedroom
le chauffage	heating
le chèque de voyage	traveller's cheque
commander	to order
la devise	currency
la douche	shower
la direction	management
l'interrupteur (m)	switch
la fenêtre	window
le lit	bed
la nuit	night
l'objet (m) de valeur	valuable
l'eau (f) chaude	hot water
l'étage (m)	floor
l'oreiller (m)	pillow
le parking	car park
la réservation	booking
le réveil automatique	early morning call
la salle de bains	bathroom
le téléphone	telephone
la serviette	towel
télévision par satellite	satellite television
la veille	the day before

Verbes pronominaux/Reflexive verbs

s'amuser	to have fun
se coucher	to go to bed
se doucher	to shower
se lever	to get up
se laver	to get washed
se réveiller	to wake up
se promener	to go for a walk
se plaindre	to complain

Mois et saisons/Months and seasons

la haute saison	high season
la demi saison	mid season
la basse saison	low season
l'automne (m)	autumn
l'été (m)	summer
l'hiver (m)	winter
le printemps (m)	spring
janvier	January
février	February
mars	March
avril	April
mai	May
juin	June
juillet	July
août	August
septembre	September
octobre	October
novembre	November
décembre	December

Maison/Home

la baignoire	bath
beau	beautiful
la campagne	countryside
le canapé-lit	sofa bed
la cheminée	fireplace
celui-ci/celui-là	this one/that one
la commode	chest of drawers
la cuisine	kitchen
la cuisinière	cooker
l'évier (m)	sink
la fermeture annuelle	annual closure
il y a	there is/are
intéressant	interesting
le lave-linge	washing machine
le lave-vaisselle	dishwasher
lequel?	which one?
le meuble	cabinet
petit	small
plus/moins/aussi	more/less/as
le réfrigérateur	fridge
le relax	garden lounger
le rez-de-chaussée	ground floor
la salle de séjour	living room
le salon de jardin	garden table/chairs

Travail en paires

1 You are booking a hotel room for your family. Create a dialogue with your partner using the prompts below. You begin.

– Say that you would like to book a room for two people and a baby (**un bébé**).
– Say that you want it for two nights.
– Explain that you would like a room with a double bed and a cot (**lit enfant**) and ask if there is a room with a bathroom.
– Ask how much it is.
– Say that you'll take it.
– Spell your name and ask if there is a car park in the hotel.
– Repeat the instructions to check that you have understood.
– Ask if breakfast is served in your room and at what time.
– Say thank you.

2 The owner of the **gîte** where you are staying on holiday has just popped in to see if all is well. Unfortunately, you have had a few problems. Tell him/her about them using the list below and listen to his/her excuses.

(Note: **une erreur** = mistake,   **brancher** = plug in,   **couvertures** = covers/blankets, **changer** = change,   **désolé** = sorry.)

a The swimming pool is smaller than the swimming pool in the brochure!

b The television does not work, there is no satellite!

c The heating does not work and there are no blankets in the bedrooms!

d The window in the kitchen is broken.

e You would like to change **gîte**.

Travail en paires

1 You are the hotel receptionist and a client is making a booking. Use the prompts below to create a dialogue with your partner. Your partner will begin.

 – Ask for how many nights.
 – Ask if they want double or single beds. (cot = **lit enfant**)
 – Say that you have a room with shower.
 – Say that it costs 80 € per night.
 – Ask in what name the booking is under.
 – Say that the car park is on the left behind the hotel.
 – Explain that breakfast is served in the restaurant between 8 a.m. and 10 a.m.
 – Finish the conversation saying "you are welcome".

2 You are the owner of a **gîte**. You have just popped in to see if your new tenants are happy. Unfortunately, they have had a few problems. Listen to their complaints and use the following instructions to reassure them.

(Note: **une erreur** = mistake   **brancher** = plug in   **couvertures** = covers
changer = change   **désolé** = sorry).

Start by apologising

a There is a mistake in the brochure.

b You need to plug in the satellite.

c The blankets are in the wardrobe in the third bedroom on the second floor. There is no heating in the **gîte** in the summer.

d Explain that you are going to look at the window.

7 Au restaurant

When you have completed this unit, you will be able to get through to someone on the telephone, arrange to meet someone, describe physical appearances and order a meal in a restaurant.

Jane est là?

1 Lire et écouter

Listen to the following short exchanges on the telephone and work out how to say the key telephone phrases given below.

a
– Oui, allô.
– Je voudrais parler à Mohammed, s'il vous plaît.
– Oui, c'est moi.
– Salut Mohammed, c'est Sandeep…

b
– Allô.
– Je pourrais parler à Janella, s'il vous plaît?
– Oui, ne quittez pas, je vous la passe.

c
– Allô.
– Je peux parler à Billy, s'il vous plaît?
– Désolé, il n'est pas là.
– Il pourrait me rappeler? C'est Lucy.
– D'accord, je vais le lui dire.

d
– Allô.
– Pourrais-je parler à Ingrid, s'il vous plaît?
– Désolé, elle n'est pas là. Vous voulez lui laisser un message?
– Non, je vais rappeler plus tard.

a Could I speak to…

b He isn't here.

c I would like to speak to…

d Hold on.

e I'll pass you over to her.

f I'll call back later.

g Would you like to leave her a message?

h Could he call me back?

i Speaking.

j I'll tell him.

Je pourrais parler à…/pourrais-je parler à … Je vais le lui dire.
Il pourrait me rappeler? Vous voulez lui laisser un message?

2 Ecouter

Listen to two short exchanges where someone is trying to get through on the telephone and fill in the gaps.

1 – Allô, oui.
   – Salut Janine, c'est Bernard.
   – Ah non, ce n'est pas Janine, c'est Isabelle!
   – Oh pardon, je **a**_____?
   – Elle n'est pas ici.
   – Je **b**_____ un message?
   – Bien sûr.

2 – Allô.
   – **a**_____ parler à Etienne, s'il vous plaît? C'est Pierre.
   – Je suis désolé, il **b**_____.
   – Ah bon, il **c**_____ rappeler?
   – Oui bien sûr, je vais **d**_____ dire.
   – Merci, au revoir.
   – Au revoir.

Ça te dirait?

3 Ecouter

Listen to a telephone conversation between two friends organising a night out and then answer the questions below.

a What does Sandrine suggest doing?
b What is her plan?
c How are they going to get in touch with Raphaël and Pierre?
d What arrangements are made? Give three details.

ça te dit/dirait de	j'ai besoin de	j'ai envie de
on pourrait aller	on se retrouve	on se voit

grammaire

Vous voulez parler <u>à Bernard</u>?	Oui, je voudrais <u>lui parler</u>.
Vous voulez laisser un message <u>à Pierre et Isabelle?</u>	Oui, je voudrais <u>leur laisser</u> un message.

Il est comment?

a

Il est grand et gros
et il a des cheveux
bruns et courts.
Il a des yeux bleus
et il porte des lunettes.
Il a une barbe
et une moustache.

b

Elle est petite et mince et
elle a des cheveux
blonds et longs.
Elle a des yeux verts
et des taches de
rousseur. Elle porte
des boucles d'oreilles.

 4 Ecouter

Sandrine phones Agnès back to get a description of Raphaël and Pierre as she has not met either of them before. Listen to their telephone conversation and write down a description of both Raphaël and Pierre.

 5 Ecouter et écrire

Listen to a dialogue between two friends in a university coffee bar and fill in the gaps.

Audrey   Salut Laurent, ça va?
Laurent   Ah, salut Audrey, ça va bien merci. Et toi?
Audrey   Bien, bien aussi. Tu **a**_____ un café?
Laurent   Euh... j'ai un **b**_____ de math à dix heures.
Audrey   Oh, ça va, il est dix heures moins le **c**_____. Tu as **d**_____
          un quart d'heure. C'est qui ton prof de maths?
Laurent   Fabien Lecomte. Tu le **e**_____?
Audrey   Non, je ne crois pas. Il est **f**_____?
Laurent   Euh... il est **g**_____ et il a des **h**_____ noirs et **i**_____.
          Il a une **j**_____ aussi.
Audrey   Et ses **k**_____?
Laurent   Alors ça, je ne sais pas!

 6 Ecrire et parler

Working in groups of three or four, everyone should write down a description of someone in the group. Include details of physical build, colour of hair and eyes and any distinguishing features. Swap the descriptions around and then read them out loud guessing who is being described.

7 Au restaurant

Tu as faim?

 7 Ecouter et lire

Look at the menu from a restaurant called "La Bonne Fourchette" and then listen to two people ordering a meal. Note down the following information:

a What each person orders for starter, main course and dessert, including any drinks.

b Note down what the French for "dish of the day" is.

"La Bonne Fourchette"

Entrée du jour *ou*
12 escargots *ou*
Assiette de crudités *ou*

Plat du jour *ou*
Plat végétarien *ou*
Truite aux amandes

Fromage *ou*
Corbeille de fruits *ou*
Coupe glacée (3 boules)

> *comme entrée/plat principal/dessert*
> *un steak saignant/à point/bien cuit*
> *Qu'est-ce que c'est, le plat du jour?*

 8 Ecouter, lire et écrire

Listen to the dialogue again and write down what the meat , fish and vegetarian options are and fill in the grid below.

9 Ecouter

Listen to a dialogue between two people in a restaurant and then say whether the statements below are true or false. (Note: **surtout** = especially; **copieux** = the dish is filling.)

a Le steak est délicieux, surtout la sauce.

b Joseph pense que la sauce est bonne.

c Le plat végétarien n'est pas très bon.

d Le plat végétarien est trop copieux.

e Sophie veut commander encore du vin.

f Joseph a soif, alors il commande de l'eau minérale.

| j'ai faim | j'ai soif |

grammaire

J'<u>en</u> prends deux   Tu <u>en</u> veux?   Il n'y <u>en</u> a plus.

10 Lire et écouter

After reading the transcript of a conversation in a restaurant, listen to the recording and correct the deliberate mistakes in the transcript. (There are seven of them.)

– Monsieur, je peux commander, s'il vous plaît?
– Oui, madame. Qu'est-ce que vous prenez?
– Comme entrée je vais prendre la salade verte et comme plat principal je prends le steak-frites.
– Et votre steak, vous le voulez comment?
– A point, s'il vous plaît.
– Et comme dessert?
– Le gâteau.
– Avec crème?
– Sans crème, s'il vous plaît. Je suis allergique à la crème.
– Très bien, je vais le noter. Et comme boisson?
– Je prends un verre de vin blanc et une bouteille d'eau minérale, s'il vous plaît.
– Et un café?
– Oui, je voudrais bien un café avec mon dessert, s'il vous plaît.

Je suis allergique à la crème.

11 Lire et traduire

Match the following phrases with their English equivalent.

a Qu'est-ce que c'est, le plat du jour? **1** I'll take two.

b Pourrais-je avoir le steak saignant? **2** There isn't any left.

c On prend encore une bouteille? **3** What is the "Dish of the Day"?

d J'en prends deux. **4** Shall we have another bottle?

e Je ne prends pas de dessert. **5** Could I have my steak rare?

f Tu as faim? **6** Would you like some?

g Vous en voulez? **7** I'm not going to have dessert.

h Il n'y en a plus. **8** Are you hungry?

12 Jeu de rôle

Working with a partner and using the menu below, play the role of waiter and customer. Order a complete meal (starter, main course and dessert). Remember to order drinks! Make sure that you swap roles. (Note: **tarte tatin** = apple tart with caramel topping).

Menu à 55 €

Soupe de poisson *ou*
Pâté et salade *ou*
Assiette de crudités

Steak-frites *ou*
Quiche végétarienne *ou*
Poulet sauce tomate

Fromage *ou*
Tarte tatin *ou*
Pâtisserie maison

Café

Extra!

 1 Ecouter

Take down the details of a message left on an answering machine. Note down the following:

a Who is calling and who the message is being left for.

b The time, place and venue of where they will meet.

c Details of the plans for the evening.

 **2 Lire**

Read the following e-mail and answer the questions below. (Note: **ensemble** = together, **se faire bronzer** = to sunbathe.)

> Marie-Claire,
>
> Merci pour ton e-mail... J'espère que tout va bien et que tu es en forme.
>
> Alors ... quoi de neuf? Moi, j'ai un nouveau copain! Il s'appelle Jacques et il a vingt-huit ans. Il est étudiant mais on travaille ensemble au supermarché le samedi. Je le connais depuis quelques mois mais on sort ensemble depuis deux semaines. Je le trouve très sympa et beau aussi! Il est assez grand, je crois qu'il fait un mètre quatre-vingt. Je suis contente parce que je suis grande aussi! Il a des cheveux noirs et bouclés et des yeux bleus. Il est très sportif, il joue au tennis au moins trois fois par semaine. Comme tu le sais, je ne fais pas trop de sport, mais je vais peut-être commencer!! Si tout va bien, on va partir en vacances ensemble cet été. On voudrait faire du camping dans le sud-ouest de la France. Jacques veut faire de la planche à voile, mais moi, je vais me faire bronzer!
>
> A bientôt j'espère.
>
> Gros bisous
>
> Stéphanie

a What news does Stéphanie have to tell Marie-Claire?

b Give a physical description of Jacques. Include at least three points.

c How long have they been together?

d Where are they planning to go for the summer holidays?

e What are each of them planning to do on holiday?

Grammaire

- **The use of the conditional to be more polite**
  The conditional form of **je peux (je pourrais)** and **je veux (je voudrais)** denotes the meaning "could/would" and is used to be more polite.

  Je <u>veux/peux</u> parler à … > Je <u>voudrais/pourrais</u> parler à …
  Il <u>peut</u> me rappeler? > Il <u>pourrait</u> me rappeler?
  Vous <u>pouvez</u> lui laisser un message? > Vous <u>pourriez</u> lui laisser un message?

- **Object pronouns *lui* and *leur***
  The object pronoun ***lui*** is used to denote both 'to him' or 'to her'. It is used to replace the person who is being referred to and is a generic term for both male and female. It is used when verbs are followed with the preposition *à*, e.g. **dire, parler, téléphoner, laisser, donner.**

  Tu téléphones à <u>Ingrid?</u> > Oui, je <u>lui</u> téléphone.
  Il va téléphoner à <u>Annie?</u> > Oui, il va <u>lui</u> téléphoner.

- **Leur** is the plural object pronoun and is used to denote "to them". It is a generic term used for both male and female.

  Elle parle <u>à Sophie et Bernadette?</u> > Oui, elle <u>leur</u> parle.

  Notice that **lui** and **leur** go in front of the verb in the infinitive when used with the near future tense.

  Vous allez laisser un message à <u>Pierre et Astrid?</u> > Oui, je vais <u>leur</u> laisser un message.

- **The use of *on***
  On is commonly used in conversation and is used to replace the first person plural ***nous***. It is conjugated as the third person singular, i.e. the same form as for ***il*** and ***elle***.

  <u>Nous</u> pouvons aller au café. > <u>On</u> peut aller au café.
  <u>Nous</u> allons au cinéma? > <u>On</u> va au cinéma?

- **The use of E*n***
  En is another pronoun, used to replace a noun when a quantity is mentioned. E.g.
  Vous avez <u>des</u> enfants? Oui, j'<u>en</u> ai trois. (but: **Vous aimez <u>les</u> enfants?**
  Oui, je <u>les</u> aime.)

  Tu veux du pain? > Oui, j'<u>en</u> veux.
  Il n'y a plus de vin. > On <u>en</u> prend encore.
  Vous allez prendre des pommes? > Oui, je vais <u>en</u> prendre trois.
  Je voudrais une cigarette > Désolé, il n'y <u>en</u> a plus.

Exercices de grammaire

The use of the conditional to be more polite

1 Make the following requests/suggestions more polite

E.g. **Je peux parler à Solange? > Je pourrais parler à Solange, s'il vous plaît?**

a Je veux parler à Monique.
b On peut aller au cinéma.
c Elle veut un apéritif?
d Il peut venir à la fin de cette semaine.
e Je peux utiliser le téléphone?

Object pronouns *lui* and *leur*

2 Insert the object pronoun **lui** or **leur** into the following sentences to replace the nouns that are underlined.

E.g. **Vous parlez <u>à Annie</u> > Oui, je <u>lui</u> parle.**

a Tu vas téléphoner <u>à ta mère.</u>
b Ils vont parler <u>à Jacques et Françoise?</u>
c Elle va dire quelque chose <u>à Mélanie.</u>
d Vous donnez de l'argent <u>à Henri?</u>
e Elles vont donner des bonbons <u>aux enfants</u>?

The use of *on*

3 Make the following text more informal using **on** instead of **nous**. Remember to change the form of the verb.

Le weekend nous aimons sortir. Souvent nous allons au restaurant parce que nous adorons la cuisine française. Après nous allons au cinéma ou en boîte ou bien nous rentrons à la maison pour regarder la télévision. Le dimanche matin nous faisons du sport, nous jouons au tennis ou au ping-pong.

The use of *en*

4 Answer the following questions using the pronoun **en**, and using the (+) or (–) signs as indicators.

E.g. **Il y a du café? (+) Oui, il y *en* a.**

a Vous prenez un dessert? (+)
b Ils ont des enfants? (–)
c Elle a des amis français? (+)
d Tu veux du chocolat? (–)
e Il mange de la viande? (+)
f Il y a du vin? (–)

Vocabulaire

Parler à quelqu'un au téléphone/Getting through to someone on the telephone

Je voudrais parler à…	I'd like to speak to…
Pourrais-je parler à…	Could I speak to…
Etienne est là?	Is Etienne there?
C'est moi.	Speaking.
Ne quittez pas.	Hold on.
Je vous le/la passe.	I'll pass you over.
Désolé, il/elle n'est pas là.	Sorry, s/he isn't here.
Pourrais-je lui laisser un message?	Could you leave him/her a message?
Je vais rappeler plus tard.	I'll ring back later.
Il/elle pourrait me rappeler?	Could s/he ring me back?
Je vais le lui dire.	I'll tell him/her.

Sortir/Making arrangements to go out

Ça te dit/dirait de …	Would you like to/do you fancy …
J'ai envie de …	I'd really like to/I fancy …
J'ai besoin de …	I need to …
On se retrouve à …	Let's meet at …
On peut …	We can …
On pourrait …	We could …
On se voit à …	See you at …

Décrire une personne/Describing someone

décrire	to describe
des cheveux: noirs/bruns/blonds/roux/longs/courts	black/brown/blonde/red/long/short hair
des yeux: verts/bleus/marron	green/blue/brown eyes
des taches (f) de rousseur	freckles
la moustache/la barbe	moustache/beard
des lunettes/des boucles d'oreilles	glasses/earrings
grand(e)/petit(e)/mince/gros(se)	big/small/slim/fat

Sortir au restaurant/Eating out

le menu	the menu
comme entrée/plat principal/dessert	for starter/main course/dessert
commander	to order
l'entrée/le plat du jour	starter/dish of the day
la viande/le poulet/le steak/les escargots (m)	meat/chicken/steak/snails
le poisson/la truite	fish/trout
végétarien	vegetarian
la pâtisserie/le gâteau	pastries/cake
la glace à la vanille/au chocolat/boule	vanilla/chocolate ice cream/scoop
saignant/à point/bien cuit	rare/medium/well done (steak)
Qu'est-ce que c'est?	What is it?
je suis allergique à	I am allergic to
l'addition (f)	the bill
avoir faim/soif	to be hungry/thirsty
encore	more

Travail en paires

1 You are trying to arrange a night out. Phone a friend and use the following information in the dialogue. Your friend will speak first.

- Say hello and ask to speak to X. Introduce yourself.
- Ask how s/he is.
- Ask if s/he wants to go out at the weekend.
- Suggest going to the cinema.
- Ask if s/he is free on Saturday evening.
- Suggest meeting outside the station at 7:30 p.m.
- Finish the conversation appropriately.

2 Use the information below to order a meal in a restaurant. Your partner is the waiter/waitress and will start the conversation. (Note: **champignons** = mushrooms).

- Ask for the menu.
- When asked, order a starter. Find out what the dish of the day is. Say that you are allergic to fish. Choose the steak.
- Say that you will have the pepper sauce.
- Say you would like the steak well done.
- Order the strawberry tart for dessert and order a glass of white wine.
- When asked, you would like a coffee after your dessert.

Saucisson sec *ou*
Salade de tomates et avocat

Plat du jour *ou*
Steak sauce au choix *ou*
Omelette aux champignons

Fromage *ou*
Fruits *ou*
Tarte aux fraises

Choix de vin rouge, blanc et rosé

Café

Travail en paires

1 You receive a phone call. Use the following information in the dialogue. You start.

- The phone rings. Say hello.
- It is a friend. Greet him/her.
- Say you are fine.
- S/he suggests a night out. Say it is a good idea and that you would like to see a film.
- Say you are free on Saturday evening. Ask what time and where.
- Confirm the time and place.
- Finish the conversation appropriately.

2 You are a restaurant waiter. Use the information below to create a dialogue with your partner who is the customer. You start the dialogue. (Note: **champignons** = mushrooms).

- Say good evening to the customer.
- Ask which starter the customer would like.
- Say that the dish of the day is "Bouillabaise" – a fish soup.
- Choice of sauce for the steak: pepper, mushroom or tomato.
- Find out how the customer would like the steak cooked.
- Ask if s/he would like some wine.
- Ask if s/he would like a coffee with the dessert.

Saucisson sec *ou*
Salade de tomates et avocat

Plat du jour *ou*
Steak sauce au choix *ou*
Omelette aux champignons

Fromage *ou*
Fruits *ou*
Tarte aux fraises

Choix de vin rouge, blanc et rosé

Café

8 Vacances et Loisirs

When you have completed this unit, you will be able to: talk about what you have done at the weekend, explain why you are late, discuss your holidays, and describe places and the weather.

Qu'est-ce que tu as fait?

1 Ecouter, lire et observer

It is Monday morning, and two friends are telling each other about their weekend. Listen to their conversation and find out why Sylvie had an excellent weekend, and why Jeanne didn't. Then read the dialogue and underline all the verb forms in the past tense (they are each in two parts; the first example has been done for you, there are 16 others). Note: **sympa** = nice, friendly.

Jeanne	Tu <u>as passé</u> un bon week-end?
Sylvie	Oui, super! Samedi soir, j'ai vu Pierre; on a mangé dans un restaurant sympa et on a dansé toute la nuit. Dimanche, j'ai dormi tard, j'ai pris un bain et j'ai lu un bon livre: un week-end très relaxant, quoi!
Jeanne	Ah oui, c'est sympa!
Sylvie	Et toi, qu'est-ce que tu as fait?
Jeanne	Oh, moi … Samedi j'ai fait des courses, mais j'ai perdu mon portefeuille, j'ai dû aller à la police …
Sylvie	Non! Est-ce qu'ils l'ont retrouvé?
Jeanne	Non, malheureusement … Et dimanche, j'ai passé la journée chez mes parents; ils ont acheté une nouvelle voiture et …
Sylvie	Vous avez fait un tour à la campagne?
Jeanne	Non, ils ont préféré rester à la maison; nous avons regardé la télévision, c'est tout.
Sylvie	Ah bon.

2 Exercice

In pairs, work out the infinitive form of the verbs you have underlined (e.g. **as passé** > **passer**).

grammaire

j'	ai	passé	Regular verbs:		Irregular verbs:	
tu	as	passé	passer>	passé	faire >	<u>fait</u>
il/elle/on	a	passé	dorm<u>ir</u> >	dorm<u>i</u>	prendre >	pr<u>is</u>
nous	avons	passé	per<u>dre</u>>	perd<u>u</u>	lire >	l<u>u</u>
vous	avez	passé			voir >	v<u>u</u>
ils/elles	ont	passé			devoir >	d<u>û</u>

 3 Ecouter

a Listen to another conversation about weekend activities and answer the following questions (Note: **plein de** = lots of, **épicé** = spicy, hot.)

1 With whom did Elise spend the weekend?
2 What kind of 'cultural things' did they do together?
3 Why didn't Jean-Marc play tennis on Saturday?
4 Why did he sleep all day on Sunday?

b Listen to the dialogue again and fill in the gaps in the summaries below.

Elise   J'**a**_____ plein de choses avec ma copine anglaise; on **b**_____ des musées, on **c**_____ une pièce de théâtre et un film.

Jean-Marc   J'**d**_____ma dissertation samedi. Le soir, j'**e**_____des amis à dîner. Ma copine Isabelle **f**_____ un plat indien très épicé. On **g**_____plein de bière et on **h**_____ toute la journée dimanche.

grammaire

Tu as <u>joué</u> au tennis?   Non, je **n'**ai **pas** <u>joué</u> au tennis.

4 Ecrire

Re-write the summaries above using the third person (i.e. **<u>Elise a fait</u> plein de choses avec sa copine anglaise, <u>elles ont visité</u>…**).

5 Parler

With a partner, practise asking and answering (in full sentences) whether or not you did the following activities last weekend. (E.g. **Tu as mangé au restaurant? > Oui, j'ai mangé au restaurant. / Non, je n'ai pas mangé au restaurant.**)

a manger au restaurant   **e** faire des courses
b danser   **f** faire du sport
c regarder la télé   **g** voir une pièce de théâtre ou un film
d travailler   **h** lire un livre

Désolé, je suis en retard...

6 Ecouter

Listen to five people apologising for being late and match their excuses with those in the list below.

a Problem with car.

b Bus was late.

c Lost track of time.

d Lost the address.

e Unfinished work.

> Qu'est-ce qui s'est passé?
> Pardon / Je suis désolé(e), j'ai perdu...
> j'ai eu un problème avec...
> je n'ai pas fini...
> je n'ai pas vu...
> j'ai dû retourner...
> Ce n'est pas grave. / Ça ne fait rien.

7 Lire et écouter

Daniel rings his friend Luc to apologise for not having come to his party. Read the dialogue and re-order the sentences. Then listen to the recording to check for the correct order. (Note: **je n'ai pas pu** = I couldn't, **les flics** = coll. for the police.)

a Ah bon! C'est grave?

b Je suis vraiment désolé, je n'ai pas pu venir hier soir parce que j'ai eu plein de problèmes!

c Allô?

d Ah, Daniel! Eh bien, qu'est-ce qui s'est passé, mon vieux?

e Eh bien, j'ai pris la voiture de mes parents et ... j'ai eu un accident.

f Oh, la voiture ... mon père est furieux!

g Non, mais j'ai dû aller chez les flics; j'ai oublié de te téléphoner, excuse-moi!

h Ah bon, qu'est-ce qui s'est passé?

i Salut Luc, c'est Daniel.

j Je comprends ... et la voiture?

8 Ecouter

Listen to a similar conversation between two friends and note down all the excuses given.

9 Traduire

Using the dialogues in exercises 7 and 8 as models, translate the following.
a I couldn't come to the party (**la soirée**); **b** because I met (**rencontrer**) an old friend in the street; **c** he suggested (**proposer de**) going to the pub; **d** we had a lot to drink; **e** I lost track of time; **f** I missed (**rater**) the last bus.

Gros bisous de Nice

10 Lire

> Salut Marcel!
> Nice est super! C'est une jolie ville,
> très animée; il y a plein de cafés et
> de restos sympas. Axèle connaît
> bien, elle a de la famille ici. Nous
> sommes arrivées hier. Ce matin, je
> suis allée à la plage mais je n'ai pas
> nagé: l'eau est trop froide!
>
> Gros bisous,
> *Laurence*

> Marcel Duchêne
> 16 rue Charcot
> 75013 Paris

Read the holiday postcard above and indicate whether the following statements are true or false.

a Laurence is holidaying on her own.

b She has just started her holiday.

c She likes Nice because it is very quiet.

d She has family there.

e She went swimming in the morning.

grammaire

je **suis** all**ée**   nous **sommes** arriv**ées**

C'est une jolie ville / une ville animée.
Il y a plein de cafés / de restaurants.

11 Parler

With a partner, tell each other about the cities you have been to and explain what they are like. You may want to use some of the following adjectives:
super, cool, sympa – nul(le) / moderne – ancien(ne), pittoresque / animé(e) – calme, tranquille / (pas) très joli(e), beau (belle) / propre – sale, pollué(e)

12 Ecouter

Listen to two friends telling each other about their holiday and fill in the gaps in the dialogue below. (Note: **pas vraiment** = not really, **rentrer** = to go/come back home.)

– Tu es parti, pendant les **a**_____ de Pâques?

– Oui, je **b**_____ allé en Irlande.

– En Irlande! **c**_____? A Dublin?

– Non, à la campagne, dans le sud-ouest.

– Super! Pendant **d**_____ de temps?

– Pendant une **e**_____.

– Il a fait beau?

– Oh, pas vraiment, mais il n'a pas fait froid. On a fait des **f**_____ fantastiques! Et toi, tu es parti?

– Oui, je suis **g**_____ à la mer, en Bretagne. J'ai **h**_____ de la planche à voile pendant deux semaines. Il a fait un temps magnifique!

– Oui, tu es tout bronzé! **i**_____ est-ce que tu es rentré?

– Eh bien, dimanche… il y a **j**_____ jours.

grammaire			
je **suis** parti(e)	nous **sommes** parti(e)s	<u>Pendant</u> combien de temps?	
tu **es** parti(e)	vous **êtes** parti(e)s	<u>Pendant</u> une semaine.	
il **est** parti	ils **sont** partis		
elle **est** partie	elles **sont** parties	<u>Quand?</u>/<u>Il y a</u> combien de temps?	
		<u>Il y a</u> trois jours.	

les vacances de Noël / de Pâques / d'été	il a fait beau / mauvais
à la mer / à la campagne / à la montagne	il a fait chaud / froid
le nord / le sud / l'est / l'ouest	

13 Ecouter

Listen to more people talking about their holiday and note down: where they have been, for how long, what the weather was like and the activities they did. (Note: **la plage** = beach.)

a Benoît:

b Sarah et Michel:

14 Jeu de rôle

With a partner, interview each other about your last holiday (where, when, for how long, weather, activities …).

Il pleut dans le nord-est

 15 Ecouter

Listen to a weather report describing what the weather is like in different regions of France, and match the symbols with the expressions.

a 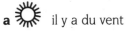 il y a du vent

b il pleut

c il y a du brouillard

d il y a du soleil

e il neige

f il y a de l'orage

g il y a des nuages

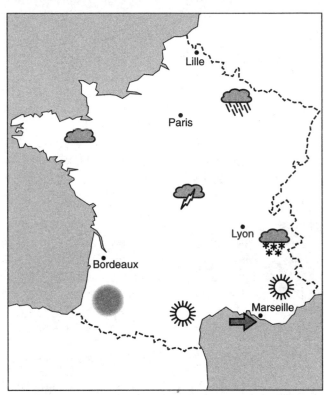

 16 Ecouter

Listen to Pierre explaining what the weather is like in Quebec in different seasons, and fill in the grid below.

a hiver	b printemps	c été	d automne

17 Parler

With a partner, describe the typical weather for the different seasons in the region/country you come from (e.g. **En hiver, il ne fait pas froid mais il pleut beaucoup; etc.**)

 94

Extra!

 1 Ecouter

Listen to four students describing their weekend and write down all the details mentioned.

a Muriel:

b Stéphane:

c Loulou:

d Bernard:

 **2 Lire**

Alain has just come back from holiday and writes a letter to his English friend Dennis. Read the letter and answer the questions below. (Note: **une balade** = **une promenade**; **la varappe** = rock-climbing.)

Cher Dennis,

Comment ça va? Tu as passé un bon été? Moi, j'ai passé de super vacances dans les Alpes! Je suis parti pendant trois semaines avec deux copains, Xavier et Eric. On a pris nos vélos et on a fait des balades fantastiques: dures, mais on a vu des paysages magnifiques! En fait, on a plus ou moins suivi la route du Tour de France. (Tu connais le Tour de France? C'est une course cycliste qui se passe chaque année.) En plus, il a fait un temps idéal: beau, mais pas trop chaud, avec quelques nuages... On a pu nager dans des petits lacs et on a même fait un peu de varappe! On a bien mangé, aussi: on a découvert des petits restos de campagne avec de la cuisine traditionnelle, et vraiment pas chers! Je suis rentré tout à fait en forme. J'ai complètement oublié les cours et les examens! Malheureusement, j'ai dû retourner travailler au bureau de mon père: je n'ai plus d'argent! J'espère que tu es en forme, toi aussi.

A bientôt,

Alain

a Where did Alain go? For how long?
b What did he do there? What was it like?
c Why does he mention the 'Tour de France'?
d What was the weather like?
e What was the food like?
f How does he feel now?
g How is he spending the rest of his holiday? Why?

Grammaire

● **Verbs: perfect tense**

a <u>Use:</u> the perfect tense is the most common of the past tenses; it is used to report events
(e.g. **Il <u>a perdu</u> son passeport! / Nous <u>sommes partis</u> pendant un mois.**)

b <u>Form:</u> as its French name ('passé composé') implies, it is made up of two parts:

the 'auxiliary' verb: **avoir**, or sometimes **être**, in the present tense

+

the 'past participle' of the verb

c <u>Past participle:</u> the past participle of regular verbs is formed as follows:
-er verbs: **-é** (e.g. **regard<u>é</u>**)   **-ir** verbs: **-i** (e.g. **fin<u>i</u>**)   **-re** verbs: **-u** (e.g. **vend<u>u</u>**)

There are also many irregular forms. Here are some of them:

fai<u>re</u> > fai<u>t</u>	av<u>oir</u> > <u>eu</u>
prendre > pr<u>is</u>	dev<u>oir</u> > d<u>û</u>
li<u>re</u> > l<u>u</u>	pouv<u>oir</u> > p<u>u</u>
v<u>oir</u> > v<u>u</u>	

d <u>Verbs with **être**:</u> some verbs are formed with **être**, including:

aller (> allé)	**rentrer (> rentré)**
arriver (> arrivé)	**rester (> resté)**
partir (> parti)	

When the auxiliary **être** is used, the past participle must agree with the subject:

<u>je</u> (m) **suis allé**	–	<u>je</u> (f) **suis allé<u>e</u>**
<u>tu</u> (m) **es allé**	–	<u>tu</u> (f) **es allé<u>e</u>**
<u>il</u> **est allé**	–	<u>elle</u> **est allé<u>e</u>**
<u>on</u> (m) **est allé<u>s</u>**	–	<u>on</u> (f) **est allé<u>es</u>**
<u>nous</u> (m) **sommes allé<u>s</u>**	–	<u>nous</u> (f) **sommes allé<u>es</u>**
<u>vous</u> (m) **êtes allé<u>s</u>**	–	<u>vous</u> (f) **êtes allé<u>es</u>**
<u>ils</u> **sont allé<u>s</u>**	–	<u>elles</u> **sont allé<u>es</u>**

e <u>Negative:</u> **ne … pas** (or other negatives like **ne … plus**) go on either side of **avoir** or **être**:
e.g. **Il <u>n'</u>a <u>pas</u> fini sa dissertation. / Vous <u>n'</u>êtes <u>pas</u> parties en vacances?**

● *Pendant* **and** *il y a*

– **Pendant** (= for) is used to refer to a specific length of time in the past (but also in the
present and in the future):
e.g. **Tu es partie <u>pendant</u> combien de temps? <u>Pendant</u> six mois.**

– **Il y a** (= ago) is used to refer to a moment in the past:
e.g. **Il a fini quand? / Il a fini <u>il y a</u> combien de temps? <u>Il y a</u> deux heures.**

Exercices de grammaire

Verbs: perfect tense (*passé composé*)

1 Avoir or **être**? Fill in the gaps with the appropriate form of **avoir** or **être**.

a Nous _____ fini notre travail.

b Je _____ arrivée hier.

c Pierre _____ parti au Québec.

d Ils _____ passé un très bon week-end.

e Ses parents _____ restés en France.

f Tu _____ vu ce film?

2 Transform the verbs from the present into the perfect tense. (E.g. **Il <u>fait</u> beau.** > **Il <u>a fait</u> beau**.)

a Je fais de la planche à voile.

b Vous aimez ce film?

c Elles ne prennent pas l'avion.

d Mes amis restent ici pendant une semaine.

e Tu (*f*) vas en vacances?

f On doit partir à dix heures.

g Nous (*m*) rentrons le 20 juillet.

h Elle ne part pas aux Etats-Unis.

3 Fill in the gaps in the text by choosing the appropriate verbs from the list below and putting them in the perfect tense. (Note: **louer** = to rent, to hire.)

louer – voir – parler – décider – passer – adorer – faire – aller – rester

J'**a**_____ à Mira hier, elle **b**_____ de super vacances! Elle **c**_____ au Maroc avec son copain. Ils **d**_____ là pendant un mois. Ils **e**_____ une voiture et ils **f**_____ le tour du pays: ils **g**_____ des endroits magnifiques! Ils **h**_____ le pays et les gens, et ils **i**_____ d'y retourner l'année prochaine.

Pendant and *il y a*

4 Pendant or **il y a?** Fill in the gaps.

a Hier, elle a travaillé _____ des heures sur sa dissertation!

b Ils sont partis de la maison _____ dix minutes.

c Le film a duré _____ combien de temps?

d Nous sommes restés en suisse _____ deux semaines.

e Il est rentré _____ combien de temps?

f Quand êtes-vous allés à Nice? _____ un mois.

Vocabulaire

Verbes/Verbs

passer	to spend (time)
rester	to stay
rentrer	to come/go back home
louer	to rent, to hire
rencontrer	to meet
rater	to miss
oublier	to forget
perdre	to lose
attendre	to wait for
connaître	to know
suivre	to follow

Les vacances/Holidays

les vacances (f) de Noël	Christmas holidays
les vacances (f) de Pâques	Easter holidays
les vacances (f) d'été	Summer holidays
la plage	beach
la balade	walk
la varappe	rock-climbing
la soirée	party
plein de	lots of
épicé(e)	spicy
les flics (m)	cops, policemen

Décrire un endroit/Describing a place

sympa	nice, friendly
nul(le)	not nice (slang)
moderne	modern
ancien(ne)	old, ancient
pittoresque	picturesque
animé(e)	lively
calme, tranquille	quiet
joli(e)	pretty
propre	clean
sale	dirty
pollué(e)	polluted

la mer	sea, seaside
la montagne	mountain
la campagne	country(side)

le nord	north
le sud	south
l'est (m)	east
l'ouest (m)	west

Le temps/The weather

il fait	beau	the weather is	nice
	mauvais		bad
	chaud		hot, warm
	froid		cold

il y a	du soleil	it is	sunny
	des nuages (m)		cloudy
	du vent		windy
	de l'orage (m)		stormy
	du brouillard		foggy

il pleut	it rains/it is raining
il neige	it snows/it is snowing

pendant	for, during
il y a	ago (also: there is/are)
(pas) vraiment	(not) really

Travail en paires

1 It is Monday morning and you are discussing the weekend with a French student. Create a dialogue with your partner using the prompts below. You begin.

– Ask your partner if s/he had a good weekend.
– Find out what s/he did with her/his cousin.
– When requested, explain that you had to work all weekend, that you cleaned the house on Saturday and that you worked on your essay on Sunday.
– Say that you haven't finished your essay, that you still (**encore**) have a lot of work to do.
– Accept the suggestion to go for a coffee.

2 You have incomplete information about your friends' holidays. Find out from your partner the missing details and complete the grid below.

	Ali	**Carla**	**Denis et Francine**
Où? (pays/région/ville)	Tunisie		Provence
Pendant combien de temps?			2 semaines
Avec qui?	famille		
Comment? (moyen(s) de transport)	voiture + bateau	avion	
Où? (logement)		amie	camping
Quoi? (activités)		tourisme, mer	

Travail en paires

1 It is Monday morning and you are discussing the weekend with a French student. Create a dialogue with your partner using the prompts below. Your partner will begin.

– Explain that you had a good weekend, that your cousin is staying with you at the moment and that you did lots of things.
– Say that your cousin loves sport, and that you saw a football match on TV on Saturday, and played tennis on Sunday. Then, ask your partner what her/his weekend was like.
– Ask your partner if s/he has finished the essay.
– React appropriately and suggest going for a coffee before the lecture.

2 You have incomplete information about your friends' holidays. Find out from your partner the missing details and complete the grid below.

	Ali	**Carla**	**Denis et Francine**
Où? (pays/région/ville)		Rome	
Pendant combien de temps?	2 mois	2 semaines	
Avec qui?		seule	2 copains
Comment? (moyen(s) de transport)			train
Où? (logement)	famille + hôtel		
Quoi? (activités)	visites (famille, amis), mer		promenades, varappe

9 Education et expérience

When you have completed this unit, you will be able to talk about your background, your education and your professional life.

Depuis combien de temps ... ?

1 Ecouter

Leila is describing her hectic life as daughter of a diplomat. Listen to the dialogue and spot the deliberate mistakes in the text below. (There are of five of them).

Je suis née à Alger en 1990. J'ai habité en Algérie pendant quatre ans puis ma mère a obtenu un poste plus intéressant en Italie. Nous avons habité à Rome pendant huit mois et je suis allée à l'école française. Ma mère travaille en Espagne depuis 1999. J'ai déménagé en France pour faire mes études et je travaille à Angers depuis six mois.

> J'ai habité en Algérie <u>pendant</u> trois ans.   J'habite à Angers <u>depuis</u> six mois.

2 Exercice

Fill in the gaps in the following sentences using either **depuis** or **pendant**.

a Elle a étudié l'anglais _____ cinq ans.
b J'apprends l'espagnol _____ dix ans.
c Il a habité à Londres _____ dix ans.
d Nous vivons à Lyon _____ un an.

3 Ecrire

Based on the information below, write a short piece in French describing Mustapha's life. (Note: **être à la retraite** = to be retired.)

Past
Born / 1975.
Lived / Tunisia / 3 years with parents.
Moved to France / in 1978.
Parents worked / Marseilles / 10 years

Present
Father / retired
Family lives in Toulouse / 4 years.
Mustapha and brother / study English / 3 years.
Brother work / 6 months / computing company

4 Parler

Make a few notes about your life (i.e. lived in Switzerland for two years etc.) and with a partner practise describing your life using **pendant** and **depuis**.

9 Education et expérience

Je me suis inscrit ...

5 Lire

Charlotte is spending two months in England to improve her English. Read her e-mail to her friend Stéphanie and answer the questions in English. (Note: **se sentir à l'aise** = to feel at ease, **s'ennuyer** = to be bored, **se présenter** = to introduce oneself.)

```
Chère Stéphanie,
Me voici donc à Liverpool depuis deux semaines. C'est une ville fascinante,
il y a énormément de choses à faire et à voir. Je me suis sentie à l'aise
immédiatement ici. Je me suis installée dans ma chambre d'étudiante et je ne
me suis pas ennuyée une minute! D'abord, je me suis inscrite en cours
d'anglais au collège et j'ai commencé à apprendre le japonais! Il y a
tellement de cours intéressants ici. J'ai appris que Joseph Bardou, notre
vieux copain, habite ici. Je l'ai vu hier matin mais je ne me suis pas
présentée ... Voilà les nouvelles en quelques lignes. Je t'embrasse et à
bientôt.

Charlotte
```

a How long has she been in Liverpool?
b How does she feel about the place?
c What two subjects is she studying?
d When did she see Joseph?

6 Ecouter

a Patrick and Angéline have just passed their **Baccalauréat** (French equivalent of 'A' levels) and are in the process of enrolling in a higher education institution of their choice. Listen to the dialogue and tick which of the following verbs you hear. (Note: **un coup de fil** = a phone call.)

se présenter	se renseigner	remplir	s'installer
s'inscrire	s'ennuyer	devenir	réussir

b Listen to the recording again and note down the following information:
  i What course Patrick has enrolled on.
  ii What course Angéline is interested in.

grammaire

Je me **suis** installé(**e**)	Nous nous **sommes** installé(**e**)s
Tu t'**es** installé(**e**)	Vous vous **êtes** installé(**e**)s
Il s'**est** installé	Ils se **sont** installés
Elle s'**est** installé**e**	Elles se **sont** installé**es**

7 Ecrire et écouter

Fill in the gaps in the following letter and then listen to the recording to check your answers. (Note: **s'amuser** = to enjoy oneself, **pas encore** = not yet, **se sentir** = to feel.)

Chère Juliette,

Je suis donc à Bristol **a**_____ deux mois mais je ne me **b**_____ pas très à l'aise ici! Les étudiants dans mon groupe ne sont pas très sympas! Je me suis **c**_____ dans ma chambre mais je **d**_____ ennuie. J'ai commencé par visiter la ville et je me suis beaucoup amusée mais je **e**_____ ici depuis deux mois et je n'ai pas encore rencontré d'autres étudiants anglais! En plus, je ne comprends pas bien l'anglais. Ils parlent trop vite! Le mois dernier, je me suis **f**_____ en cours d'anglais au collège. J'ai vu d'autres étudiants français au café hier soir et je **g**_____ suis présentée. Je vais les retrouver ce soir!

Viens me voir bientôt. Je t'embrasse bien fort,

Daniella

grammaire

Je me suis <u>beaucoup</u> amusée.   Je ne me sens pas à l'aise.

8 Ecouter et écrire

a Listen to three students (Florence, Hugo and Beate) all of whom have recently moved to London. Find out the following information. (Note: **s'améliorer** = to improve, **se faire des amis** = to make friends.)

i How long each of them has been in London.
ii Where and with whom they live.
iii What they think of people in London.
iv Their impressions of London.

b Write a summary in French about each student.

9 Jeu de rôle

With a partner describe your background and specific events in your life using the language used in this unit and the previous one i.e. negatives, **pendant/depuis**. You may need to spend a bit of time with a dictionary preparing your statement.

Voici mon CV ...

10 Ecouter

Listen to Adeline describing her student life and state whether the following statements are true or false:

a She has been studying IT since 1999.
b She has been living in Paris for three years.
c She studied English for five years.
d Her parents moved to Italy two years ago.
e She goes and visits them every two months.

11 Lire

Read Adeline's curriculum vitæ and work out what the following are in French:

a surname **b** place of birth **c** 'A' levels **d** Degree **e** MA **f** distinction **g** IT skills **h** clerical worker **i** bilingual **j** work placement **k** date of birth **l** company

---

C.V.

Nom: Dubout
Prénom: Adeline
Adresse: 67 rue Lamarck 75018 Paris   *Téléphone:* 01 42 64 53 03
Date de naissance: 24 03 1977   *Lieu de naissance:* Bilbao
Nationalité: française

Diplômes

1995	Baccalauréat Economie (mention Très Bien)
1997	DEUG Administration Economique et Sociale
1998	Licence Administration Economique et Sociale
1999	Maîtrise Economie et Environnement

Expérience professionnelle

1995	Stage de trois mois à la Société Nestlé, Croydon, Angleterre
1996 –1998	Employée de bureau. Société d'Import-Export, Paris
1999 – à ce jour	Assistante. Conseil Economique et Social, Paris

Langues: Bilingue français-espagnol
              Anglais – parlé, lu et écrit

Connaissances en informatique: Excel, Quattro Pro, Power Point

---

12 Lire et écouter

Amanda and Sonia are talking about exams. With a partner, re-order the sentences and check the sequence by listening to the dialogue (Note: **se débrouiller** = to manage (well), **passer des examens** = to take exams, **réussir** = to pass, **une note** = a mark.)

a Mais c'est une très bonne note! Tu as de la chance. Moi, j'ai passé des examens la semaine dernière et je ne sais pas si je les ai réussis.

b Si, mais je ne me suis pas très bien débrouillée. J'ai eu 12 sur 20 seulement.

c Salut Amanda! Ça va?

d Non, je ne l'ai pas vue. Où est-elle?

e Bof! J'ai eu les résultats de mon examen de math ce matin.

f Cinq, la semaine dernière et trois avant.

g Combien d'examens est-ce que tu as passés?

h Est-ce que tu as vu la liste des résultats?

i Tu n'as pas réussi?

j D'accord.

k Dans le hall. On y va?

grammaire

Tu as réussi **tes examens**?   Non, je ne sais pas si je **les** ai réussi**s**.

Est-ce que tu as vu **la liste** des résultats?   Non, je ne **l'**ai pas vu**e**.

Combien d'**examens** est-ce que tu as passés?

 13 Ecrire

You are working for a recruitment agency and you have spoken to three candidates all looking for a job as an English language teacher in a summer school. You took some notes and your manager is asking you to write a short summary in French describing the experience of each candidate. Use the information below. (Note: **une mention** = a distinction, **formation d'enseignant(e)** = teacher training, **enseigner** = to teach.)

Candidate 1

Julia / from Birmingham / has degree in Italian literature / in 1997 enrolled on a teacher training course / passed with distinction / moved to London six months ago / has taught for two months.

Candidate 2

John / born in Manchester / got a Degree in English literature / spent five years in Europe / worked as barman and English teacher / worked in London as a teacher for two years.

Candidate 3

Carmen / bilingual Spanish-English / did a Master's Degree / enrolled on teacher training course last year / passed with distinction / has no teaching experience...

J'ai un entretien ...

14 Exercice

Match the sentences in French with their English equivalent.

a I have got an interview
b I did not pass my exam.
c We did a work placement.
d She has already worked in this area.

1 Je n'ai pas réussi mon examen.
2 Nous avons fait un stage.
3 Elle a déjà travaillé dans ce secteur.
4 J'ai un entretien.

15 Ecouter et écrire

Listen to a conversation between Odile and Samuel talking about a job interview and fill the gaps with the missing words. (Note: **passer un entretien** = to have an interview, **recevoir** = to receive.)

Samuel	Salut Odile, tu vas bien?
Odile	Très bien, merci. J'ai **a**_____ une lettre ce matin et je vais **b**_____ un entretien.
Samuel	Super! Pour quelle société?
Odile	C'est pour une société de marketing.
Samuel	Tu as déjà **c**_____ dans ce secteur?
Odile	Oui. Je travaille à mi-temps **d**_____ un an aux Galeries Lafayette à Paris. L'année dernière j'ai aussi fait un **e** _____ de trois mois chez Marks et Spencers à Londres.
Samuel	Tu as passé des examens de marketing?
Odile	Oui. Cet été, j'ai **f** _____ mon diplôme!
Samuel	Félicitations!
Odile	Merci, et toi? Tu as **g**_____ tes examens?
Samuel	J'ai **h**_____ un an à l'université. Je vais finir ma licence l'année prochaine.
Odile	En quoi?
Samuel	En **i**_____.
Odile	Et qu'est-ce que tu vas faire après?
Samuel	Je voudrais faire une **j**_____.
Odile	Et bien, **k**_____ chance!
Samuel	Et toi aussi pour ton entretien! Salut!

16 Parler

Imagine that you have an interview for a job. With a partner, describe your past working experience and your qualifications. State why you would like the job and why you think you are the best candidate.

Extra!

 1 Lire

Read the following covering letter for a job application and answer the questions below.

> le 31 juillet 2000
>
> Monsieur,
>
> Suite à votre annonce parue dans le Guardian International du 30 juillet 2000, je me permets de vous proposer ma candidature pour le poste de responsable de marketing. Je pense posséder toutes les qualifications et l'expérience requises.
>
> J'ai quitté l'Université de Warwick en 1997 avec une licence en études commerciales, avec mention très bien. En octobre 1997 j'ai passé un diplôme de marketing et je l'ai obtenu en été 1998. Au cours de mes études supérieures, je me suis spécialisé dans le secteur 'études de marchés' et j'ai fait un stage de six mois chez Nestlé à Vevey en Suisse. A l'université j'ai suivi un cours de français intensif pendant un an donc je parle couramment.
>
> Vous trouverez ci-joint mon curriculum vitae.
>
> En attendant une réponse, recevez Monsieur, l'expression de mes salutations distinguées.
>
> Joseph Brown

a What post is Joseph applying for?
b Give details of his qualifications.
c What specialist knowledge does he have?
d Give details of time spent abroad.
e What knowledge of foreign languages does he have?

 2 Ecouter

Listen to two people talking about their qualifications and work experience and fill in the grid below.

	Qualifications	Work experience	Knowledge of languages	IT skills
Man				
Woman				

Grammaire

- ### *Pendant* and *depuis*

  Pendant is used to describe how long something lasted (something which is finished).
  E.g. **J'ai habité à Londres pendant 3 ans**. (*I lived in London for three years but do not live there any more*). Note that the perfect tense is used.

  Depuis is used to describe something that has lasted and is still occuring.
  E.g. **J'habite à Londres depuis 3 ans**. (*I have lived in London for three years and I still live there*). Note that the present tense is used.

- ### Reflexive verbs in the perfect tense

  All reflexive verbs use **être** as auxiliary in the perfect tense. E.g. **se renseigner = il s'<u>est</u> renseigné.** Note: the past participle agrees with the subject of the verb.
  E.g. **je me suis renseigné(e)**
  　　　tu t'es renseigné(e)
  　　　il / elle s'est renseigné(e)
  　　　nous nous sommes renseigné(e)s
  　　　vous vous êtes renseigné(e)s
  　　　ils / elles se sont renseigné(e)s

  Note the word order with:

  – the negative:
  　　　Je <u>ne</u> me suis <u>pas</u> inscrit à l'université.
  　　　Elle <u>ne</u> s'est <u>plus</u> ennuyée.
  　　　Nous <u>ne</u> nous sommes <u>jamais</u> sentis à l'aise.

  – adverbs:
  　　　Je me suis <u>beaucoup</u> amusé en France.
  　　　Il s'est <u>assez</u> ennuyé à Paris.

- ### Object pronouns and the perfect tense

  With verbs using **avoir** as auxiliary in the perfect tense, there is no agreement with the subject. E.g.
  j'ai mangé　elle a mangé　　　　　nous avons mangé　elles ont mangé

  However, when the direct object is placed before the verb, the past participle must agree with the direct object. This can happen:

  – with pronouns (which go before the verb). E.g.
  Est-ce que tu as vu <u>Paul et Martin</u>?　Oui, je <u>les</u> ai vu<u>s</u> hier.
  Est-ce qu'il a contacté <u>l'entreprise</u>?　Oui, il <u>l'</u>a contacté<u>e</u> hier.

  – with questions, when there is an inversion. Eg.
  Combien d'<u>examens</u> as-tu passé<u>s</u>?

Exercices de grammaire

Pendant and *depuis*

1 Translate the following sentences into French:

   a I lived in Australia for three years.
   b They have been working in England for two months.
   c She studied English at school for five years.
   d They have been learning French for three months.
   e How long did you live there for?

Reflexive verbs in the perfect tense

2 The following outline information describes the lives of Claudia and Aziz when they were students. Use it to write a summary. (Note: **se mettre** = to begin.)

   a Claudia / s'inscrire / université / Paris / in 1998
   b Aziz / se renseigner / pour entrer / école de commerce.
   c Ils / s'amuser / beaucoup / Paris.
   d Claudia / se mettre à / apprendre l'espagnol.
   e Aziz / se mettre à / faire de la natation.
   f Claudia et Aziz / s'installer / appartement / près de la Sorbonne.

3 Answer the following questions in the negative:

   a Est-ce que tu t'es inscrit à l'université?
   b Est-ce qu'elle s'est renseignée pour les cours de japonais?
   c Est-ce que vous vous êtes installés dans votre nouvelle maison?
   d Est-ce qu'elles se sont ennuyées?
   e Est-ce que Jacques s'est amusé?
   f Est-ce qu'elles se sont senties à l'aise en France?

4 Answer the questions by replacing the underlined words with a direct object pronoun. Make sure that the past participle agrees with the pronoun.
   E.g. **Est-ce qu'elle a aimé <u>cette ville</u>?   Oui, elle <u>l</u>'a aimé<u>e</u>.**

   a Est-ce que tu as passé <u>ton entretien</u>?
   b Est-ce que tu as envoyé <u>ton CV</u>?
   c Est-ce qu'elle a obtenu <u>le poste</u>?
   d Est-ce qu'il a réussi <u>ses examens</u>?
   e Est-ce qu'elles ont contacté <u>l'entreprise</u> pour le poste?
   f Est-ce que vous avez rencontré <u>la directrice</u>?

9 Éducation et expérience

Vocabulaire

Verbes pronominaux/Reflexive verbs

s'ennuyer	to be bored
s'installer	to settle
s'inscrire	to enrol
s'amuser	to enjoy oneself
se spécialiser	to specialise
se débrouiller	to cope/manage
se présenter	to introduce oneself
se sentir à l'aise	to feel at ease
se renseigner	to find out/enquire
se mettre à	to start doing something

Examens et qualifications/Exams and qualifications

passer un examen	to sit an exam
réussir	to pass
échouer	to fail
obtenir	to gain/get
le baccalauréat (bac)	'A' levels (equivalent)
la maîtrise	Master's degree
la licence	Bachelor's degree
le doctorat	PhD, doctorate
la fac (coll.)	university
la formation d'enseignant	teacher training
améliorer	to improve
la note	mark
le résultat	result
la mention	distinction
le diplôme	diploma

Etudes/Studies

les lettres (f) modernes	humanities
les sciences (f)	sciences
l'ingénierie (f)	engineering
les études (f) commerciales	business studies
la gestion	management
la littérature	literature
l'informatique (f)	computing
le marketing	marketing

Le curriculum vitæ/CV

la formation	education/training
l'expérience (f) professionnelle	work experience
divers	miscellaneous
le stage	work placement
suivre un cours	to do a course
le cours intensif	intensive course
le séjour à étranger	stay abroad
la langue étrangère	foreign language
parler couramment	to speak fluently
l'outil (m) informatique	computing
le permis de conduire	driving licence
être à la retraite	to be retired
passer un coup de fil	to make a phone call
remplir un formulaire	to fill in a form
fournir	to provide/supply
recevoir	to receive
obliger de	to have to
déménager	to move
vivre	to live
l'internet (m)	internet
l'entretien (m)	interview
le tour du monde	world trip
bilingue	bilingual
connaissance	knowledge
depuis	for/since
pendant	for/during
longtemps	a long time
l'assistant(e)	assistant
le chercheur(euse)	researcher
le poste	job/position
la société	company
l'entreprise (f)	firm

Travail en paires

A

1 You have just moved to Paris for a six-month work placement. You are having a drink with one of your work colleagues. Use the following information in your conversation. Your partner will start.

– You have been living in Paris for two months.
– You are a student and you are going to be working in Paris for six months.
– Your colleague comments on your French. Say you have been learning for two years.
– You are living in a flat near the river. It is very nice and you have settled in well.
– You like Paris and you like the French a lot.
– You have been having fun. You have met lots of people and you go out a lot in the evenings to bars and cafés.

2 You have asked one of your work colleagues to shortlist a candidate for an interview. Your partner has the CV. Ask the following questions. You start.

– Ask your colleague who s/he has chosen.
– Find out his nationality and age.
– Find out if he has a degree. If so, what subject and when did he finish University.
– Find out if he has a Master's Degree.
– Find out if he speaks English.
– Find out if he has IT skills.
– Find out what he is currently doing.
– Find out what other work experience he has.

Travail en paires

1 You are going out for a drink with a colleague from work. S/he is English and has only been at the company for a couple of months. You start.

– Ask how long s/he has been in Paris.
– Ask how long s/he is staying.
– Say that s/he speaks very good French. Ask how long s/he has been learning.
– Find out where s/he lives and ask if s/he likes the flat.
– Ask if s/he likes Paris.
– Ask if s/he has been having a good time and ask what s/he does in the evenings.

2 You have been asked to compile a shortlist for an interview panel. You have selected the following CV as you think it is appropriate. Your partner is your manager and wants to know more information about the candidate. Use the CV below to answer any questions you are asked. Your partner will start.

Nom: Lucas Rocher
Adresse: 12 rue de la Craffe, 56000 Nancy
Nationalité: française
Date de naissance: 15/10/78 à Nancy

Formation:
Diplôme d'ingénieur, obtenu juillet 2000, Ecole Nationale de Paris
Licence en biochimie 1996–1999, La Sorbonne, Paris
Baccalauréat scientifique (mention bien), obtenu en juillet 1996, Lycée Georges Pompidou, Nancy

Expérience professionnelle:
Depuis septembre 2000: Ingénieur chez SOFICAM, Nancy
Janvier–juillet 1998: Stage de six mois chez BELLCANADA, Calgary, Canada
Mai–septembre 1996: Caissière à l'hypermarché de Vandoeuvre, Nancy

Divers:
Bonne connaissance de l'outil informatique (Word/Wordperfect/Excel)
Anglais parlé courant: séjour au Canada

10 Au travail!

When you have completed this unit, you will be able to socialise using some colloquial French, ask for and give help, give instructions and ask permission, give your opinion and describe your intentions.

A plus!

 1 Lire et écouter

a Read the conversation between Babette and a colleague of hers at the campsite where she is going to work for the summer. Find in the dialogue the equivalent of the following sentences/phrases:

i	Qu'est-ce que tu fais comme travail?	**v**	On m'a donné.
ii	Où est-ce que tu vas travailler?	**vi**	C'est bien.
iii	Je dois partir.	**vii**	C'est horrible!
iv	Tu as de la chance!	**viii**	Les enfants.

Dominique	Salut, je m'appelle Dominique. Et toi?
Babette	Moi, c'est Babette.
Dominique	Tu vas bosser où?
Babette	A la crèche.
Dominique	Veinarde! C'est super d'être avec les mômes.
Babette	Et toi, c'est quoi ton boulot?
Dominique	Moi, on m'a refilé l'organisation des jeux le soir. C'est l'enfer! (...) Oh, il est trois heures! Bon, je me casse.
Babette	OK, à plus!

b Listen to the dialogue paying particular attention to pronunciation.

Au revoir!	A demain!
A tout de suite!	A la semaine prochaine!
A tout à l'heure! ("A tout!")	A bientôt!
A plus tard! ("A plus!")	A la prochaine!
A ce soir!	A un de ces jours! ("A un de ces quatre!")

Il est interdit de...

2 Lire et observer

Look at the following signs (**panneaux**) and match them with the French instructions below.

a

c

e

b

d

f

1 Interdit aux animaux
2 Ne pas stationner

3 Défense de fumer
4 Accès interdit

5 Attention au feu
6 Ne pas plonger

3 Ecouter

Listen to six short dialogues that take place on a campsite. Note down where the conversation takes place and what the problem is.

	Place	Problem
a		
b		
c		
d		
e		
f		

il est interdit de / il est défendu de fumer
interdit de / défense de plonger
ne pas stationner

4 Lire, écrire et écouter

Read the following dialogue between the campsite owner and a tourist and fill in the gaps (one word per gap). Then listen to the recording to check your answers. (Note: **déplacer** = to move.)

Propriétaire	Monsieur, la voiture bleue là-bas, c'est à vous?
Touriste	Oui, c'est à **a** _____ . Il y a un problème?
Propriétaire	Oui, je suis **b** _____ mais il est **c** _____ de stationner devant la réception.
Touriste	Ah bon! Ce n'est pas indiqué.
Propriétaire	Ah si, monsieur, il y a un grand panneau devant la porte... vous voyez? **d** _____ -vous déplacer votre voiture, s'il vous plaît?
Touriste	Je **e** _____ rester quelques minutes?
Propriétaire	Désolé monsieur, mais c'est **f** _____ . Vous bloquez l'**g** _____ au camping!

5 Ecrire et parler

Using one of the signs in exercise 2, imagine a scenario similar to the one in exercise 4. Write a dialogue with your partner and practise reading it out loud.

6 Ecouter

The same tourist is having a few problems trying to find an appropriate place to park his car. Listen to the dialogue that ensues and answer the questions below.

- **a** Why does the campsite owner ask the tourist to move his car again?
- **b** Where does the owner suggest he move the car to?
- **c** Why can't he park there?
- **d** Where does he finally park his car?

grammaire

Où est-ce que je mets <u>la voiture</u>?	Mettez-<u>la</u> là.
Je <u>la</u> mets ici?	Non, ne <u>la</u> mettez pas là, mettez-<u>la</u> ici.

7 Traduire

Write a note to one of the tourists on the campsite asking them to move their car, by expressing the following in French:

Could you move your car because I cannot get out. Please put it beside your caravan or in the car park. Thank you.

Qu'est-ce qui s'est passé?

 8   Ecouter

You hear an ambulance in the campsite and you rush to see if you can be of any help. There, you meet Nathan who explains what has happened. Listen to the dialogue and state whether the following statements are true or false. (Note: **pas grand-chose** = not a lot; **le type** = the guy; **renverser** = to knock down; **grave** = serious; **reculer** = to reverse; **Je m'en vais** = I'm going (away).)

a A serious accident has happened on the campsite.
b Nathan once helped the man described.
c A child has been knocked down but is now OK and sitting down.
d Nicolas attends the campsite's crêche.
e The parents are in a restaurant.
f The grandmother is looking after Nicolas.

grammaire

C'est le type <u>que</u> tu as aidé l'autre jour.
C'est Nicolas <u>qui</u> vient à la crèche tous les matins. / Tu vois l'enfant <u>qui</u> est assis là?

 9   Ecouter

When working in a holiday resort, you may encounter emergency situations. Re-order the sentences in the following two dialogues and then listen to them to check your answers. (Note: **les pompiers** = fire brigade; **perdre connaissance** = to lose consciousness.)

Conversation a

a Vous êtes sûr? Je vais voir …
b Oh! C'est rien. C'est le résident qui fait un barbecue!
c Alors? Qu'est-ce qui s'est passé?
d Mademoiselle, il faut appeler les pompiers, j'ai vu de la fumée sortir de la caravane 12.

Conversation b

a D'accord, je m'en occupe tout de suite.
b Appelez le SAMU, s'il vous plaît, ma fille a mangé des fruits de mer et elle est allergique.
c C'est grave?
d Oui, elle a perdu connaissance.

 10 Jeu de rôle

With a partner, imagine a dialogue based on the situations described below. Take it in turn to play the distressed client and the helpful employee.

a Your daughter has been knocked down by a car.
b Your tent is on fire.

Moi, je trouve que ...

 11 Lire et écouter

Emma, Robert and Yvan have just been to a local concert. Read their conversation, then listen to the recording and correct the deliberate mistakes in the transcript (there are ten of them).
(Note: **trop de monde** = too many people; **un groupe** = band; **l'endroit** = place.)

Yvan	Eh bien, c'était pas génial, hein?
Emma	Moi, j'ai trouvé ça bien… Bon, ce ne sont pas des stars, mais ils jouent bien et leur musique est bonne, je trouve.
Robert	Vous ne pensez pas qu'il y avait trop de monde?
Emma	Oui, c'est vrai, la salle était vraiment trop petite.
Yvan	A mon avis, les concerts en province sont toujours mauvais. Il faut aller dans les grandes villes pour ça.
Robert	Ah non, je suis pas d'accord, j'ai vu de fantastiques concerts dans des petites villes de province, justement, c'était plus sympa et moins commercial.
Emma	Moi, je crois que si on aime un groupe, ça n'a pas d'importance l'endroit où on le voit.
Robert	Oui, c'est vrai.

A mon avis,…
(Moi,)   je trouve que…   … c'est / c'était très bien
         je pense que…
         je crois que…
(Moi,)   j'ai trouvé ça super / formidable / génial / nul / mauvais / pas terrible /
         ennuyeux / etc.
         Et toi, tu as aimé?
         Je suis d'accord. / C'est vrai.   Je ne suis pas d'accord. / Ce n'est pas vrai.

grammaire

moi, toi, lui, elle, nous, vous, eux, elles	c'est	c'était
	il y a	il y avait

12 Parler

With a partner, read the statements below and state your own opinion.
'E.g. – **Moi, je trouve que les Parisiens ne sont pas très polis. Et toi? – Je suis d'accord.**)

a Les Parisiens sont des gens très polis.
b Il y a de très bons restaurants à Londres.
c La musique folk, c'est pour les vieux!
d Il n'y a rien de bon au cinéma en ce moment.
e Kate Winslet est une excellente actrice!
f Le français est facile à apprendre.

Je voudrais partir ...

 13 Ecouter

Listen to four friends talking about their future plans and indicate whether the following statements are true or false.

a Micky n'a pas encore fini ses études.
b Serge ne veut pas aller en Thaïlande.
c Serge a l'intention de travailler dans une école.
d Isabelle n'a pas envie de travailler tout de suite.
e Isabelle va faire des études d'ingénieur.
f Alex va travailler dans un magasin de télévisions.

> Je voudrais...
> J'aimerais...
> J'ai envie de...   (...faire le tour
> Je pense...   du monde)
> J'ai l'intention de...

 14 Ecrire

Write in full sentences Muriel's plans for the future, which are listed below. Try to use as many different expressions of intention as possible (e.g. **Muriel <u>a l'intention de</u> continuer ses études, elle <u>voudrait</u> ...**).

a continuer ses études / faire une maîtrise en traduction
b voyager pendant un an
c passer quelques mois en Angleterre / améliorer son anglais
d travailler comme free-lance / acquérir de l'expérience
e essayer d'obtenir un poste à la Commission européenne

 15 Parler

With a partner, interview each other about your plans for the future.

118

Extra!

 1 Ecouter

Listen to a conversation between four students at the campsite and note down the following information for each of them: how long they have been at the campsite / what job they do there / where they come from / what subject they study.

a Babette
b Richard
c Stéphanie
d Jean-Marc

 2 Lire

Read the following information about what to do in case of emergency while in France and answer the questions below.

Les pharmacies
Pour un problème mineur, vous pouvez directement demander conseil dans les pharmacies. La nuit ou pendant le week-end, l'adresse de la pharmacie de garde est indiquée dans le journal local ou en vitrine dans les autres pharmacies.

Les pompiers   *Numéro de téléphone: 18*
Les pompiers interviennent pour les feux, les accidents, les noyades, les blessures. Ils ont la réputation de pouvoir résoudre tous les problèmes domestiques! Par exemple: le chat qui ne peut plus descendre de l'arbre... Attention! Il ne faut pas abuser!

Le SAMU   *Numéro de téléphone: 15*
Il s'agit du service d'aide médicale d'urgence. On les contacte pour les accidents graves. Ils sont en contact avec les hôpitaux.

La police et la gendarmerie   *Numéro de téléphone: 17*
La police intervient pour les accidents, les cambriolages, les agressions. A la campagne, les gendarmes remplacent la police qui travaille principalement dans les villes.

a In which circumstances would you go directly to the chemist's in France?
b Where can you find out about emergency chemists at the weekend?
c How are firemen perceived in France?
d In which circumstances would you get in touch with the SAMU?
e What is the difference between the **Police** and the **Gendarmes**?

Grammaire

- **Object pronouns and the imperative**

  With the imperative (see Unit 4), object pronouns come after the verb.

  E.g. **Où est-ce que je mets ma voiture? Mettez-<u>la</u> là.**

  When there is a negative, object pronouns come before the verb.

  E.g. **Je la mets là? Non, ne <u>la</u> mettez pas là, mettez-la ici.**

  Note: when **me** and **te** come after the verb, they are replaced by **moi** and **toi**.

  E.g. **Suivez-<u>moi</u>! (**But: **Vous <u>me</u> suivez?) Arrête-<u>toi</u>! (**But: **Tu <u>t</u>'arrêtes?)**

- *ne... pas* **and the infinitive**

  With the infinitive, both parts of **ne ... pas** come in front of the verb.

  E.g. <u>**Ne pas**</u> **fumer.**

  Je préfère <u>ne pas</u> sortir.

- *qui* **and** *que*

  When explaining whom or what you are talking about, the relative pronouns **qui** and **que** can be used for linking the two parts of the sentence.

  E.g. **C'est un enfant <u>qui</u> vient à la crèche. (**Rather than: **C'est un enfant. Il vient à la crèche.)**

  C'est le type <u>que</u> tu as aidé. (Rather than: **C'est le type. Tu l'as aidé**.)

  – **qui** is used when the person or thing referred to is the subject of the verb.

  E.g. **C'est un enfant <u>qui</u> vient à la crèche.**

  l'enfant vient à la crèche: enfant = subject of **vient**

  – **que** is used when the person or thing referred to is the object of the verb.

  E.g. **C'est le type <u>que</u> tu as aidé.**

  tu as aidé <u>le type</u>: type = object of **as aidé**

  (Note: **que > qu'** in front of a vowel: e.g. **C'est le type <u>qu'</u>ils ont aidé.)**

- **moi, toi, lui...**

moi	**nous**
toi	**vous**
lui/elle	**eux/elles**

  These pronouns are used:

  – to emphasise the subject pronouns **je, tu, il, elle, nous, vous, ils, elles**:

  e.g. <u>**Moi**</u>**, je trouve que c'est bien.**

  <u>**Lui**</u>**, il habite à Bordeaux.**

  – after prepositions like **chez, avec, pour**, etc.:

  e.g. **Je travaille avec <u>eux</u>.**

  Pierre vient chez <u>nous</u> ce soir.

Exercices de grammaire

Object pronouns and the imperative

1 Answer the questions both in the positive and in the negative, replacing the words underlined with a pronoun: e.g. **Je mets <u>ma voiture</u> au parking? (Tu)**
> **Oui, mets-<u>la</u> au parking. / Non, ne <u>la</u> mets pas au parking.**

a J'appelle <u>les pompiers?</u> (Vous)
b Je ferme <u>la porte?</u> (Tu)
c Je monte <u>la tente</u> là-bas? (Tu)
d J'emmène <u>les enfants</u> à la piscine? (Vous)
e Je laisse <u>le sac</u> dans la voiture ? (Tu)
f Je finis <u>le dernier morceau de gâteau?</u> (Vous)

Ne... pas and the infinitive

2 Transform the following instructions, using **ne pas** + infinitive
E.g. **Défense de fumer. > Ne pas fumer.**

a Défense de passer.
b Il est interdit de stationner.
c Défense d'ouvrir la fenêtre.
d Il est défendu de jouer à la balle.
e Il est interdit de nourrir les animaux.
f Il est défendu de marcher sur la pelouse.

Qui and que

3 Fill in the gaps, choosing between **qui** or **que** (or **qu'**).
a C'est la voiture _____ tu aimes bien.
b C'est un chanteur _____ vient du Québec.
c Ce sont les gens _____ sont installés là-bas.
d J'ai beaucoup aimé le concert _____ on a vu.
e Tu as parlé à la fille _____ travaille au bar?
f Vous avez vu le barbecue _____ ils ont acheté?

Moi, toi, lui...

4 Fill in the gaps in the dialogue, choosing between **moi, toi, lui, elle, nous, vous, eux** or **elles**.
– Tu as aimé la soirée chez Tom?
– Bof! Je n'aime pas beaucoup aller chez **a**_____; ses parents sont toujours là et on ne peut pas s'amuser, avec **b**_____. Et **c**_____, tu as aimé?
– **d**_____, je les trouve sympas, ses parents, surtout sa mère.
– Oui, **e**_____, elle est cool, c'est vrai ... Tiens, je t'ai apporté ce CD.
– C'est pour **f**_____?
– Oui, oui, c'est pour **g**_____.

10 Au travail!

Vocabulaire

Dire au revoir/Saying goodbye

A tout de suite!	See you in a minute!
A tout à l'heure!	See you later!
A plus tard!	See you later!
A ce soir!	See you this evening!
A demain!	See you tomorrow!
A la semaine prochaine!	See you next week!
A bientôt!	See you soon!
A la prochaine!	See you next time!
A un de ces jours!	See you around!

Langage familier/Colloquial language

bosser	to work
refiler	to give
le (la) môme	kid
le type	guy
le boulot	job
le fric	money
veinard(e)	lucky
C'est l'enfer!	It's hell!
Je m'en vais.	I'm going away.
Je me casse!	I'm off!
J'en ai marre	I'm fed up!
A tout! / A plus!	See you later!
pas grand-chose	not a lot
trop de monde	too many people

Instructions/Instructions

Il est interdit de…/ Il est défendu de…	Refrain from…/ It is forbidden to…
Interdit de stationner/ Défense de stationner	No parking
Ne pas fumer	No smoking
Attention (à)	Caution / Be careful
être admis(e)	to be allowed

En cas d'urgence/In case of emergency

le panneau	sign
l'accident (m)	accident
grave	serious
le feu	fire
la fumée	smoke
renverser	to knock down
déplacer	to move
reculer	to reverse
perdre connaissance	to lose consciousness
les pompiers	fire brigade
le SAMU	mobile accident unit
le poste de secours	first-aid post

Opinions/Opinions

A mon avis,…	In my opinion,…
Je trouve que…	I find that…
Je pense que…	I think that…
Je crois que…	I believe that…
(ne pas) être d'accord	to (dis)agree
formidable/génial(e)	great/super
pas terrible	not very good
ennuyeux(euse)	boring

Intentions/Intentions

Je voudrais…/J'aimerais…	I would like…
Je pense…	I am thinking of…
J'ai envie de…	I feel like…
J'ai l'intention de…	I intend to…

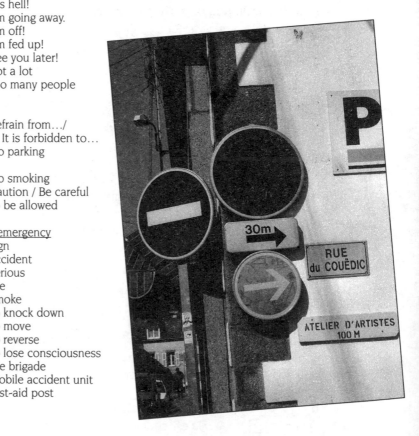

Travail en paires

1 It is Monday afternoon and you need to park your car. You are not sure about the parking restrictions in the area so you ask a passerby for help. Use the following prompts in your conversation. You start.

- Attract the attention of a passerby and ask if you can park here.
- Ask why not during the week?
- Ask if there is a car park nearby.
- Ask if s/he knows if you have to pay.
- Ask him/her to repeat the directions to the car park.
- Thank him/her appropriately.

2 You are discussing your holiday plans with a friend who has plans of his/her own. Using the following information, state your intentions and opinions and ask about your friend's plans. Your partner will start.

August

Going on holiday to West of France.

One of the best places for windsurfing.

Went there last year and enjoyed it.

Really liked the food.

Hope the weather is good.

Weather was excellent last year. Warm and windy, good for water sports.

December

Going to the States on a skiing holiday.

Have been to the States before.

Never been skiing before.

Think skiing is difficult.

Hope there is a lot of snow.

Travail en paires

1 You are stopped by someone in a car who wants to know about the parking restrictions in the area. Use the following information in your conversation. Your partner will start the conversation.

– Say that parking is not allowed between 0800 and 1800 on weekdays but it is allowed at the weekend.
– During the week parking is only permitted for residents.
– Tell him/her that there is a car park nearby and give directions; turn right at the end of the road, it is on the left by the supermarket.
– Say you are not sure if it is free, you think that you have to pay.
– Respond to his/her question.
– Finish the conversation appropriately.

2 You are discussing your holiday plans with a friend who has plans of his/her own. Using the following information, state your intentions and opinions and ask about your friend's plans. You start.

August
Going on holiday to Ireland for two weeks.
Went to Spain last year but didn't really enjoy it, it was too hot and there were too many people.
You have been to Ireland before, three years ago.
You really love the pubs and think in general that the night life is really good.
The people are also very friendly.

December
Not going on holiday.
Going to stay at home with friends and family.
Really like to be at home for Christmas.
Perhaps spend a weekend in Scotland.
Love the weather – it is always wet and windy!

Exercices supplémentaires
SUPPLEMENTARY EXERCISES

Toi et moi

 1 Lire

The following questions may be used to find out information about someone.
Match them with the appropriate response.

e.g. Tu t'appelles comment?
a Vous travaillez à Paris?
b Tu es belge ou suisse?
c Où travaillez-vous?
d Vous êtes française?
e Tu es vendeur?

1 A Paris.
2 Non, je suis belge.
3 Non, réceptionniste.
4 Je suis suisse.
5 Jeanne Meunier.
6 Non, à Calais.

 2 Lire et écouter

Read a dialogue between two people meeting at a party in Paris and re-order the
jumbled text. Then, listen to the recording to check your answer.

a – Ah! Et vous travaillez à Paris?
b – Moi, c'est Fiona.
c – Non, je suis irlandaise.
d – Bonsoir!
e – Je m'appelle Marc. Et vous?
f – Oui, je suis professeur d'anglais.
g – Bonsoir!
h – Ah! Vous êtes anglaise?

 3 Traduire

Translate the following sentences into French.

a Hi! How are you?
b Goodbye, Sir.
c I am German (*feminine*).
d Are you (*formal*) American (*masculine*)?
e Are you (*informal*) a student (*feminine*)?
f I live in London but I am from Glasgow.

4 Lire et écrire

Transpose the following passages from the first person singular **je** to the third person singular **il** or **elle**.

E.g. **Je m'appelle Béatrice et je suis française. > Elle s'appelle Béatrice et elle est française.**

a Je m'appelle Natasha. Je suis américaine. J'habite à New York mais je suis de Chicago. Je suis étudiante en histoire de l'art.

b Je m'appelle Bob. Je suis irlandais. J'habite à Belfast mais je suis de Dublin. Je suis technicien.

c Je m'appelle Malika. Je suis marocaine. J'habite à Lille mais je suis de Paris. Je suis serveuse.

d Je m'appelle Luca. Je suis italien. Je suis de Milan mais j'habite à Rome. Je suis acteur.

5 Parler

Listen to the prompts in English on the recording and practise asking the appropriate questions at a conference.

6 Lire

Read an interview with an exchange student, published in the student paper of a French university, and try to understand as much as you can without a dictionary (you don't need to understand every word) so as to answer the questions below.

> – Roberto, tu as vingt ans, tu es étudiant en philosophie, tu viens de Naples; pourquoi est-ce que tu études ici, en France?
> – Parce que j'adore la France! J'aime les Français, j'aime la cuisine française, la littérature, le cinéma, … et bien sûr la philosophie: Descartes, Rousseau, Sartre, etc. Et je fais du français depuis l'âge de onze ans. Ma mère est suisse, mais elle ne parle pas français, elle vient de Zurich. Je suis très content en France, les études sont intéressantes et j'ai un travail: je suis serveur dans un restaurant italien!

a How old is Roberto?
b What does he study?
c Where does he come from?
d Why does he like France?

e When did he start studying French?
f Why doesn't his mother speak French?
g Why does he like his studies?
h What sort of job does he do?

7 Ecrire

Imagine: you have decided to join an internet chat-room for learners of French and you send your first message, introducing yourself to the other members. Write your message, giving as much information as possible.

Les autres

 ## 1 Lire et écouter

Match the following questions with the appropriate answer then listen to the recording to check your answers.

E.g. Tu as quel âge?
1 Tu es mariée?
2 Vous avez des enfants?
3 Il est divorcé?
4 Il a quel âge?
5 Tu as des amis ici?
6 Ah, tu as un fils?
7 Elle a dix ans?

a Oui, un fils.
b Oui, et il a deux enfants.
c Il a douze ans.
d Oui, trois ou quatre.
e Non, mais j'ai un copain.
f Non, douze ans.
g Oui, il s'appelle David.
h J'ai 20 ans.

 ## 2 Lire, écrire et écouter

Read the following dialogue between two students who are talking about their friends and their family and fill in the gaps. Listen to the recording to check your answers.

Laurence	Ah, tu habites à Lyon?
Justin	Oui, et toi? Où **a** _____ -tu?
Laurence	A Lyon avec mon frère.
Justin	Il est **b** _____?
Laurence	Non, il travaille dans un café. Et toi, tu as un frère?
Justin	Non, **c** _____ une sœur. Elle s'appelle Danielle.
Laurence	Elle est mariée?
Justin	Oui, **d** _____ mari s'appelle Henri.
Laurence	Il travaille?
Justin	Non, il **e** _____ étudiant en philosophie.
Laurence	Ah voici mon copain, au bar avec sa sœur!

 ## 3 Lire et écrire

Go back to exercise 10 (page 15) (about Hervé's family tree) and correct the false statements in that exercise, then write them out in full sentences. (There are six of them).

 ## 4 Traduire

How do you say the following sentences in French?

a He's nineteen years old.
b How old are they?
c Do you have brothers and sisters?
d We live with our brother.
e They have a son and a daughter.
f Her daughter is six.
g My boyfriend works with his father.
h Do you live with your parents?

5 Ecrire

Using the language you have met so far, write a few sentences about your family.
E.g: **J'ai un fils …**

6 Parler

Imagine: you are studying town planning in France and you are conducting a
survey in the streets of Calais. Listen to the prompts in English on the recording
and then practise asking the appropriate questions about work, family and home.
(Note: flat = **un appartement**, house = **une maison**, sorry! = **pardon!**)

7 Lire et écrire

You have received the letter below from your new penfriend. Read it and write a
suitable response.

Cher…,/Chère…,

C'est moi, Alain, ton correspondant français. J'ai dix-huit ans, j'habite à Lille et je suis
étudiant en informatique. J'habite avec mes parents, ma soeur Julie et ma grand-mère.
J'ai une copine, elle s'appelle Tania, elle est russe et elle a dix-neuf ans. Elle est à
l'université avec moi. Sa famille habite à Moscou. Et toi, quel âge as-tu? Tu as des
frères et des soeurs? Tu habites avec tes parents? Tu as un copain/une copine? Ecris-moi
vite!

A bientôt,

Alain

8 Lire et écrire

Re-order the following jumbled sentences.

a sandwich/vous/un/voulez?
b boire/chose/veux/quelque/à/tu?
c pour/merci/non/moi/pas.
d café/veux/un/tu?
e moi/chaud/un/chocolat/pour.

9 Ecrire

You are in a cafeteria and have just bumped into an old friend, Brigitte. Imagine
what type of conversation might ensue, then write a dialogue in French between
you and Brigitte. For guidance, look at the following prompts in English.

Say hello. Ask how she is.
Offer her a drink.
Ask if she would also like something to eat, etc.

3 La routine

1 Ecouter

Around the world, different people are doing different things at different times. Listen to the tape to find out about them and fill in the grid below in English.

	Place	Time	Activity
a Mr and Mrs Durand			
b Marianne Pottier			
c Alain Laforêt			
d Michel Dubinge			
e Samia Tarouch			
f Marcel Dijan			

2 Lire

Read the letter below from an English student to her French penfriend and fill in the gaps with the missing words. (Note: **devoirs** = assignment.)

Chère Assia,

Comment vas-tu? Bien, j'espère.

Je **a**_____ étudiante depuis octobre et j'aime l'université. Le jeudi je **b** _____ les cours à 11 heures et je **c**_____ à 3 heures. Je prends **d**_____ déjeuner à la cafétéria de l'université avec Daniel. Je mange toujours **e**_____ spaghettis, c'est délicieux! L' **f**_____-midi nous allons à la bibliothèque pour finir **g**_____ devoirs de la semaine. Ensuite, nous **h**_____ le train pour aller à la piscine. Je vais à la piscine le lundi soir, le jeudi après-midi et le samedi matin. Aujourd'hui, je **i**_____ le ménage et demain je **j**_____ à Londres. Je prends le train à 6 heures et **k** j'_____ à 11 heures. J'aime beaucoup ma vie d'étudiante ici. Ecris-moi vite!

Sandy

3 Ecouter, lire et écrire

a Read through the descriptions below in a lonely hearts column then listen to the same five people describing themselves and decide who is who.

1 Jeune femme, 22 ans, intelligente et active, aime lire, aller au théâtre et faire du sport (squash, aérobic).

2 Homme, 45 ans, intelligent et riche, aime le théâtre, l'opéra, la musique classique et les promenades dans la nature.

3 Jeune homme, 28 ans, tendre et sportif, aime écouter de la musique, faire du sport et sortir en boîte.

4 Femme, 39 ans, dynamique et aventureuse, aime le travail, les voyages, les hommes et l'aventure.

5 Homme, 62 ans, tendre, sens de l'humour, aime faire la cuisine et le ménage, aller au théâtre et à l'opéra.

b Using the above extract again, play cupid and find a suitable partner for the following people:

  i Jeanne, 29, very dynamic, loves sport.
  ii Louis, 40, hardworking, loves travelling.
  iii Jules, 25, very bright, loves culture.
  iv Marie, 59, very gentle, loves opera.
  v Isabelle, 42, sophisticated, loves playing the piano.

c Using the extract as a model, write your own advertisement.

4 Lire et écrire

Look at the following sentences and according to the plus or minus signs, write in the correct form of either **aimer bien** (+), **aimer** (++), **aimer beaucoup** (+++), **ne pas aimer beaucoup** (–), **ne pas aimer** (– –) or **détester** (– – –) e.g.

Vous +++ faire du vélo.   >   Vous aimez beaucoup faire du vélo.

a Je ++ jouer à la pétanque.
b Tu – – faire du sport.
c Elle + aller à la piscine.

d Vous +++ faire des courses.
e Nous – – jouer au tennis.
f Ils – – – aller à la gym.

5 Exercice

Match the problem in English with the appropriate advice in French.
(Note: **essayer** = to try.)

1 I watch too much television.
2 I have not got any food.
3 I can't do it.
4 I have not got any money.
5 I am not very fit.
6 I am really tired.

a Tu dois aller au supermarché.
b Vous devez aller au lit.
c Tu dois faire du sport.
d Vous devez arrêter.
e Vous devez aller à la banque.
f Vous devez essayer.

4 En ville

 1 Lire

Put the sentences below in the right order to form a dialogue.

a C'est où, la Rue George Sand?
b Non, c'est à dix minutes environ.
c Mais, je vous en prie.
d Pardon, monsieur?
e Oui, dans la Rue George Sand.
f Oui?
g C'est loin?
h Alors, vous prenez la troisième rue à gauche, puis la première à droite, et c'est là.
i Merci beaucoup!
j Est-ce qu'il y a un supermarché près d'ici?

2 Exercice

Find the odd one out.

a rue / avenue / place / garage / boulevard
b tourner / lire / prendre / traverser / aller
c boulangerie / épicerie / supermarché / bibliothèque / boucherie
d entre / devant / puis / derrière / sur

3 Exercice

What was the question? Find an appropriate question for each of the answers below. (E.g. La Rue des Mimosas? C'est la deuxième à droite. > Pardon, vous savez où est la Rue des Mimosas?)

a L'Office du Tourisme? Alors, vous prenez la deuxième rue à gauche, et c'est en face, sur la gauche.
b Oui, il y a une poste à 2 minutes d'ici, dans la Rue des Combattants.
c Ah non, elle n'est pas à côté de la gare, elle est en face.
d Non, c'est à 5 minutes.
e De rien, au revoir.

 4 Ecouter et parler

On holiday in France, you have just arrived in a little town. You go into the tourist office to get a map and find out about your hotel, restaurants and other places of interest. Listen to the prompts in English before taking your turn in the conversation. (Note: a map of the town = **un plan de la ville**.)

 5 Lire et écouter

Read the following dialogue, a conversation in a shop, and fill in the gaps (one word for each gap). Then listen to the recording to check your answers.
(Note: **la cabine (d'essayage)** = changing room.)

– Bonjour, je peux vous **a**_____?
– Oui, je **b**_____ essayer ce pantalon.
– Oui. Vous **c**_____ voulez en quelle **d**_____ : noir, bleu ou beige?
– Vous ne **e**_____ avez pas en blanc?
– Non, désolé.
– Bon, je vais essayer **f**_____ beige.
– Voilà. La cabine est **g**_____ côté de la caisse.
– Merci. (...)
– Ça va?
– Oui, il est parfait. Je le **h**_____.

6 Exercice

Look at the following list of clothes and using the (+) or (–) signs as indicators, state whether or not you like each item.

E.g. Vous aimez la jupe? (+)   >   Oui, je l'aime.
        Tu aimes le pantalon? (–)   >   Non, je ne l'aime pas.

a Vous aimez la chemise? (+) **d** Ils aiment l'écharpe? (+)
b Tu aimes le manteau? (–) **e** Est-ce qu'il aime le gilet? (+)
c Est-ce qu'elle aime la veste? (–) **f** Vous aimez les chaussures? (–)

 7 Traduire

Translate the following statements into French.

a The skirt? No, I do not like it.
b This dress? Yes, I prefer it.
c Do you like it?
d Yes, I like it.
e Do you like this pair of trousers?
f She likes the yellow shirt and I like it too.

 8 Lire

Unscramble the following sentences.

a pantalon / j' / le / aime / noir
b gris / pull / préfère / je / ce
c chaussures / jaunes / aimes / ces / tu / ?
d je / les / ne / pas / aime
e vous / jupe / préférez / cette / rose / ?
f verte / aime / cette / il / veste / pas / n'

5 En train

1 Exercice

What was the question? Match the appropriate question with each of the answers below.

(E.g. **Seconde classe, SVP. > Première ou seconde classe?**)

a Pendant les vacances? Eh bien, je vais aller en Espagne, chez mon copain.

b Oui, à San Francisco.

c Attendez ... il part à 10h32.

d Alors ... il arrive à Lille à 20h56.

e Ça fait 124 euros.

f Quai numéro 3.

g J'y vais en métro, en général.

h Vous devez aller à la porte numéro 12.

1 Comment allez-vous au travail?

2 C'est sur quel quai?

3 A quelle heure part le train?

4 Qu'est ce que tu vas faire pendant les vacances?

5 Je dois aller où?

6 Ça fait combien?

7 A quelle heure arrive le train?

8 Ils habitent aux Etats-Unis?

2 Lire

The sentences in the dialogue below have been jumbled up. Re-order them.

a Le train part à14h35.

b Je voudrais un billet, aller-retour, pour Avignon, s'il vous plaît. C'est combien?

c Alors, 45 euros.

d Seconde classe, pardon.

e Alors, c'est le quai numéro 3.

f Alors, c'est un peu plus loin, sur votre gauche là-bas.

g Bon. Merci beaucoup. Au revoir.

h Oui. Et à quelle heure part le prochain train, s'il vous plaît?

i Un aller-retour pour Avignon, c'est ...

j Et c'est quel quai?

k Quai 3 ... où est-ce que c'est?

3 Parler

You are at the coach station in Limoges and you want to go to Guéret. Listen to the prompts in English before taking your turn in the conversation.

4 Lire

Read your friend Stéphane's letter, which has been ripped up. Put the pieces together.

> Cher Ben,

> Ensuite, nous allons voir un ami qui habite à Madrid, nous allons prendre le train rapide pour y aller. Il faut réserver à l'avance pour avoir une place. Matthias veut aller au Portugal pour voir son copain Carlos.

> Comment vas-tu?
> Je suis à Paris jusqu'à dimanche et après … les vacances! Je suis très content. Je vais partir avec mes deux copains Dino et Matthias. Dino est de Rome et Matthias habite en Corse avec ses parents mais il étudie à Paris.

> Il habite à côté de Lisbonne, alors nous allons prendre le car, c'est moins cher! Carlos est en vacances et il va nous faire visiter les petits villages portugais en vélo. C'est une bonne idée mais je ne suis pas très sportif! Et toi? Qu'est-ce que tu vas faire et où vas-tu aller pendant les vacances? Tu peux venir avec nous si tu veux.

> Nous voulons aller dans le sud de l'Europe pour commencer. Je vais prendre le train avec Dino jusqu'à Irún en Espagne et Matthias va arriver en avion à Bilbao. Il faut aller le chercher à l'aéroport. Nous voulons visiter le Pays basque et aller à la plage pendant quelques jours.

> A bientôt.
> Stéphane

5 Ecouter

Fill in the gaps in the text below and listen to the recording to check your answers.

Ce soir je vais **a** _____ au cinéma avec mes amis. D'habitude nous **b**_____ allons **c**_____ métro mais cette semaine il y a une **d**_____ du métro à Paris. Alors il **e** _____ trouver un autre moyen de transport et **f**_____ pouvons y aller **g**_____ voiture. Le film commence **h**_____ 20h30 mais il **i**_____ partir de la maison vers 19h parce qu'il y a beaucoup de circulation. Nous prenons la voiture de **j**_____ copine Céline parce que ma voiture est **k**_____ panne. J'espère que nous allons arriver **l**_____ l'heure.

6 A l'hôtel

 1 Lire et écouter

Read the following dialogue and fill in the gaps. Listen to the recording to check your answers.

– Bonjour, je **a**_____ réserver trois chambres.
– C'est à **b**_____ nom?
– Au **c**_____ de Poussin.
– Pour **d**_____ de nuits?
– Pour trois nuits.
– Pour combien de **e**_____?
– Pour six.
– Vous voulez des **f**_____ simples?
– Oui, s'il vous **g**_____. Combien ça fait?
– La chambre **h**_____ 100 euros, alors 3 chambres ça **i**_____ 300 euros.
– Vous **j**_____ les cartes de crédit?
– Oui, pas de problème.

 2 Ecrire et parler

In a hotel, how would you say the following sentences in French?

a Is there a private car park?
b Where is the lift, please?
c What time is breakfast?
d I have a problem with my room.
e There aren't any towels in the bathroom.
f The lift on the third floor does not work.

 3 Lire

Find the odd one out.

a chambre/douche/barbecue/téléphone
b salon/piscine/cuisine/wc
c janvier/printemps/juin/août

d réserver/prendre/se lever/vouloir
e réservation/piscine/sauna/parking

 4 Ecouter et écrire

Listen to four people spelling difficult names on the phone and write them down.

a … **c** …
b … **d** …

5 Lire et écrire

Read Paula's letter. She wrote it some time ago to book some rooms in a hotel. Use it as a model to book a room for your next holiday. You should use the following information to formulate your response.

– one room for three people.
– one double bed/one single bed.
– bathroom if possible.
– from 3rd August until 6th August.
– Is there satellite television/a restaurant in the hotel?
– How much is the set mcal?

Paula Daniels
50 Bowlers Street
Londres

Londres, le 14 juin 2001

Monsieur,

Je voudrais réserver deux chambres pour deux personnes du 15 août au 23 août. Je voudrais une chambre avec deux lits simples et salle de bains et une chambre avec un lit pour deux personnes. Si possible avec vue sur la mer. Est-ce qu'il y a un parking dans l'hôtel?
Avec mes remerciements, je vous prie de croire, monsieur, à mes salutations distinguées.

Paula Daniels

---

6 Ecrire

Your French friend is going to spend a fortnight in your house in your absence. Describe the layout of your house. Give details about the different floors, and the furniture in each room. You can also explain what is wrong in the house (broken/not working, etc.).

7 Ecouter et parler

Take part in a conversation at a hotel reception. In the first part you will be making a booking and in the second part a complaint. Take your turn in the conversation when you are prompted in English.

7 Au restaurant

1 Exercice

Find the French for:

a
– Hello.
– May I speak to Helen, please?
– Hold on, I'll pass you over.
– Thanks.

b
– Hello
– Is Janet there?
– Sorry, she isn't here.
– Can I leave a message?

c
– Hello.
– Hello, I'd like to speak to Bruce, please.
– Sorry he isn't here.
– Could he call me back?
– OK, I'll tell him.

d
– Hello
– Could I speak to Emer, please?
– Speaking.
– Hello, it's Carol.

2 Ecrire

Fill in the gaps in the following telephone conversation. Some gaps may have more than one word. Then listen to the recording to check your version.

– Allô.
– Salut, Carl, **a** _____ Claudia.
– Salut, ça va?
– Oui bien merci. **b** _____ tu fais ce week-end?
– Euh … rien.
– Ça te **c** _____ de sortir samedi soir?
– Oui, pourquoi pas.
– On **d** _____ aller au cinéma.
– Bonne idée.
– A quelle heure?
– On **e** _____ devant le cinéma à 7h?
– Entendu. A samedi soir.
– Oui, à samedi, au revoir.

3 Parler

You are meeting some work colleagues at Charles de Gaulle airport. You have never met them before and do not know what they look like. You ask a work colleague to describe them.

Listen to the prompts in English before taking your turn.

 4 Ecrire

Put the following descriptions into full sentences.

a Isabelle: 25 ans, française, petite, cheveux blonds, longs, yeux bleus
b Alan: 33 ans, anglais, grand, mince, cheveux bruns, yeux verts, moustache, barbe
c Joshua: 50 ans, américain, très grand, gros, cheveux noirs, courts, yeux bleus, lunettes
d Juliette: 17 ans, irlandaise, grande, mince, cheveux roux, yeux verts, taches de rousseur

 5 Lire

Match the following requests with the most appropriate answer.

1 Qu'est-ce que c'est l'entrée du jour?
2 Comment voulez-vous votre steak?
3 Vous avez choisi?
4 Vous voulez du gâteau?
5 Tu en veux?
6 Vous avez une entrée végétarienne?
7 Vous prenez du vin?

a Non, je ne mange jamais de dessert.
b Oui, un petit peu s'il te plaît.
c Essayez l'assiette de crudités.
d Oui, on en prend une bouteille.
e Pas encore.
f Saignant s'il vous plaît.
g C'est de la soupe.

6 Exercice

Find the odd one out.

a gâteau / steak / glace / pâtisserie / fruit
b saucisson / agneau / steak / truite / poulet
c tomate / pomme / carotte / oignon / salade
d dessert / addition / entrée / plat principal

 7 Lire et écouter

Put the jumbled sentences below in the right order to form a dialogue, then listen to the recording to check your answers.

a Et comme plat principal, monsieur?
b D'accord, je la prends.
c Oui, monsieur, vous avez choisi?
d Et comme dessert?
e Je ne prends pas de dessert.
f Oui, euh … qu'est-ce que c'est l'entrée du jour?
g C'est une salade niçoise. C'est très bon.
h Très bien. Vous prenez du vin peut-être?
i Comme plat principal, je vais prendre la truite aux amandes, s'il vous plaît.
j Un verre de vin blanc, s'il vous plaît.
k Monsieur, s'il vous plaît?

8 Vacances et Loisirs

 1 Traduire

Translate the following statements into French.

a We have had an excellent weekend.
b What did you (= **tu**) do on Saturday night?
c I couldn't come because I had to work.
d They (*m*) have had a problem with their car.
e Lucie loved Paris, she visited all the museums.
f I haven't seen the film, but I have read the book.

 2 Ecrire

Write a summary of what you have done during the week, using the information in the diary below. Use the following verbs: **avoir**, **étudier**, **dîner**, **travailler**, **faire**, **voir**, **jouer**.

Lundi 17	10h00-12h00 cours d'anglais / 2h00-5h00 séminaire
Mardi 18	Etude à la bibliothèque
Mercredi 19	9h00-10h30 cours de chimie / 8h00 dîner chez Marc
Jeudi 20	Travail à la maison: dissertation
Vendredi 21	9h30-12h30 cours de maths / courses en ville
Samedi 22	3h00 match de foot
Dimanche 23	Tennis avec Mimi

 3 Lire et écrire

Unscramble the following sentences.

a raté / ils / dernier / le / ont / métro
b restaurant / un / mangé / j' / bon / dans / ai
c as / que / qu' / tu / ce / fait / est / ?
d très / nous / week-end / passé / avons / bon / un
e voiture / il / sa / a / eu / avec / problème / un
f pas / a / venir / n' / pu / nous / elle / avec

4 Lire et écrire

Read the letter below and fill in the gaps (one missing word for each gap).

Salut Sylvie!

Comment ça va? Est-ce que tu as reçu ma carte d'Inde? Je suis partie pendant un mois, avec **a**_____ copain Alex. On est d'abord **b**_____ à Delhi; c'est une ville fascinante mais très **c**_____ et polluée. On a aussi **d**_____ le Taj Mahal à Agra, à l'est de Delhi. Après, on a **e**_____ le train pour aller à Goa, sur la côte. C'est très touristique, mais on **f**_____ pu nager et se faire bronzer. Il a **g**_____ très chaud pendant deux semaines et puis la saison des pluies a commencé. On a **h**_____ les derniers jours à l'hôtel. On a lu, on a **i**_____ du poisson et des fruits de mer et on **j**_____ allés au marché: on a trouvé **k**_____ de jolies choses pour les amis. On a vraiment adoré **l**_____ Inde; on a **m**_____ d'y retourner l'année prochaine, peut-être dans le sud cette fois. Et toi, qu'est-ce que tu **n**_____ fait cet été? Réponds-moi vite!

Bisous,

Carole

5 Ecrire

Imagine that you are Sylvie. Write a reply to Carole's letter, explaining how you spent the summer months. Your letter should contain the following:

– thank Carole for her letter;
– you have also been to India, two years ago, and you loved it;
– this year, you stayed in Lille during the summer because you had to work;
– you found a job in a restaurant and you worked there for one month;
– in August, you had to study because you have exams next week;
– fortunately, you met an old friend and you did lots of things together in the evenings, so you had a good summer.

6 Ecouter et parler

You have just come back from a holiday in Cornwall and you are talking about it with a friend who has also been away. Listen to the prompts in English before taking your turn in the conversation.

9 Education et expérience

 1 Parler

You have recently moved to Lille and are talking to a friend about your first impressions of life in France. Listen to the prompts in English before taking your turn.

 2 Lire et écrire

Re-order the jumbled sentences.

a six / à / mois / travaillent / Brighton / ils / depuis.

b ans / à / habité / j' / Londres / ai / pendant / six.

c en / ai / commencé / études / 1996 / j' / mes.

d je / terminées /dernière / année / les / ai / l'.

e trouvées / ai / je / intéressantes / très / les.

f langues / je / inscrite / en / suis / me / de / cours /

g France / en /suis / bien / me / je / installé.

 3 Ecouter

Three people are having interviews in a recruitment agency. Listen to them talking about their training and professional life and make notes using the grid below.

	Degree	Work experience	Plans for future
Nadine			
Kofi			
Elizabeth			

4 Ecouter et ecrire

Listen to Samina talking about her education and work experience and fill in the missing gaps.

J'ai **a**_____ mes études en juillet 2000. J'ai une **b**_____ de sciences naturelles et de 1996 à 1999, j'ai **c**_____ une maîtrise de biologie marine à l'université de Nice. **d** _____ septembre 2000 je travaille aux Etats-Unis comme chercheur. Je suis bilingue français-arabe, et j'ai aussi une bonne **e**_____de l'anglais. Il y a trois ans, je **f**_____ suis **g**_____ en cours d'espagnol. J'ai **h**_____ à tous mes examens et je dirais que je le parle bien et je **i**_____ débrouille à l'écrit. J'aime aussi faire du sport, surtout de la planche àvoile et de la natation.

5 Ecrire

Using the headings below, write your own CV.

Nom:

Date de naissance:

Nationalité:

Adresse:

Formation:

Expérience professionnelle:

Divers:

Centres d'intérêt:

10 Au travail

 1 Lire

Express the following sentences in more colloquial language, changing the words underlined.

  a Je vais chercher <u>les enfants</u>.
  b On m'a <u>donné</u> de l'argent.
  c Je <u>m'en vais</u>.
  d Jc <u>travaille</u> au bar.
  e A un de ces <u>jours</u>!
  f Qu'est-ce que tu fais comme <u>travail</u>?
  g A <u>plus tard</u>.
  h C'est <u>horrible</u>.

 2 Parler

You are being introduced to a colleague who works in a campsite. Listen to the prompts in English before taking your turn in the conversation.
(Note: **poste de secours** = first-aid post.)

 3 Ecouter

Listen to a conversation between a tourist and a campsite owner and answer the questions below.

  a Where can tourists park their cars?
  b What are the campsite restrictions regarding pets?
  c What time does the restaurant shut?
  d What are the restrictions on the use of the swimming pool?
  e What is the restriction regarding music?

 4 Lire et écrire

Unscramble the following sentences.

  a de / ici / interdit / fumer / est / il
  b voitures / derrière / la / les / mettez / autres
  c est / indiqué / ce / pas / n'
  d les / c' / travailler / est / de / mômes / sympa / avec
  e au / désolé / monsieur / bloquez / l' / accès / camping / vous
  f défendu / est / jouer / de / il / la / de / musique
  g la / là / mettez / ne / pas

5 Lire

Dennis is about to finish his degree and writes a letter to his French friend Alain. Read the letter and answer the questions below it. (Note: **un mémoire** = dissertation, **j'en ai marre (de)** = I'm fed up (with), **le fric** = money (slang).)

Salut Alain!

Comment ça va? Moi, je bosse dur en ce moment: les examens commencent bientôt et en plus, j'ai deux dissertations à finir et je dois rendre mon mémoire de fin d'études! Mais, encore deux mois, et c'est FINI! J'ai des difficultés à imaginer la vie après l'université, mais je suis vraiment impatient de faire autre chose. Je trouve que les études universitaires durent trop longtemps. J'en ai marre d'étudier, j'ai envie de voir le monde et de travailler, de gagner de l'argent et d'être enfin indépendant! J'espère trouver du boulot dans une autre ville, plus petite que Londres. Ici, c'est trop grand, il y a trop de gens, trop de pollution et tout coûte cher. Mais avant ça, j'ai l'intention de prendre de longues, longues vacances! Le seul problème, c'est le fric. Il va falloir que je travaille pendant l'été pour gagner assez d'argent pour acheter un billet d'avion pour une destination exotique ... Et toi, quelles nouvelles? Est-ce que tu en as aussi marre de la fac? Quels sont tes projets pour l'année prochaine? Ecris-moi, si tu as le temps.

A bientôt,

Dennis

a Why is Dennis very busy at the moment?
b When is he going to finish his studies?
c How does he feel about his studies?
d What does he want to do afterwards?
e What does he think about London?
f What does he need to do during the summer? Why?

 6 Ecrire

Imagine that you are Alain. Write a reply to Dennis's letter, including the following:

– thank Dennis for his letter;
– tell him about your studies: whether you find them interesting/hard/etc. and how many years/months you still have to do;
– explain whether or not you plan to stay in the town/city you are in at the moment; say how you find the place;
– tell him about your plans for the future: what you intend to do after university and, before that, what your plans are for the next holiday;
– say you hope to see him again (**revoir**) soon.

GUIDE TO GRAMMATICAL TERMS

Language learners often feel unsure about grammatical terms. The following list gives some simple definitions. Examples are underlined, terms used which are defined elsewhere in the list are given in bold. Examples are drawn from English: reference is made to French only when something distinctive about that language needs to be noted. This Guide is concerned only with the meanings of grammatical terms: there is a French Grammar Summary beginning on page 148.

Adjective   A word used to describe a noun ('an <u>interesting</u> woman'; 'the curry is <u>hot</u>'). See also **demonstrative adjective**, **possessive adjective**.

Adverb   A word which describes the action of a **verb** ('she sings <u>beautifully</u>', 'he cooks <u>well</u>') or modifies (= gives further information about) an **adjective** ('it's a <u>really</u> expensive car') or another adverb ('she sings <u>really</u> well').

Agree   In English, **adjectives** don't change their form but in French they have to agree with the noun they are describing in **gender** and **number**: if the noun is feminine, the adjective must be in the feminine form, if the noun is plural, so is the adjective.

Article   <u>The</u> (called the definite article), <u>a</u> or <u>an</u> (the indefinite article).

Auxiliary verb   A **verb** combining with another verb to form a compound tense. ('She <u>has</u> gone' = auxiliary verb 'to have' here used to form the perfect tense by combining with the **past participle** of the verb 'to go'.)

Comparative   Form of an **adjective** ('that room is <u>bigger than this one</u>'; 'they've bought a <u>more expensive</u> car') or adverb ('it happens <u>more often</u> than you think') expressing a greater degree. See also **superlative**.

Conjunction   A word which joins parts of a sentence ('he was tired <u>and</u> he wanted to go home'; 'they arrived early <u>because</u> they wanted a good place').

Demonstrative adjective   These 'point out' **nouns** (<u>this</u> chair/<u>these</u> chairs; <u>that</u> house/<u>those</u> houses).

Direct object   The word which directly undergoes the action of the verb. In the sentence 'she sent her mother a present', what she sent was a present, so that is the direct object. She didn't send her mother! See also **indirect object**.

Gender   In French, all **nouns** have a grammatical **gender**, masculine or feminine, and **adjectives** have to **agree**.

Imperative   Verb form used in giving commands and instructions ('<u>Turn</u> left now!').

Indirect object   A secondary **object**. In the sentence 'she sent her mother a present', the **direct object**, the thing which is sent, is the present. It was sent to her mother, the indirect object.

Infinitive   The basic form of a **verb** ('<u>to sing</u>'; '<u>to write</u>').

Irregular verb   Verb that doesn't follow a standard pattern.

Noun   Word denoting a person ('student'), thing ('book') or abstract idea ('happiness').

Number   Whether a word is **singular** or **plural**.

Object   The **noun** or **pronoun** which undergoes the action of the **verb**. 'We bought a house'; 'I saw him'.

Object pronoun   Pronoun used when it's the **object** of the **verb**. Me, you, him, her, it, us, them.

Past participle   Part of the **verb** which combines with an **auxiliary verb** to form the Perfect tense ('they have arrived'; 'I have seen').

Plural   More than one: the plural of 'man' is 'men'.

Possessive adjective   e.g. 'my house', 'your friend', 'his car' etc.

Preposition   e.g. 'on the table', 'under the chair', 'to the station', 'for the teacher' etc.

Pronoun   Word taking the place of a **noun**. 'Peter saw the waitress' becomes 'he saw her'.

Reflexive verb   In French, a **verb** formed with an extra pronoun (called a reflexive pronoun).

E.g. se laver (to get washed): je me lave, il se lave, vous vous lavez etc.

Regular verb   **Verb** that follows a standard pattern.

Relative pronoun   **Pronoun** used to refer back to a noun earlier in the sentence, e.g. 'the man *who* lives there is very old'; 'the book *which* he chose …'; 'the woman/film *that* he saw…'.

Singular   One rather than many: the singular of 'bananas' is 'banana'.

Subject   Who or what carries out the action of the verb. 'A student sent me this email'; 'we are travelling next week'; 'the letter arrived yesterday'.

Subject pronoun   Pronoun used when it's the **subject** of the **verb**: I, you, he, she, it, we, they.

Tense   Form taken by a **verb** to show when the action takes place, e.g. Present tense: 'they live in New York'; Past tense: 'they lived in New York'; Future tense: 'they will live in New York' etc.

Verb   Word indicating an action ('they ate their dinner') or state ('the book lay on the table'). Different **tenses** are used to show when something happened. See also **irregular verb**, **reflexive verb**, **regular verb**.

GRAMMAR SUMMARY

In this section, you will find a summary of the grammar points covered in the book, as well as some supplementary information and verb tables. For a more detailed explanation of the different points, please refer to the grammar pages in each unit (given in brackets). If you are not familiar with grammatical terms, you will probably find the 'Guide to Grammatical Terms' on the previous two pages very useful as an introduction to this section.

The noun group

Nouns

1. *Masculine and feminine* (see page 8)

In French, nouns are masculine (m) (e.g. **le jour**) or feminine (f) (e.g. **la nuit**). Their ending can sometimes give an indication of their gender. The following are generally <u>feminine</u>:
- most nouns ending in **-e**: e.g. **la piscine**, **la chose**;
- nouns ending in   **-ie**: e.g. **l'épicerie**, **la biologie**;
                     -ion: e.g. **l'opinion**, **l'éducation**;
                     -té: e.g. **la nationalité**, **la société**.

The following are generally <u>masculine</u>:
- nouns ending in   **-c**, **-f**, **-l**, **-r**: e.g. **le vol**, **le bar**;
                     -age: e.g. **le chômage**, **le garage**;
                     -ment: e.g. **le renseignement**, **le changement**.

But there are many exceptions: e.g. **le musée**, **la mer**, etc.
Most words used to refer to people have a masculine and a feminine form, the feminine form usually having an extra **-e** at the end: e.g. **l'ami**, **l'amie**.

2. *Plural*

Most nouns form their plural (i.e. when they refer to more than one person or thing) by adding an **-s** (e.g. **le livre**, **les livres**).
Notable exceptions are:
- nouns ending in **-s**, **-x**, or **-z**, which do not change: e.g. **le pays**, **les pays**;
- nouns ending in **-au**, **-eau** or **-eu**, which take an **-x**: e.g. **le bateau**, **les bateaux**;
- nouns ending in **-al** or **-ail**, which have their plural in **-aux**: e.g. **le journal**, **les journaux**.

Determiners

3. *Articles* (see pages 20, 32 and 72)

There are three main kinds of articles:
Le is used to refer to a person or thing which is known by the person you are talking to, either because it is specific (e.g. **la France**; **le livre qui est sur la table**) or because it is generic (e.g. **le mardi** – every Tuesday; **j'aime les maths** – maths in general). The different forms are:

- **le** with a masculine word (e.g. **le pain**);
- **la** with a feminine word (e.g. **la chemise**);
- **l'** with a word starting with a vowel, masculine or feminine (e.g. **l'enfant**);
- **les** with a plural word, masculine or feminine (e.g. **les lunettes**).

Un is used when the person or thing referred to is not specified (e.g. **un livre**; **il a des amis français**). The different forms are:
- **un** with a masculine word (e.g. **un cours**);
- **une** with a feminine word (e.g. **une lettre**);
- **des** with a plural word, masculine or feminine (e.g. **des chaussures**).

Du is used to refer to an uncountable quantity (e.g. **j'ai mangé du poulet** – compare with **j'aime le poulet** and **j'ai acheté un poulet**). The different forms are:
- **du** with a masculine word (e.g. **du vent**);
- **de la** with a feminine word (e.g. **de la chance**);
- **de l'** with a word starting with a vowel, masculine or feminine (e.g. **de l'eau**);
- **des** with a plural word, masculine or feminine (e.g. **des frites**).

4. Demonstratives (see page 46)

Ce is used when referring to a person or thing by pointing them out. The different forms are:
- **ce** with a masculine word (e.g. **ce pull**);
- **cet** with a masculine word starting with a vowel (e.g. **cet après-midi**);
- **cette** with a feminine word (e.g. **cette année**);
- **ces** with a plural word, masculine or feminine (e.g. **ces gens**).

5. Possessives (see page 20)

Like the articles and the demonstratives, they agree with the noun that follows, i.e. the person or thing they refer to (e.g. **mon vélo**, **mes disques**). For the different forms, see page 20.
Note: possession can also be expressed using **le**, **la**, **l'**, **les** + **de**: e.g. **C'est la copine de Paul? Non, c'est sa soeur.**

6. Interrogatives

Quel is used to ask information about someone or something. The different forms are:
- **quel** with a masculine word (e.g. **Quel âge as-tu?**);
- **quelle** with a feminine word (e.g. **Quelle heure est-il?**);
- **quels** with a masculine word in the plural (e.g. **Quels sont tes plats préférés?**);
- **quelles** with a feminine word in the plural (e.g. **Quelles boucles d'oreille voulez-vous essayer?**).

7. Adjectives (see pages 46 and 72)

Adjectives are used to describe a person or a thing (e.g. **un type sympa**, **un travail ennuyeux**). Most adjectives come after the noun in French, but there are many exceptions. For example, a number of short and common adjectives come before the noun:

bon(ne)	**grand(e)**	**long(ue)**	**vieux(vieille)**	**beau(belle)**
mauvais(e)	**petit(e)**	**court(e)**	**jeune**	**joli(e)**
nouveau(elle)	**gentil(le)**	**premier(ère)**		
gros(se)	**haut(e)**	**deuxième**		

Some adjectives can be placed before the noun to give a particular emphasis: e.g. **C'est une excellente idée!**

Adjectives agree in gender (masculine or feminine) and number (singular or plural) with the noun they describe (e.g. **des étudiantes chinoises**). The most common patterns for the endings are as follows:

masculine singular	feminine singular	masculine plural	feminine plural
grand	**grande**	**grands**	**grandes**
jeune	**jeune**	**jeunes**	**jeunes**
premier	**première**	**premiers**	**premières**
vendeur	**vendeuse**	**vendeurs**	**vendeuses**
acteur	**actrice**	**acteurs**	**actrices**
anglais	**anglaise**	**anglais**	**anglaises**
furieux	**furieuse**	**furieux**	**furieuses**
ancien	**ancienne**	**anciens**	**anciennes**

But many common adjectives are irregular: e.g. **long, longue**; **blanc, blanche**.

Note: the following adjectives, which come before the noun, have a different form in the masculine singular when the noun starts with a vowel or a silent **h**:
- **beau** > **bel** (e.g. **un bel homme**)
- **nouveau** > **nouvel** (e.g. **le nouvel an**)
- **vieux** > **vieil** (e.g. **un vieil ordinateur**)

Comparisons: to compare one person or thing with another, the following structure is used:
        plus (more) / **moins** (less) / **aussi** (as) + adjective + **que**
For example, **Ce film est plus long** (longer) **que l'autre.**
        A la campagne, la vie est moins chère (less expensive) **qu'à Paris.**
        Tu trouves que le vin italien est aussi bon (as good) **que le vin français?**
Note that **plus** and **bon** cannot be used together, **meilleur** (better) is used instead: e.g. **Elle a eu des meilleurs résultats que l'année passée.** (Similarly, **mieux** is used instead of **plus** and the adverb **bien**: e.g. **Je travaille mieux à la bibliothèque qu'à la maison.**)

8. Pronouns (see pages 46, 58, 84, 108 and 120)

Pronouns are used instead of nouns to avoid:
- mentioning the noun if it is obvious whom or what is being talked about: e.g. **Tu habites à Paris?**
- repeating the noun if it has already been mentioned: e.g. **Tu connais Marie? Oui, bien sûr, je la** (= Marie) **connais bien.**

There are many pronouns to choose from, depending on their function in the sentence, the words that introduce them and the person or thing they refer to.

Here are those covered in this book:

function	singular	plural	examples
subject	je, tu, il, elle, on	nous, vous, ils, elles	<u>On</u> va au cinéma. <u>Vous</u> venez avec nous?
object – direct (i.e. not introduced by a preposition)	me, te, le, la	nous, vous, les	Je <u>la</u> vois tous les jours. Tu peux <u>nous</u> appeler la semaine prochaine?
object – indirect introduced by **à** <u>person</u> <u>thing</u> or <u>place</u>	me, te, lui y	nous, vous, leur y	Il <u>t'</u>a parlé? Nous <u>y</u> allons demain.
object – indirect introduced by an expression of quantity <u>person</u> or <u>thing</u>	en	en	J'<u>en</u> ai trois, et vous?
introduced by a preposition like **chez**, **pour**, **avec**, etc. (come <u>after</u> the verb) <u>person</u>	preposition + **moi, toi, lui, elle**	preposition + **nous, vous, eux, elles**	Je ne suis jamais allée chez <u>eux</u>. C'est pour <u>moi</u> ou pour <u>lui</u>?

Qui and **que** are called <u>relative pronouns</u> and are used to give details about a person or a thing without repeating the noun in a separate sentence. For example, **On a logé chez un ami. <u>Cet ami</u> habite à Paris depuis dix ans. > On a logé chez un ami <u>qui</u> habite à Paris depuis dix ans.**

• **Qui** is used when the person or thing being referred to is the subject of the verb. For example, **Elle travaille dans une <u>école</u>. <u>L'école</u> est près de chez elle. > Elle travaille dans une école <u>qui</u> est près de chez elle.**

• **Que** is used when the person or thing being referred to is the object of the verb. For example, **Hier, on a vu un <u>film</u>. On a adoré <u>ce film</u>. > Hier, on a vu un film <u>qu'</u>on a adoré.**

The verb group

Verbs

9. Verb conjugation (see pages 8, 20 and 32)

Verbs are made of two parts: a stem and an ending: e.g. **aim-er**, **je regard-e**, **vous sort-ez**.

Different endings are used depending on the person (1st, 2nd, 3rd), the number (singular, plural), the tense (present, past, future), etc. Some verbs follow a regular pattern of endings, but many don't.

It can be helpful to classify verbs in four groups, according to their ending in the infinitive (the form you would find in the dictionary, e.g. **habiter**):

- verbs ending in **-er**: all regular, except for **aller**;
- verbs ending in **-ir**: regular verbs follow either the **finir** pattern or the **partir** pattern; there are also some irregular verbs;
- verbs ending in **-re**: some follow the **perdre** pattern, but many are irregular;
- verbs ending in **-oir**: all irregular.

See the verb tables pages 154 to 157 for the different conjugations.

10. Verb construction (see pages 60, 72 and 108)

Verbs can be constructed in different ways. They can:

- come on their own, with no complement: e.g. **Elle dort. Mes amis sont arrivés.**
- come with: – a direct object: e.g. **Je prends le bus. Marc la connais.**
  - an indirect object: e.g. **Ils parlent à leurs amis. Tu lui a téléphoné?**
  - an infinitive: e.g. **Nous devons partir. Le film va commencer.**
- be reflexive: e.g. **Vous vous levez à quelle heure? Je m'ennuie!**
- be impersonal (only used with **il**): e.g. **Il pleut. Il faut réussir!**

11. The present tense (see pages 32, 46 and 60)

The present tense is used to refer to:

- a current or usual action / situation: e.g. **J'habite à Bruxelles.**
- an action / situation in the process of happening: e.g. **Anne n'est pas là, elle fait des courses.**
- an action / situation in the future: e.g. **Le train part dans cinq minutes.**
- instructions: e.g. **Vous prenez la première à droite.**

So, depending on the context, it will be translated in different ways. For example,

– **En général, on mange à une heure.** > We usually <u>eat</u> at one o'clock.

– **On mange!** > We're <u>eating</u>!

– **Ce soir, on mange au restaurant.** > Tonight, we<u>'re eating</u> at the restaurant.

For the different forms of the present tense, see the verb tables pages 154 to 157 and the unit pages mentioned above.

12. The perfect tense (see pages 96 and 108)

The perfect tense ('passé composé') is used to refer to a past event, seen as completed. It is generally made up of the present tense of **avoir** (the auxiliary), followed by the past participle of the verb: e.g. **Hier, j'ai joué au football. Ils ont voyagé pendant deux mois.**

A few verbs form the perfect tense with **être**. They are:
* the following 14 verbs (most easily remembered in pairs):

aller – **venir**
arriver – **partir**
entrer – **sortir**
monter – **descendre**
passer – **retourner**
tomber – **rester**
mourir – **naître**

* all reflexive verbs.

When the auxiliary **être** is used, the past participle must agree with the subject of the verb: e.g.
<u>**Ta mère**</u> **est arriv<u>ée</u>.** <u>**Ils**</u> **se sont bien amus<u>és</u> au Portugal.**

For the different forms of the perfect tense and use with negatives and pronouns, see the unit pages mentioned above as well as the verb tables pages 154 to 157.

13. *The imperative* (see pages 46 and 120)

The imperative is used to give instructions or tell someone to do something. It is generally formed like the present tense, but without the pronouns **tu** or **vous**: e.g. <u>**Attends**</u>**!** <u>**Continuez**</u> **tout droit!**

14. <u>Adverbs</u>

Adverbs can be used to describe an action / situation: e.g. **Il vient <u>rarement</u> ici.** Many adverbs end in **-ment** (similarly in English, many end in -ly). This ending is usually added to the feminine form of the adjective: e.g. **lente-ment**, **heureuse-ment**.

However, many adverbs do not end in **-ment**, including some very common ones: e.g. **bien**, **mal**, **beaucoup**, **peu**, **souvent**, **vite**, etc.

15. <u>Prepositions</u> (see pages 32 and 60)

Prepositions are used to introduce a complement:
* to a verb: e.g. **jouer <u>de</u> la guitare**, **aller <u>chez</u> quelqu'un**;
* to a noun: e.g. **une chambre <u>avec</u> salle de bains**; **un verre <u>de</u> vin**;
* to an adjective: e.g. **content(e) <u>de</u> quelque chose**, **facile <u>à</u> faire**.

When **le** and **les** follow **à** and **de**, they always combine to form **au / aux** and **du / des** – see page 32.

Verb tables

Auxiliaries

Infinitive	Present	Perfect	Imperfect	Future	Conditional
être	je suis	j'ai été	j'étais	je serai	je serais
	tu es	tu as été	tu étais	tu seras	tu serais
	il/elle/on est	il/elle/on a été	il/elle/on était	il/elle/on sera	il/elle/on serait
	nous sommes	nous avons été	nous étions	nous serons	nous serions
	vous êtes	vous avez été	vous étiez	vous serez	vous seriez
	ils/elles sont	ils/elles ont été	ils/elles étaient	ils/elles seront	ils/elles seraient
avoir	j'ai	j'ai eu	j'avais	j'aurai	j'aurais
	tu as	tu as eu	tu avais	tu auras	tu aurais
	il/elle/on a	il/elle/on a eu	il/elle/on avait	il/elle/on aura	il/elle/on aurait
	nous avons	nous avons eu	nous avions	nous aurons	nous aurions
	vous avez	vous avez eu	vous aviez	vous aurez	vous auriez
	ils/elles ont	ils/elles ont eu	ils/elles avaient	ils/elles auront	ils/elles auraient

Regular verbs

Infinitive	Present	Perfect	Imperfect	Future	Conditional
aimer	j'aime	j'ai aimé	j'aimais	j'aimerai	j'aimerais
	tu aimes	tu as aimé	tu aimais	tu aimeras	tu aimerais
	il/elle/on aime	il/elle/on a aimé	il/elle/on aimait	il/elle/on aimera	il/elle/on aimerait
	nous aimons	nous avons aimé	nous aimions	nous aimerons	nous aimerions
	vous aimez	vous avez aimé	vous aimiez	vous aimerez	vous aimeriez
	ils/elles aiment	ils/elles ont aimé	ils/elles aimaient	ils/elles aimeront	ils/elles aimeraient
finir	je finis	j'ai fini	je finissais	je finirai	je finirais
	tu finis	tu as fini	tu finissais	tu finiras	tu finirais
	il/elle/on finit	il/elle/on a fini	il/elle/on finissait	il/elle/on finira	il/elle/on finirait
	nous finissons	nous avons fini	nous finissions	nous finirons	nous finirions
	vous finissez	vous avez fini	vous finissiez	vous finirez	vous finiriez
	ils/elles finissent	ils/elles ont fini	ils/elles finissaient	ils/elles finiront	ils/elles finiraient
partir	je pars	je suis parti(e)	je partais	je partirai	je partirais
	tu pars	tu es parti(e)	tu partais	tu partiras	tu partirais
	il/elle/on part	il/elle/on est parti(e)(s)	il/elle/on partait	il/elle/on partira	il/elle/on partirait
	nous partons	nous sommes parti(e)s	nous partions	nous partirons	nous partirions
	vous partez	vous êtes parti(e)s	vous partiez	vous partirez	vous partiriez
	ils/elles partent	ils/elles sont parti(e)s	ils/elles partaient	ils/elles partiront	ils/elles partiraient

Infinitive	Present	Perfect	Imperfect	Future	Conditional
perdre	je perds tu perds il/elle/on perd nous perdons vous perdez ils/elles perdent	j'ai perdu tu as perdu il/elle/on a perdu nous avons perdu vous avez perdu ils/elles ont perdu	je perdais tu perdais il/elle/on perdait nous perdions vous perdiez ils/elles perdaient	je perdrai tu perdras il/elle/on perdra nous perdrons vous perdrez ils/elles perdront	je perdrais tu perdrais il/elle/on perdrait nous perdrions vous perdriez ils/elles perdraient

Irregular verbs

Infinitive	Present	Perfect	Imperfect	Future	Conditional
aller	je vais tu vas il/elle/on va nous allons vous allez ils/elles vont	je suis allé(e) tu es allé(e) il/elle/on est allé(e)(s) nous sommes allé(e)s vous êtes allé(e)s ils/elles sont allé(e)s	j'allais tu allais il/elle/on allait nous allions vous alliez ils/elles allaient	j'irai tu iras il/elle/on ira nous irons vous irez ils/elles iront	j'irais tu irais il/elle/on irait nous irions vous iriez ils/elles iraient
appeler	j'appelle tu appelles il/elle/on appelle nous appelons vous appelez ils/elles appellent	j'ai appelé tu as appelé il/elle/on a appelé nous avons appelé vous avez appelé ils/elles ont appelé	j'appelais tu appelais il/elle/on appelait nous appelions vous appeliez ils/elles appelaient	j'appellerai tu appelleras il/elle/on appellera nous appellerons vous appellerez ils/elles appelleront	j'appellerais tu appellerais il/elle/on appellerait nous appellerions vous appelleriez ils/elles appelleraient
boire	je bois tu bois il/elle/on boit nous buvons vous buvez ils/elles boivent	j'ai bu tu as bu il/elle/on a bu nous avons bu vous avez bu ils/elles ont bu	je buvais tu buvais il/elle/on buvait nous buvions vous buviez ils/elles buvaient	je boirai tu boiras il/elle/on boira nous boirons vous boirez ils/elles boiront	je boirais tu boirais il/elle/on boirait nous boirions vous boirez ils/elles boiraient
connaître	je connais tu connais il/elle/on connaît nous connaissons vous connaissez ils/elles connaissent	j'ai connu tu as connu il/elle/on a connu nous avons connu vous avez connu ils/elles ont connu	je connaissais tu connaissais il/elle/on connaissait nous connaissions vous connaissiez ils/elles connaissaient	je connaîtrai tu connaîtras il/elle/on connaîtra nous connaîtrons vous connaîtrez ils/elles connaîtront	je connaîtrais tu connaîtrais il/elle/on connaîtrait nous connaîtrions vous connaîtriez ils/elles connaîtraient
devoir	je dois tu dois il/elle/on doit nous devons vous devez ils/elles doivent	j'ai dû tu as dû il/elle/on a dû nous avons dû vous avez dû ils/elles ont dû	je devais tu devais il/elle/on devait nous devions vous deviez ils/elles devaient	je devrai tu devras il/elle/on devra nous devrons vous devrez ils/elles devront	je devrais tu devrais il/elle/on devrait nous devrions vous devriez ils/elles devraient

Infinitive	Present	Perfect	Imperfect	Future	Conditional
dire	je dis tu dis il/elle/on dit nous disons vous dites ils/elles disent	j'ai dit tu as dit il/elle/on a dit nous avons dit vous avez dit ils/elles ont dit	je disais tu disais il/elle/on disait nous disions vous disiez ils/elles disaient	je dirai tu diras il/elle/on dira nous dirons vous direz ils/elles diront	je dirais tu dirais il/elle/on dirait nous dirions vous diriez ils/elles diraient
écrire	j'écris tu écris il/elle/on écrit nous écrivons vous écrivez ils/elles écrivent	j'ai écrit tu as écrit il/elle/on a écrit nous avons écrit vous avez écrit ils/elles ont écrit	j'écrivais tu écrivais il/elle/on écrivait nous écrivions vous écriviez ils/elles écrivaient	j'écrirai tu écriras il/elle/on écrira nous écrirons vous écrirez ils/elles écriront	j'écrirais tu écrirais il/elle/on écrirait nous écririons vous écririez ils/elles écriraient
faire	je fais tu fais il/elle/on fait nous faisons vous faites ils/elles font	j'ai fait tu as fait il/elle/on a fait nous avons fait vous avez fait ils/elles ont fait	je faisais tu faisais il/elle/on faisait nous faisions vous faisiez ils/elles faisaient	je ferai tu feras il/elle/on fera nous ferons vous ferez ils/elles feront	je ferais tu ferais il/elle/on ferait nous ferions vous feriez ils/elles feraient
lire	je lis tu lis il/elle/on lit nous lisons vous lisez ils/elles lisent	j'ai lu tu as lu il/elle/on a lu nous avons lu vous avez lu ils/elles ont lu	je lisais tu lisais il/elle/on lisait nous lisions vous lisiez ils/elles lisaient	je lirai tu liras il/elle/on lira nous lirons vous lirez ils/elles liront	je lirais tu lirais il/elle/on lirait nous lirions vous liriez ils/elles liraient
mettre	je mets tu mets il/elle/on met nous mettons vous mettez ils/elles mettent	j'ai mis tu as mis il/elle/on a mis nous avons mis vous avez mis ils/elles ont mis	je mettais tu mettais il/elle/on mettait nous mettions vous mettiez ils/elles mettaient	je mettrai tu mettras il/elle/on mettra nous mettrons vous mettrez ils/elles mettront	je mettrais tu mettrais il/elle/on mettrait nous mettrions vous mettriez ils/elles mettraient
pouvoir	je peux tu peux il/elle/on peut nous pouvons vous pouvez ils/elles peuvent	j'ai pu tu as pu il/elle/on a pu nous avons pu vous avez pu ils/elles ont pu	je pouvais tu pouvais il/elle/on pouvait nous pouvions vous pouviez ils/elles pouvaient	je pourrai tu pourras il/elle/on pourra nous pourrons vous pourrez ils/elles pourront	je pourrais tu pourrais il/elle/on pourrait nous pourrions vous pourriez ils/elles pourraient
prendre	je prends tu prends il/elle/on prend nous prenons vous prenez ils/elles prennent	j'ai pris tu as pris il/elle/on a pris nous avons pris vous avez pris ils/elles ont pris	je prenais tu prenais il/elle/on prenait nous prenions vous preniez ils/elles prenaient	je prendrai tu prendras il/elle/on prendra nous prendrons vous prendrez ils/elles prendront	je prendrais tu prendrais il/elle/on prendrait nous prendrions nous prendrions ils/elles prendraient

Infinitive	Present	Perfect	Imperfect	Future	Conditional
savoir	je sais tu sais il/elle/on sait nous savons vous savez ils/elles savent	j'ai su tu as su il/elle/on a su nous avons su vous avez su ils/elles ont su	je savais tu savais il/elle/on savait nous savions vous saviez ils/elles savaient	je saurai tu sauras il/elle/on saura nous saurons vous saurez ils/elles sauront	je saurais tu saurais il/elle/on saurait nous saurions vous sauriez ils/elles sauraient
venir	je viens tu viens il/elle/on vient nous venons vous venez ils/elles viennent	je suis venu(e) tu es venu(e) il/elle/on est venu(e)(s) nous sommes venu(e)s vous êtes venu(e)s ils/elles sont venu(e)s	je venais tu venais il/elle/on venait nous venions vous veniez ils/elles venaient	je viendrai tu viendras il/elle/on viendra nous viendrons vous viendrez ils/elles viendront	je viendrais tu viendrais il/elle/on viendrait nous viendrions vous viendriez ils/elles viendraient
voir	je vois tu vois il/elle/on voit nous voyons vous voyez ils/elles voient	j'ai vu tu as vu il/elle/on a vu nous avons vu vous avez vu ils/elles ont vu	je voyais tu voyais il/elle/on voyait nous voyions vous voyiez ils/elles voyaient	je verrai tu verras il/elle/on verra nous verrons vous verrez ils/elles verront	je verrais tu verrais il/elle/on verrait nous verrions vous verriez ils/elles verraient
vouloir	je veux tu veux il/elle/on veut nous voulons vous voulez ils/elles veulent	j'ai voulu tu as voulu il/elle/on a voulu nous avons voulu vous avez voulu ils/elles ont voulu	je voulais tu voulais il/elle/on voulait nous voulions vous vouliez ils/elles voulaient	je voudrai tu voudras il/elle/on voudra nous voudrons vous voudrez ils/elles voudront	je voudrais tu voudrais il/elle/on voudrait nous voudrions vous voudriez ils/elles voudraient

VOCABULARY

à	to, at	Antilles (f. pl.)	West Indies
d'abord	(at) first	août	August
tout d'abord	first of all	s'appeler	to be called
accès (m.)	access	apéritif (m.)	aperitif
accident (m.)	accident	appareil (m.)	appliance, telephone
d'accord	fine, OK	appartement (m.)	flat, appartment
être d'accord	to agree	appel (m.)	call, phone call
ne pas être d'accord	to disagree	appeler	to call, to telephone
acheter	to buy	appétit (m.)	appetite
acteur (trice)	actor, actress	bon appétit	enjoy your meal
actuellement	at the moment	apprendre	to learn
addition	the bill	appuyer	to push, to press
adorer	to adore, to love	après	after, afterwards
adresse (f.)	address	d'après	according to
aérobic (m.)	aerobics	après-midi (m.or f.)	afternoon
aéroport (m.)	airport	architecte	architect
affaire (f.)	business	architecture (f.)	architecture
africain(e)	African	argent (m.)	money
Afrique (f.)	Africa	argent de poche (m.)	pocket money
Afrique du Sud (f.)	South Africa	Argentine (f.)	Agentina
âge (m.)	age	argentin(e)	Argentine
agence (f.)	agency	armoire (f.)	wardrobe
agneau (m.)	lamb	s'arrêter	to stop
agréable	pleasant	arrivée (f)	arrival
aider	to help	arriver	to arrive, to happen
aimer	to like, to love	ascenseur (m.)	lift
Algérie (f.)	Algeria	assez	enough, rather
algérien(ne)	Algerian	assiette (f.)	plate
Allemagne (f.)	Germany	assistant(e)	assistant
allemand(e)	German	athlétisme (m.)	athletics
aller	to go	attendre	to wait for
aller simple (m.)	single ticket	faire attention	to be careful
allergique à	allergic	aucun(e)	any, more, no
aller-retour (m.)	return ticket	aujourd'hui	today
allô	hello (on the phone)	au revoir	goodbye
améliorer	to improve	aussi	also, too
ami(e)	friend	aussi … que	as …. as
s'amuser	to have fun, enjoy oneself	autobus (m.)	bus
an (m.)	year	automne (m.)	autumn
ancien(ne)	former, ancient	autour de	around
anglais(e)	English	autre	other
Angleterre (f.)	England	être en avance	to be early
animal (m)	animal	avant	before
animal domestique	pet	avec	with
animé(e)	lively	avenir (m.)	future
année (f.)	year	à l'avenir	in the future
annoncer	to announce	avenue (f.)	avenue
annuler	to cancel	avion (m.)	airplane

avis (m.)	opinion	bonjour	hello
à mon avis	in my opinion	bonne nuit	good night
avocat(e)	lawyer	bonsoir	good evening
avoir	to have	bord (m.)	edge, side
avril	April	au bord de la mer	at the seaside
		bosser (coll.)	to work
baccalauréat (bac) (m.)	A-levels (equivalent)	boucher(ère)	butcher
baignoire (m.)	bath tub	boucherie (f.)	butcher's shop
bain (m.)	bath	boucles d'oreille (f. pl.)	earrings
salle de bains (f.)	bathroom	boulanger(ère)	baker
balade (f.)	walk, stroll, ramble	boulangerie (f.)	baker's shop
banque (f.)	bank	boule (f.)	scoop, ball
bar (m.)	bar	boulevard (f.)	boulevard
barbe (f.)	beard	boulot (m.) (coll.)	job, work
bar-tabac (m.)	newsagent, tobacconist's shop	bout (m.)	end, tip
		bouteille (f.)	bottle
bas(se)	low	bricolage (m.)	DIY
en bas	downstairs, at the bottom	faire du bricolage	to do DIY
bateau/ferry (m.)	boat, ferry	briller	to shine
bâtiment (m.)	building	britannique	British
beau (belle)	beautiful, handsome	bronzer	to tan
beau-fils (m.)	son-in-law, step-son	se faire bronzer	to sunbathe
beau-frère (m.)	brother-in-law, step-brother	brouillard (m.)	fog
		bruit (m.)	noise
belle-fille (f.)	daughter-in-law, step-daughter	brûlure (f.)	burn
		brun(e)	brown (hair)
belle-mère (f.)	mother-in-law, step-mother	bureau (m.)	office
belle-sœur (f.)	sister-in-law, step-sister	bureau de tourisme (m.)	tourist information office
beaucoup	a lot	bus (m.)	bus
bébé (m.)	baby		
beige	beige	ça	that, it
belge	Belgian	ça va?, ça va	how are you?, (I'm) fine
Belgique (f.)	Belgium	c'est ça	that's right
besoin (m.)	need	cabine d'essayage (f.)	changing room
avoir besoin (de)	to need	café (m.)	black coffee, pub
beurre (m.)	butter	café crème (m.)	white coffee
bibliothèque (f.)	library	caisse (f.)	check out till
bien	well, good	calme	quiet
bien sûr	of course	campagne (f.)	countryside
bientôt	soon	camping (m.)	campsite
à bientôt!	see you soon!	faire du camping	to go camping
bienvenue!	welcome!	Canada (m.)	Canada
bière (f.)	beer	canadien(ne)	Canadian
bilingue	bilingual	canapé-lit (m.)	sofa bed
billet (m.)	ticket	car (m.)	coach
biologie (f.)	biology	carré (m.)	square
biscuit (m.)	biscuit	carrefour (m.)	crossroads
blanc(he)	white	carte (f.)	map, card, menu
bleu(e)	blue	en cas de	in the event of
blond(e)	blonde	casquette (f.)	cap
boire	to drink	casser	to break
boisson (f.)	drink	se casser (coll.)	to leave
boîte de nuit (f.)	nightclub	Je me casse! (coll.)	I'm off!
aller en boîte	to go clubbing	cathédrale (f.)	cathedral
bon(ne)	good, mild (weather)	cause (f.)	cause

159

à cause de	because of	ciel (m.)	sky
ce (cet, cette), ces	it, this, that, these, those	cinéma (m.)	cinema
ceci	this	cinq	five
cela	that	cinquante	fifty
célibataire	single	circulation (f.)	traffic
celui-ci, celui-là	this one, that one	circuler	to run (trains)
(celle-ci, celle-là)		citron (m.)	lemon
cent	one hundred	citron pressé (m.)	fresh lemon juice
centre (m.)	centre	classe (f.)	class
centre-ville (m.)	town centre	clair(e)	light, clear
certificat (m.)	certificate	client(e)	customer
chacun(e)	each one	climat (m.)	climate
chaise (f.)	chair	coca (m.)	coca-cola
chaise roulante (f.)	wheelchair	coin (m.)	corner
chambre (f.)	bedroom	au coin de	at the corner of
champignon (m.)	mushroom	collège (m.)	(lower) secondary school
chance (f.)	luck	collègue	colleague
bonne chance	good luck!	commander	to order
changement (m.)	change	comme	like, as
changer	to change	commencer	to begin, to start
chanter	to sing	comment	how
chanteur(euse)	singer	commerce (m.)	trade, business, shop
chaque	each	centre commercial (m.)	shopping centre
charcuterie (f.)	cold meats, delicatessen	commode (f.)	chest of drawers
château (m.)	castle	complet(ète)	full, complete
chaud	hot, warm	complètement	completely
avoir chaud	to be hot	composter	to validate, to punch (ticket)
chauffage (m.)	heating		
chauffeur (m.)	driver	comprendre	to understand, to include
chaussettes (f. pl.)	socks	compris(e)	included
chaussures (f. pl.)	shoes	comptable (m.)	accountant
chemin (m.)	path, way	comptabilité (f.)	accountancy
cheminée (f.)	fireplace	compte (m.)	account
chemise (f.)	shirt	compter	to count
chemisier (m.)	blouse	conduire	to drive
chèque (m.)	cheque	confortable	comfortable
chèque de voyage (m.)	traveller's cheque	congé (m.)	leave, time off
cher(ère)	expensive	connaissance (f.)	knowledge
chercher	to look for	connaître	to know (someone)
chercheur(euse)	researcher	continuer	to continue
cheveux	hair	contre	against
chez	at somebody's house	par contre	however
chez moi	at my house	copain (m.)	boyfriend, friend
chic	smart	copine (f.)	girlfriend, friend
chimie (f.)	Chemistry	correspondance (f)	connection, (tube, train)
Chine (f.)	China	Corse (f.)	Corsica
chinois(e)	chinese	costume (m.)	suit
chocolat (m.)	chocolate	côte (f.)	coast, chop
chocolat chaud (m.)	hot chocolate	côté (m.)	side
choisir	to choose	à côté de	next to
chômage (m.)	unemployment	côté couloir	aisle seat
être au chômage	to be unemployed	côté fenêtre	window seat
chômeur(euse)	unemployed person	se coucher	to go to bed, to lie down
chose (f.)	thing	couleur (f.)	colour
cigarette (f.)	cigarette	couramment	fluently

cours (m.)	lecture, course
cours intensif (m.)	intensive course
courses (f. pl.)	shopping
faire des courses	to go shopping
court(e)	short
cousin(e)	cousin
coûter	to cost
couverture (f.)	cover, blanket
crèche (f.)	nursery
crème (f.)	cream
croire	to believe
croissant (m.)	croissant
croque-monsieur (m.)	toasted ham and cheese sandwich
crudités (f. pl.)	raw vegetables
cuiller (f.)	spoon
cuisine (f.)	kitchen
cuisiner	to cook
cuisinier(ère)	cook
cuisinière	cooker
cuit(e)	cooked
bien cuit	well done (steak)
culturel(le)	cultural
curieux(euse)	nosy
curriculum vitæ (m.)	CV
dame (f.)	lady
Danemark (m.)	Danemark
danois(e)	danish
dans	in
danse (f.)	dance
danser	to dance
date (f.)	date
de	of, from
se débrouiller	to cope, to manage
décembre	December
décider	to decide
décrire	to describe
déjeuner (m.)	lunch
demain	tomorrow
à demain!	see you tomorrow!
demander	to ask for
déménager	to move house
dentiste	dentist
départ (m.)	departure
département (m.)	department (administrative area)
déplacer	to move
depuis	for, since
dernier(ère)	last
derrière	behind
désirer	to want
descendre	to go down
désolé(e)	sorry
desert (m.)	dessert

au-dessous de	below, underneath
au-dessus de	above
destination (f.)	destination
à destination de	going to
détester	to detest
deux	two
deuxième	second
devant	in front of
devenir	to become
devoir	to have to, must
différent(e)	different
difficile	difficult
dimanche (m.)	Sunday
dîner	to dine, to have dinner
dîner (m.)	evening meal
diplôme (m.)	diploma, certificate
dire	to say
directeur(trice)	director, manager
direction (f.)	management
disque (m.)	disc, record
dissertation (f.)	essay
divers(e)	miscellaneous
divorcé(e)	divorced
dix	ten
dix-huit	eighteen
dix-neuf	nineteen
dix-sept	seventeen
docteur (m.)	doctor
doctorat (m.)	PhD doctorate
domicile	residence
c'est dommage	it's a pity
donc	therefore, so
dormir	to sleep
dormir à la belle étoile	to sleep out in the open
douche (f.)	shower
se doucher	to shower
douze	twelve
draps (m. pl.)	bed linen
droit (m.)	law
droit(e)	straight
droite (f.)	right
à droite	on the right
du, de la, des	of the, some
durer	to last
eau (f.)	water
eau minérale (f.)	mineral water
échouer	to fail
école (f.)	school
écologie (f.)	ecology
économie (f.)	economics
écossais(e)	Scottish
Ecosse	Scotland
écouter	to listen to
écrire	to write

éducation (f.)	education
église (f.)	church
électricien(ne)	electrician
elle (f.)	she, her
elles (f. pl.)	they, them
emploi (m.)	job
employé(e)	employee
en	in, of it, of them
encore	more, yet, still
endroit (m.)	a place
enfant (m.)	child
enfant unique (m.)	only child
enfer (m.)	hell
c'est l'enfer! (coll.)	it's hell!
enfin	finally, well
s'ennuyer	to be bored
ennuyeux(euse)	boring
enseignement (m.)	teaching
enseigner	to teach
ensemble	together
ensuite	next, then
entendre	to hear
entier(ère)	entire, whole
entre	between
entrée (f.)	starter, entrance
entreprise (f.)	firm, company
entrer	to come in, to go in
entretien (m.)	interview
envie (f.)	urge, craving
avoir envie (de)	to feel like, to fancy, to want
envoyer	to send
épeler	to spell
épicé	spicy
épicerie (f.)	grocer's shop
épicier(ère)	grocer
équipe (f.)	team
équipé	equipped
équitation (f.)	horse-riding
escalade (f.)	climbing
escargot (m.)	snail
Espagne (f.)	Spain
espagnol(e)	Spanish
espérer	to hope
essayer	to try
essence (f.)	petrol
est (m.)	east
étage (m.)	floor
Etats-Unis (m. pl.)	United States
été (m.)	summer
étoile (f.)	star
étranger(ère)	foreign
être	to be
étude (f.)	study
études (f. pl.)	studies

études (f.) commerciales	business studies
étudiant(e)	student
étudier	to study
euro (m.)	euro
Europe (f.)	Europe
européen(ne)	European
évier (m.)	sink
examen (m.)	exam
exemple (m.)	example
expérience (f.) professionnelle	work experience
exposition (f.)	exhibition
exprès	on purpose
fac (f.) (coll.)	university
en face de	opposite
de toute façon	in any case, anyway
faim (f.)	hunger
avoir faim	to be hungry
faire	to do, to make
ça fait	it is, it comes to
il faut	it is necessary
famille (f.)	family
fatigué(e)	tired
fauteuil (m.)	armchair
faux(sse)	false, untrue
femme (f.)	woman, wife
fenêtre (f.)	window
jour férié	public holiday
fermer	to close
fermeture annuelle (f.)	annual closure
fête (f.)	party, public holiday
feu (m.)	fire
feux (m. pl.)	traffic lights
février	February
fille (f.)	girl, daughter
fils (m.)	son
fin (f.)	end
finalement	finally, in the end
finir	to finish
flèchettes (f. pl.)	darts
flic (m.) (coll.)	policeman
fois (f.)	time
foncé(e)	dark
football (m.)	football
footing (m.)	jogging
formation (f.)	education/training
formidable	great
fort(e)	strong, loud
fournir	to provide/supply
franc (m.)	franc
français(e)	French
France (f.)	France
francophone	French-speaking
frère (m.)	brother

fric (m.) (coll.)	money	à quelle heure?	at what time?
frites	chips	heureusement	fortunately
froid(e)	cold	heureux(se)	happy
avoir froid	to be cold	hier	yesterday
fromage (m.)	cheese	histoire (f.)	history
fruit (m.)	fruit	hiver (m.)	winter
fumée (f.)	smoke	homme (m.)	man
fumer	to smoke	hôpital (m.)	hospital
(non)-fumeurs	(non) smoking	horaire (m.)	timetable
	compartment	hôtel (m.)	hotel
furieux(euse)	furious	hôtel de ville (m.)	town hall
		huit	eight
gagner	to earn, to win		
gallois(e)	Welsh	ici	here
garage (m.)	garage	idée (f.)	idea
gare (f.)	station	bonne idée!	good idea!
gare routière (f.)	coach station	identité (f.)	identity
gâteau (m.)	cake	il (m.)	he, it
gauche	left	ils (m. pl.)	they
à gauche	on the left	il y a	ago, there is, there are
génial(e)	great, super	image (f.)	image
gens (m. pl.)	people	imperméable (m.)	rain coat
gentil(le)	kind, nice	important(e)	important
géographie (f.)	geography	impossible	impossible
gestion (f.)	management	Inde (f.)	Indian
gestion d'entreprise (f.)	business management	indien(ne)	Indian
gilet (m.)	cardigan	infirmier(ère)	nurse
gîte (m.)	self-catering	information (f.)	information
	accommodation	informatique (f.)	computing
glace (f.)	ice cream	ingéniérie (f.)	engineering
goûter	to taste	ingénieur (m.)	engineer
grand(e)	big, tall	s'inscrire	to enrol
Grande-Bretagne (f.)	Great Britain	s'installer	to settle
grand-mère (f.)	grandmother	intelligent(e)	intelligent
grand-père (m.)	grandfather	intention (f.)	intention
grands-parents (pl.)	grandparents	avoir l'intention (de)	to intend to
gratuit(e)	free (no charge)	interdire	to forbid
grave	serious	intéressant(e)	interesting
grec(que)	Greek	internet (m.)	internet
Grèce (f.)	Greece	interrupteur (m.)	switch
grève (f.)	strike	inviter	to invite
grillé(e)	grilled	Irak (m.)	Irak
gris(e)	grey	iraquien(ne)	Iraqi
gros(se)	big, fat	Irelande (f.)	Ireland
groupe (m.)	group	irlandais(e)	Irish
guichet (m.)	ticket office	Italie (f.)	Italy
guitare (f.)	guitar	italien(ne)	Italian
gym (f.)	gym		
		jamaïcain(e)	Jamaican
s'habiller	to get dressed	Jamaïque (f.)	Jamaica
habiter	to live	jamais	never
comme d'habitude	as usual	jambon (m.)	ham
haut(e)	high	janvier	January
heure (f.)	hour	Japon (m.)	Japan
être à l'heure	to be on time	japonais(e)	Japanese

jardin (m.)	garden	licence (f.)	Bachelor,s degree
jaune	yellow	lieu (m.)	place
je	I	au lieu	instead of
jean (m.)	jeans	ligne (f.)	line
jeu (m.)	game	limonade (f.)	lemonade
jeudi	Thursday	linguistique (f.)	linguistics
jeune	young	lire	to read
joli(e)	pretty	liste (f.)	list
jouer	to play	lit (m.)	bed
jour (m.)	day	lit double (m.)	double bed
à un de ces jours (coll.)	see you around!	lit simple (m.)	single bed
journal (m.)	newspaper	litre (m.)	litre
journaliste	journalist	littérature (f.)	literature
journée (f.)	day	livre (m.)	book
bonne journée!	have a good day!	livre (f.)	pound
juillet	July	location (f.)	hire, rental
juin	June	loger	to accommodate, to stay
jupe (f.)	skirt	loin	far, far away
jus (m.)	juice	loisir	leisure
jusqu'à	until, up to	Londres	London
juste	just, correct	long(ue)	long
		longtemps	a long time
kilo (m.)	kilo	louer	to rent, to hire
kilomètre (m.)	kilometer	lourd(e)	heavy
kilométrage (m.)	mileage	lui, leur	(to) him, (to) her, (to) them
kir (m.)	Kir (white wine and	lundi (m.)	Monday
blackcurrant)		lune (f.)	moon
		lunettes (f. pl.)	glasses
là	there	lycée (m.)	upper secondary school
là-bas	over there		
lac (m.)	lake	madame (f.)	madam, Mrs
laisser	to leave	mademoiselle (f.)	miss
laisser un message	to leave a message	magasin (m.)	shop
lait (m.)	milk	grand magasin (m.)	department store
langage (m.) familier	colloquial language	magazine (m.)	magazine
langue (f.) étrangère	foreign language	magnifique	brilliant
lave-linge (f.)	washing machine	mai	May
laver	to wash	main (f.)	hand
se laver	to get washed	maintenant	now
lave-vaisselle (m.)	dishwasher	mais	but
le, (la, les)	the	maison (f.)	house
le, la	it, him, her	à la maison	at home
les	them	maîtrise (f.)	Masters degree
lecture (f.)	reading	mal (m.)	pain, bad
léger(ère)	light	mal	badly
légume (m.)	vegetable	pas mal	not bad (pretty good)
lendemain (m.)	the day after	malade	ill
lequel?/laquelle?	which one?	malheureusement	unfortunately
lettre (f.)	letter	manger	to eat
lettre de		manteau (m.)	coat
recommandation (f.)	reference letter	marchand(e)	shopkeeper
lettres modernes (f. pl.)	humanities	marche (f.)	step
se lever	to get up	marché (m.)	market
librairie (f.)	bookshop	marcher	to walk, to function
libre	free	ça marche?	does it work?

mardi (m.)	Tuesday	monsieur (m.)	Sir, Mr
mari (m.)	husband	montagne (f.)	mountain
marié(e)	married	monter	to go up
marketing (m.)	marketing	montrer	to show
Maroc (m.)	Morroco	morceau (m.)	piece, bit
marocain(e)	Moroccan	mot (m)	word
marrant(e)	funny	moto (f.)	motorbike
en avoir marre (coll.)	to be fed up	mourir	to die
marron	brown (eyes)	moustache (f.)	moustache
mars	March	moyen(ne)	average
match (m.)	match	moyen de transport (m.)	means of transport
mathématiques (f. pl.)	mathematics	musée (m.)	museum
matin (m.)	morning	musique (f.)	music
matinée (f.)	morning		
mauvais(e)	bad	nager	to swim
me	(to) me, myself	naissance (f.)	birth
mécanicien(ne)	mechanic	naître	to be born
médecin (m.)	doctor	natation (f.)	swimming
médicament (m.)	medecine, medication	faire de la natation	to go swimming
meilleur(e)	better	nationalité (f.)	nationality
même	same, even	ne … jamais	never
ménage (m.)	housework, household	ne … pas	not
mention (f.)	distinction	ne … plus	no longer, no more
menu (m.)	menu	ne … que	only
mer (f.)	sea, seaside	ne … rien	nothing
au bord de la mer	at the seaside	neige (f.)	snow
merci	thank you	il neige	it snows, it is snowing
mercredi (m.)	Wednesday	neuf	nine
mère (f.)	mother	neveu (m.)	nephew
météo (f.)	weather forecast	ni	neither
métier	job, career	nièce (f.)	niece
mètre (m.)	metre	Noël (m.)	Christmas
métro (m.)	tube, underground	noir(e)	black
mettre	to put	nom (m.)	name
se mettre à (faire)	to start (doing)	nom de famille (m.)	surname
meuble (m.)	a piece of furniture	au nom (de)	in the name of
midi	midday, noon	nombre (m.)	number
mignon(ne)	cute, attractive	non	no
milieu (m.)	middle	non-fumeurs	non smoking
mille	thousand	nord (m.)	north
million (m.)	million	note (f.)	mark
mince	slim	notre, nos	our
minuit	midnight	nous	we, (to) us, ourselves
minute (f.)	minute	nouveau(elle)	new
à mi-temps	part-time	novembre	November
mode (f.)	fashion	nuage (m.)	cloud
moderne	modern	nuit (f.)	night
moi	me	nul(le) (coll.)	not nice
moins	less	numéro (m.)	number
mois (m.)	month		
moitié (f.)	half	objet (m.)	object
môme (m.) or (f.)	kid	objet (m.) de valeur	valuable
mon, ma, mes	my	être obligé(e) de	to have to
monde (m.)	world	obtenir	to gain, to get
beaucoup de monde	a lot of people	s'occuper de	to deal with, to take care of

165

octobre	October	pension (f.)	guest house
oeil (m.) (yeux pl.)	eye	demi-pension (f.)	half-board
oeuf (m.)	egg	perdre	to lose
offrir	to offer	perdre connnaisance	to lose consciousness, to
oiseau (m.)	bird	faint	
on	one/we	père (m.)	father
oncle (m.)	uncle	permettre	to allow
onze	eleven	permis de conduire (m.)	driving licence
opéra (m.)	opera	personne (f.)	person
opinion (f.)	opinion	personnes handicapées	
orage (m.)	storm	(f. pl.)	disabled people
orange (f.)	orange	pétanque (f.)	boules
orange pressée (f.)	fresh orange juice	petit(e)	little, small, short (person)
ordinateur (m.)	computer	petit déjeuner (m.)	breakfast
oreille (f.)	ear	petite-fille (f.)	granddaughter
oreiller (m.)	pillow	petit-fils (m.)	grandson
ou	or	peu	not much
où	where	un (petit) peu	a (little) bit
oublier	to forget	à peu près	more or less, about
ouest (m.)	west	peut-être	perhaps
Ouganda (m.)	Ouganda	pharmacie (f.)	chemist's shop
ougandais(e)	Ugandan	pharmacien(ne)	chemist
oui	yes	philosophie (f.)	philosophy
outil informatique (m.)	computer package	photographie (f.)	photography
ouvert(e)	open	piano (m.)	piano
ouvrir	to open	pièce (f.)	room/play
		pied (m.)	foot
pain (m.)	bread	à pied	on foot
en panne	broken down, out of order	ping-pong (m.)	table tennis
pantalon (m.)	trousers	pique-nique (m.)	picnic
Pâques (m.)	Easter	piquer (coll.)	to steal
par	through	piscine (f.)	swimming pool
parc (m.)	park	pittoresque	picturesque
parce que	because	place (f.)	seat, square
pardon	excuse me, sorry, pardon	plan (m.)	map
parents (pl.)	parents	se plaindre	to complain
parfois	sometimes	planche à voile (f.)	windsurfing
parking (m.)	car park	plat(e)	flat, smooth
parler	to speak	plat (m.)	dish
partir	to leave	plat du jour (m.)	dish of the day
pas	not	plat principal (m.)	main course
pas du tout	not at all	plein(e)	full
pas grand-chose	not a lot	plein de	lots of
pas mal de	quite a lot of	à plein temps	full-time
passer	to pass by, through	il pleut	it rains, it's raining
passer un coup de fil		pluie (f.)	rain
(coll.)	to make a phone call	plus	more
passer un examen	to sit an exam	plus ou moins	more or less
pâtisserie (f.)	pastry / cake shop	plus tard	later
payer	to pay	à plus tard!	see you later!
pays (m.)	country	plusieurs	several
Pays-Bas (m. pl.)	Netherlands	pneu crevé (m.)	flat tyre
Pays de Galles (m.)	Wales	à point	medium done
pendant	for, during	pointure (f.)	shoe size
penser	to think	poisson (m.)	fish

poivre (m.)	pepper	quart d'heure (m.)	quarter of an hour
police (f.)	police	quartier (m.)	neighbourhood, area
policier(ère)	policeman (woman)	quatorze	fourteen
politique (f.)	politics	quatre	four
pollué(e)	polluted	à un de ces quatres!	
pomme (f.)	apple	(coll.)	see you around!
pompiers (m. pl.)	fire brigade	quatre-vingt-dix	ninety
pont (m.)	bridge	quatre-vingts	eighty
porte (f.)	door	quatrième	fourth
portefeuille (m)	wallet	que (conjunction)	that, than
porter	to carry, to wear	que (pronoun)	that, what, which,
Portugal (m.)	Portugal	qu'est-ce que c'est?	what is it?
portugais(e)	Portuguese	Québec (m.)	Quebec
possible	possible	québécois(e)	Quebecois
poste (f.)	post office	quel(le)	what, which
poste (m.)	job, position	quelque	some
poste de secours (m.)	first-aid post	quelque chose	something
pot (m.) (coll.)	drink	quelquefois	sometimes
poulet (m.)	chicken	quelques	a few
pour	for	quelqu'un	someone
pourboire (m.)	tip (money)	question (f.)	question
pourquoi	why	qui	who, whom
pousser	to push	quinze	fifteen
pouvoir	to be able, can	quitter	to leave
préférer	to prefer	quoi	what
premier(ère)	first		
prendre	to take	radio (f.)	radio
prénom (m.)	first name	randonnée (à pied) (f.)	walking, hiking
près	near	rapide	fast
se présenter	to introduce oneself	rappeler	to call back, to call again
prêt(e)	ready	rater	to miss
prêter	to lend	réceptionniste	receptionist
printemps (m.)	spring	recevoir	to receive
prix (m.)	price	recommander	to recommend
problème (m.)	problem	refiler (coll.)	to give
prochain(e)	next	réfrigérateur (m.)	fridge
à la prochaine!	see you next time!	refuser	to refuse
proche	near	regarder	to watch, to look at
professeur (m.)	teacher	région (f.)	region
profession (f.)	occupation	relax (m.)	garden lounger
projet (m.)	plan, project	relaxant	relaxing
promenade(f.)	walk	remplir un formulaire	to fill in a form
se promener	to go for a walk	rencontrer	to meet
proposer	to suggest	rendez-vous (m.)	appointment
propre	clean	renseignements (m. pl.)	information
en provenance de	coming from	se renseigner	to find out, make enquiries
psychologie (f.)	psychology	rentrer	to come, go back (home)
puis	then	renverser	to knock down
pull (m.)	jumper	réparer	to repair
		repas (m.)	meal
quai (m.)	platform	répéter	to repeat
qualification (f.)	qualification	répondre	to answer
quand	when	réponse (f.)	answer
quarante	forty	se reposer	to rest, to relax
quart (m.)	quarter	réservation (f.)	booking

réserver	to book
responsable	person in charge
responsable de	responsible (for)
restaurant (m.)	restaurant
reste (m.)	remainder, rest
rester	to stay
résultat (m.)	result
retard (m.)	delay
être en retard	to be late
retourner	to go back
retraite (f.)	retirement
être à la retraite	to be retired
se retrouver	to meet up
réussir	to succeed, to pass
se réveiller	to wake up
réveil automatique (m.)	early morning call
revenir	to come back
rez-de-chaussée	ground floor
rien	nothing
de rien	don't mention it, that's OK
rivière (f.)	river
robe (f.)	dress
rond(e)	round
rond-point (m.)	roundabout
rose	pink
rouge	red
route (f.)	road
roux(sse)	ginger (hair)
Royaume-Uni (m.)	United Kingdom
rue	road, street
rugby (m.)	rugby
russe	Russian
sac (m.)	bag
saignant(e)	rare (steak)
saison (f.)	season
basse saison (f.)	low season
demi-saison (f.)	mid season
haute saison (f.)	high season
salade (f.)	salad
sale	dirty
salle (f.)	room
salle de bains (f.)	bathroom
salle à manger	dining room
salle de séjour (f.)	living room
salon (m.)	sitting room
salut!	hi!, goodbye! (informal)
samedi (m.)	Saturday
SAMU	mobile accident unit
sandwich (m.)	sandwich
sans	without
sauce (f.)	sauce
sauce au poivre	pepper sauce
saucisse (f.)	sausage
saucisson (m.)	salami, cured meat
sauf	except
saumon (m.)	salmon
savoir	to know (something)
savon (m.)	soap
science (f.)	science
sciences commerciales (f. pl.)	business studies
sciences de l'éducation (f. pl.)	education
sciences politiques (f. pl.)	politics
se	himself, herself, themselves
sec (sèche)	dry
second(e)	second
secrétaire	secretary
seize	sixteen
séjour (m.)	stay, living room
séjour à l'étranger	stay abroad
sel (m.)	salt
selon	according to
semaine (f.)	week
à la semaine prochaine!	see you next week!
Sénégal (m.)	Senegal
sénégalais(e)	Senegalese
sens (m.)	direction, sense
sentir	to feel
se sentir à l'aise	to feel at ease
séparé(e)	separated
sept	seven
septembre	September
serré(e)	tight
serveur(euse)	waiter(tress)
serviette (f.)	towel
servir	to serve
seul(e)	alone
seulement	only
si	if
s'il te plaît, s'il vous plaît	please (informal, formal)
simple	simple
sinon	otherwise, or else
six	six
ski (m.)	ski, skiing
faire du ski	to go skiing
ski nautique (m.)	water skiing
snack bar (m.)	snack bar
SNCF	French national railways
s'occuper de	to look after
société (f.)	company
sociologie	sociology
sœur (f.)	sister
soif (f.)	thirst
avoir soif	to be thirsty
soir (m.)	evening

à ce soir	see you this evening
soirée (f.)	evening
soixante	sixty
soixante-dix	seventy
soleil (m.)	sun
son, sa, ses	his, her
sortie (f.)	exit, way out
sortir	to come/go out
soupe (f.)	soup
sous	under
souvent	often
se spécialiser	to specialise
sport (m.)	sport
faire du sport	to play sport
sportif(ve)	keen on sport, good at sport
stage (m.)	work placement
stagiaire	person on work placement
station de métro (f.)	underground station
station service (f.)	petrol station
steak (m.)	steak
sucre (m.)	sugar
sud	south
Suède (f.)	Sweden
suédois(e)	Swedish
suffisant(e)	sufficient
suggérer	to suggest
Suisse (f.)	Switzerland
suisse	Swiss
suivant(e)	next, following
suivre	to follow
suivre un cours	to do a course
super	super, brilliant, great
supermarché (m.)	supermarket
sur	on
sûr(e)	sure, certain
bien sûr	of course
surtout	above all, especially
sympa	nice, friendly
tableau (m.)	picture
taches de rousseur (f. pl.)	freckles
taille (f.)	size
tante (f.)	aunt
taper	to type
tard	late
tarte (f.)	pie
tarte aux pommes	apple pie
tartine (f.)	buttered bread
tasse (f.)	cup
taxi (m.)	taxi
tchèque	Czech
te	(to) you, yourself
technicien(ne)	technician

tee-shirt (m.)	tee-shirt
téléphone (m.)	telephone
téléphoner à	to telephone
télévision (f.)	television
télévision par satellite (f.)	satellite television
tellement	so much
temps (m.)	time, weather
de temps en temps	from time to time
tenir	to hold, to keep
tennis (m.)	tennis
tente (f.)	tent
terminer	to finish
terrasse (f.)	terrace
terre (f.)	ground
pas terrible	not very good
test (m.)	test
tête (f.)	head
TGV (m.)	high speed train
thé (m.)	tea
théâtre (m.)	theatre
ticket (m.)	ticket
timbre (m.)	postage stamp
toi	you
toilettes (f. pl.)	toilets
faire sa toilette	to wash
tomate (f.)	tomato
tomber	to fall
ton, ta, tes	your (informal)
tôt	early
toujours	always
tour (m.)	turn, tour (of a city)
tour (f.)	tower
tour du monde (m.)	world trip
tourisme (m.)	tourism
tout de suite	immediately
à tout de suite	see you in a minute
tout droit	straight ahead
tout(e), tous(tes)	every, all
tous les jours	everyday
tout le monde	everyone
traducteur(trice)	translator
traduction (f.)	translation
train (m.)	train
tranquille	quiet
transport (m.)	transport
travail (m.)	work
travailler	to work
traverser	to cross
treize	thirteen
trente	thirty
très	very
trois	three
trop (de)	too (much)
trop de monde	too many people

trouver	to find	vin (m.)	wine
se trouver	to be situated, to find oneself	vingt	twenty
		vingtième	twentieth
truite (f.)	trout	violon (m.)	violin
tu	you (singular, informal)	visite (f.)	visit
type (m.) (coll.)	guy	visiter	to visit
		vitesse (f.)	speed
un(e)	a, one	vivre	to live
une fois	once	vocabulaire (m.)	vocabulary
uniforme (m.)	uniform	voici	here is, here are, here you are
université (f.)	university		
usine (f.)	factory	voilà	there you are, here you are
utile	useful		
utiliser	to use	voile (f.)	sailing
		voir	to see
vacances (f.pl.)	holidays	voisin(e)	neighbour
vanille (f.)	vanilla	voiture (f.)	car, carriage
varappe (f.)	rock climbing	vol (m.)	flight
varié(e)	varied	volley (m.)	volleyball
végétarien(ne)	vegetarian	à volonté	help yourself
veille (f.)	day before	votre, vos	your (formal or plural)
veinard(e) (coll.)	lucky	à votre disposition	available
vélo (m.)	bike	à votre service	you are welcome
en vélo	by bike	vouloir	to want, to wish
vendeur(euse)	sales assistant	vous	you (formal or plural), yourselves
vendre	to sell		
vendredi (m.)	Friday	voyage (m.)	trip
venir	to come	voyager	to travel
vent (m.)	wind	vrai(e)	real, true
vérifier	to check	vraiment	really
verre (m.)	glass	vue (f.)	view
vers	towards	vue sur la mer (f.)	sea view
vert(e)	green		
veste (f.)	jacket	week-end (m.)	weekend
vêtements (m. pl.)	clothes		
vétérinaire (m.or f.)	vet	y	there
viande (f.)	meat	yaourt (m.)	yoghurt
vie (f.)	life	yoga (m.)	yoga
vieux (vieille)	old		
village (m.)	village	zéro	zero, nought
ville (f.)	town, city		

ANSWERS

UNIT 1

1 b 1c; 2a; 3b.

3 je suis; je m'appelle; c'est

4 Spanish; French; Irish; African; Italian; Indian; Senegalese; Scottish; Greek; German; English; Welsh.
secretary; nurse; doctor; teacher; director; student; lawyer; journalist; waiter/waitress; receptionist; technician; sales assistant

5 Italian; lawyer; Spanish; technician; Greek; teacher; Indian; journalist; Welsh; student; Irish; secretary.

7 a masculine; **b** feminine; **c** feminine; **d** masculine or feminine; **e** masculine; **f** masculine or feminine; **g** masculine; **h** masculine; **i** feminine; **j** masculine.

8 a Electra: Greek; student of philosophy; Rhodes; London; **b Ravi**: Indian; doctor; Bombay; Manchester; **c Mesenge**: Senegalese; student of physics; Dakar; Nice; **d Matthias**: Swiss; receptionist; Zurich; London; **e Silva**: Spanish; student of English; Barcelona; Oxford; **f Steve**: Welsh; waiter; Cardiff; Brussels

10 a appelle; **b** moi; **c** suis; **d** à; **e** suis; **f** de; **g** directeur; **h** vendeuse

11 a Oui, c'est moi. **b** Je suis sénégalaise. **c** Je suis de Dakar. **d** Je suis vendeuse.

12 a Vous êtes Joseph Toure? **b** Vous êtes français? **c** Vous êtes d'où? **d** Qu'est-ce que vous faites?

13 f; d; b; c; a; e; h; g.

14 a Comment tu t'appelles? **b** Qu'est-ce que tu fais? **c** Tu es anglaise? **d** Tu es d'où? **e** Où est-ce que tu habites? **f** Tu travailles?

16 a Jacques Vandevelde; **b** belge; **c** à Liège; **d** étudiant; **e** Isabelle Chamfraud; **f** canadienne; **g** à Montréal; **h** étudiante

Extra!

1

	Name	Nationality	Town of residence	Subject of study	Job
a	Clément Dufond	French	Bastia	politics	no
b	Gérard Denis	Belgian	Brussels	English or languages	yes, in a bar
c	Nathalie Martin	French	Nice	biology	no
d	Sylvie Lebon	French	Poitiers	languages	no
e	Arthur Dumarre	Swiss	Lausanne	German and economics	yes, part-time placement
f	Béa Lemercier	Swiss	Geneva	history	yes, waitress in restaurant

2 a Paris; **b** law; **c** waitress; **d** engineer; **e** Versailles.

Exercices de grammaire

1 a espagnol; **b** irlandaise; **c** sénégalais; **d** galloise; **e** suisse; **f** belge; **g** grec; **h** infirmière; **i** réceptionniste; **j** secrétaire; **k** directeur; **l** vendeuse; **m** professeur; **n** étudiante

2 a Elle ne s'appelle pas Mary. Elle est étudiante. Elle n'est pas américaine. Elle habite à Rome. Elle ne travaille pas au bureau.
b Il s'appelle Laurent. Il n'est pas infirmier. Il est français. Il n'habite pas à Toulouse. Il travaille dans un café.

3 a Tu es Hélène? **b** Tu viens d'où? **c** Qu'est-ce qu'elle fait? **d** Est-ce qu'il travaille? **e** Tu habites où? **f** Tu es américaine?

4 a Elle habite à Marseille? **b** Qu'est-ce qu'il fait? **c** Tu es étudiant à Londres? **d** Est-ce que vous êtes de Rome? **e** Comment tu t'appelles? **f** Il travaille dans un café.

UNIT 2

3 1; 3; 4; 7; 9; 12; 14; 15; 18; 25; 30; 44; 60

5 salut!; tu travailles; j'ai un copain; une copine; congolais; français

7 **a** her son; **b** her boyfriend and his daughter; **c** doctor; **d** four years old

8 **a** ta; **b** quel; **c** ans; **d** Où; **e** à; **f** est; **g** étudiante; **h** travaille

10 **a** V; **b** F; **c** F; **d** F; **e** V; **f** F; **g** F; **h** V; **i** V; **j** F

11 f; b; d; a; c; e

12 **a** Ce sont mes copines; **b** Ils travaillent à Londres; **c** Ils habitent à Paris; **d** Ce sont tes copains?; **e** Ils ont treize ans; **f** Mes amies sont étudiantes.

13 **a** F; **b** F; **c** F; **d** V; **e** V; **f** F

14 **a** 2; **b** 1; **c** 3

15 **a** ça; **b** ma; **c** veux; **d** un; **e** un; **f** quelque chose; **g** merci; **h** un

Extra!

1 Possible answers
François: 1 brother/1 sister Isabelle lives in Belgium/lots of friends in Brussels
Anne Marie: 1 younger sister/lots of friends everywhere: Bordeaux, Lille, Limoges, Nancy, Lyons/1 brother Arnaud from Lyons
Gabriella: 1 sister goes to university in Lyons/2 brothers still at school (college)/mother does not work/father works at the train station/not many friends/best friend lives near her

2 **a** 21; **b** She is a student there; **c** four; **d** no; **e** four sisters; **f** Southport; **g** She is nosy.

Exercices de grammaire

1 **a** habite; **b** ont; **c** s'appelle; **d** a; **e** est; **f** travaille; **g** s'appelle; **h** a; **i** est; **j** est; **k** habite; **l** travaille; **m** a.

2 **a** ma; **b** nos (plural); **c** notre/mon; **d** sa; **e** leur (plural); **f** ton; **g** son

3 **a** ta; **b** notre; **c** des; **d** un; **e** le/mon; **f** son; **g** un/le; **h** un/mon; **i** votre; **j** un/ton

UNIT 3

2 **a** Je fais la cuisine; **b** Nous regardons la télé; **c** Je fais une dissertation pour le cours de philo; **d** Rien de spécial, nous lisons; **e** J'écoute la musique; **f** Je mange.

4 **1** e; **2** g; **3** d; **4** h; **5** a; **6** j; **7** b; **8** f; **9** c; **10** i

5 **a** Bertrand; **b** the swimming pool; **c** guitar lesson; **d** going clubbing; **e** Alain, his sister and a girlfriend; **f** cycling

8 **a** a quarter past two; **b** twenty five to eleven; **c** half past five; **d** a quarter to midnight; **e** ten past eight; **f** nine o'clock

10 **a** lundi; **b** mardi; **c** mercredi; **d** jeudi; **e** vendredi; **f** samedi; **g** dimanche

11 **a** open from 9 a.m. to 1 p.m., from Monday to Friday; **b** closed at the weekend; **c** open from midday to 4 p.m. on Tuesdays and Thursdays; **d** closed on Saturday afternoon from 1 p.m. to 3 p.m. **e** open in the evening from 6 p.m. to 9 p.m.

12 **a** je prends; je commence; je termine; je travaille; je vais; je pars; j'arrive; je finis; je mange
b **i** V; **ii** F; **iii** V; **iv** F; **v** V; **vi** V; **vii** F; **viii** V

14 **a** j'aime bien le sport; **b** j'aime beaucoup la planche à voile; **c** je n'aime pas beaucoup le football; **d** j'aime beaucoup le théâtre

15 **a** aller; **b** jouer; **c** jouer; **d** faire; **e** faire; **f** jouer

16 **a** does not like going swimming, likes to play football and rugby, likes to go to the cinema; **b** does not like to dance, likes to play sport a lot, likes cycling and wind-

surfing; **c** likes to go to the gym, to go shopping, to listen to music, hates going to the theatre; **d** does not like to watch television, likes to play cards, really likes to do yoga but does not like cooking

Extra!

1   Possible answers
    Ricardo: lots of work/does sport/phones his friends/goes for walks/goes cycling
    Anne: nurse, works nights/will go to friend's birthday party/will go to a club/will go to a restaurant
    Daniella: lots of work/student of German and Italian/gets home late/only goes out at the week-end/goes swimming with her boyfriend

2   **a** to go shopping with her friends; **b** at nine o'clock; **c** has lunch; **d** goes to the gym; goes swimming; **e** She goes to a restaurant and then to see a film or to a bar or nightclub; **f** at midday

Exercices de grammaire

1   **a** Nous jouons du piano; **b** Tu joues au tennis; **c** Je vais au cinéma; **d** Vous allez à l'université? **e** Ils/elles jouent aux cartes; **f** Tu vas à la piscine?

2   **a** aime; **b** vais; **c** faire; **d** n'aime pas; **e** sors; **f** allons; **g** aimons; **h** n'est pas; **i** préfère; **j** aime; **k** adore.

3   **a** Vous aimez faire du sport?; **b** Elle n'aime pas faire de la natation; **c** Nous aimons bien jouer aux cartes; **d** Il n'aime pas aller au cinéma; **e** J'aime regarder la télévision.

4   **a** Il doit aller à l'église le dimanche matin; **b** Je dois sortir ce soir; **c** Ils doivent aller au lit; **d** Tu dois boire quelque chose; **e** Nous devons travailler cet après-midi; **f** Vous devez faire du sport.

UNIT 4

1   **a** 6; **b** 3; **c** 4; **d** 5; **e** 7; **f** 8; **g** 1; **h** 2

2   **a** la gare; **b** l'Hôtel de ville; **c** une station de métro; **d** la poste

3   **a** bibliothèque; supermarché.
    b Vous prenez la deuxième rue à droite, et c'est là, à gauche; Vous prenez la première rue à droite, et c'est là à droite.

4   **a** Statue du Petit Quinquin; **b** hôpital militaire; **c** Eglise St Maurice; **d** la gare

6   **a** next to; **b** between; **c** opposite; **d** in front of; **e** on the corner of; **f** behind

7   **a** F: Le restaurant est à côté de la boucherie; **b** F: La bibliothèque est dans la Rue des Alliés; **c** F: Entre la poste et le musée, il y a un théâtre; **d** V; **e** F: Le bar-tabac est au coin de la Rue Dauphine et de l'Avenue Gambetta; **f** V; **g** V; **h** F: Il y a un arrêt d'autobus devant la gare.

9   **a** a black coat; **b** a white or green shirt; **c** He doesn't like it; **d** blue, pink, red and yellow; **e** the coat, the green shirt and the pink shirt.

10 **a** €75; **b** chemise; **c** €95; **d** gilet rouge; **e** €250; **f** chemise bleue; **g** chemise blanche; **h** €180

11 Je voudrais ce pull **rouge**; **90** euros; Moi, je voudrais cette **jupe** bleue et ces deux tee-shirts **blancs**; Et ce **manteau**; Et tu n'aimes pas la **veste** verte là?; Non, je n'aime pas beaucoup les **vestes**; elle coûte **200** euros; Regarde ce **pantalon**; il est **vert**-rose.

13 **a i** a pair of trousers, a shirt and maybe shoes; **ii** black trousers, a grey shirt and black shoes; **b i** Tu aimes ce pantalon?; **ii** Moi aussi; **iii** J'aime les deux; **iv** Je préfère les noires; **v** Tu veux les essayer?

14 **a** jupe; **b** noire; **c** aime; **d** jupe; **e** la; **f** ce; **g** deux; **h** les; **i** bleue; **j** droite

Extra!

1 **a** F; **b** V; **c** F; **d** V; **e** F; **f** F

2 **a** blue dress and pink dress; **b** jumper and skirt; **c** 65 euros; **d** blue skirt and white raincoat

Exercices de grammaire

1 **a** prends/prenez; **b** vas/allez; **c** tournes/tournez; **d** traverses/traversez; **e** prends/prenez; **f** continue/continuez

2 **a** la; **b** de la; **c** de l'; **d** du; **e** de l'; **f** du; **g** la; **h** la; **i** le

3 **a** l'; **b** la; **c** la; **d** les; **e** l'

4 **a** cette; **b** ces; **c** ce; **d** cette; **e** ces; **f** cet

5 **a** les chemises roses; **b** les tee-shirts blancs; **c** les pantalons rouges; **d** les jupes bleues; **e** les gilets gris; **f** les robes jaunes

UNIT 5

1 le Portugal; Porto; la Suisse; l'Italie; Rome; la Grèce; les Pays-Bas; le Danemark; l'Espagne; Madrid

2 **a** à; **b** au; **c** en; **d** en; **e** en; **f** aux; **g** à; **h** en

4 **a** 10.11; **b** three 2nd class tickets; **c** 10.52; **d** platform 2

6 **a** réservation; **b** deux; **c** à; **d** partir; **e** 9 heures; **f** correspondance; **g** arrive; **h** 126; **i** non-fumeurs; **j** réservation; **k** composter

9 1 d; 2 e; 3 b; 4 g; 5 c; 6 f; 7 a

10 **a** the 07.58 from Paris-Nord; **b** the 08.00 or the 08.09; **c** the 07.58 or the 08.28

11 1 b; 2 a; 3 c

12 **a** vas; **b** partir; **c** train; **d** cher; **e** vendredi; **f** 100; **g** aéroport; **h** beaucoup

15 **a** 3; **b** 5; **c** 4; **d** 1; **e** 2

16 c; g; d; b; a; f; e

17 **a** broken down car; **b** late at the airport; **c** run out of petrol; **d** strike/train cancelled

Extra!

1

	train no.	from	to	platform	track	delay
a	993	Nantes	–	2	4	–
b	625	–	Marseille	6	8	–
c	289	–	Lyon	–	–	25 mins
d	418	Paris	Avignon	7	14	–
e	472	–	Grenoble	–	–	10 mins
f	325	Macon	Valence	–	–	15 mins
g	591	Saint-Etienne	–	8	10	–

2 **a** 4; **b** underground and bus; **c** Saturdays 9 a.m.–5 p.m.; **d** 0h12; **e** every minute

Exercices de grammaire

1 **a** au; **b** aux; **c** en; **d** en; **e** au; **f** en; **g** au; **h** aux; **i** en; **j** en; **k** en; **l** au; **m** en; **n** en

2 **a** Je vais prendre le train pour Milan; **b** Nous allons prendre l'avion pour Rome; **c** Ils vont partir pour Naples; **d** Elle va prendre le bateau pour la Corse; **e** Tu vas visiter la ville pour acheter des souvenirs?; **f** Nous allons aller en Corse pour faire de la randonnée.

3 **a** veulent; **b** peut; **c** faut; **d** voulez; **e** veut; **f** pouvons; **g** faut; **h** peuvent

4 **a** Comment est-ce que tu vas à Bordeaux? J'y vais en voiture; **b** Est-ce qu'ils vont en France mardi? Ils y vont lundi; **c** Est-ce qu'elle va au supermarché tous les jours? Elle y va tous les jours; **d** Comment est-ce que vous allez au travail? Nous y allons à pied; **e** Est-ce que tu vas à Paris en avion? J'y vais en Eurostar.

UNIT 6

1 **a** voudrais; **b** vous; **c** combien; **d** deux; **e** une; **f** fait

2 **conversation 1:** 1; 2; 2; 85; **conversation 2:** 2; 1; 1; 95; **conversation 3:** 3; 2; 4; 97

4 Stankevitch; Herbolin; Rebayi

5 1 f; **2** e; **3** a; **4** c; **5** d; **6** b

6 **a** 4; **b** 6; **c** 5; **d** 1; **e** 7; **f** 3; **g** 8; **h** 2

7 **a** shower not working/water cold/press red switch; **b** no pillows/normally are in the wardrobe/also problem with satellite/will check

8 La douche ne marche pas./ Il n'y a pas d'eau chaude./ Le chauffage ne fonctionne pas.

9 **a** Elle se lève tard, elle se lave et il y a un problème avec la douche; **b** Elle va à la reception. Elle se plaint; **c** Elle se promène près de la Tour Eiffel et de Notre-Dame; **d** Elle s'amuse beaucoup; **e** Elle rentre à l'hôtel. Elle se couche tard.

10 **a** de 6h à 9h; **b** chambre ou restaurant; **c** 8,30 euros

11 **a** morning call/available; **b** swimming-pool is open; **c** the following cards; **d** traveller's cheques and cash; **e** 24 hours a day; **f** is served; **g** satellite TV is available; **h** management is not responsible

12 **a** F; **b** T; **c** T

13 **a** ouvert; **b** décembre; **c** janvier; **d** du; **e** au; **f** basse; **g** septembre; **h** novembre.

15 dans la brochure; entre les deux; est plus grand; le premier

16 extra sofa in the lounge/washing machine is not in the kitchen any more, it is in the bathroom/added a TV set and a phone in the first bedroom/ added a cot in the second bedroom/ swimming pool works between 9 a.m. and 8 p.m.

Extra

1 1 Saint Denis; 2 Beau site; 3 Beau site; 4 Saint Denis; 5 Les Pinsons; 6 Saint Denis/Les Pinsons.

2 Possible answers
Customer 1: wants to book rooms for next week for three days (Friday to Sunday)/one double room with toilet and one single room/wants sea view, satellite TV and fridge/will arrive Friday around 3 p.m.
Customer 2: problems/shower is not working/no hot water/only cold/window does not close/noisy in the street/wife can't sleep/TV is not working

Exercices de grammaire

1 **a** me; **b** me; **c** nous; **d** nous; **e** nous; **f** se; **g** se; **h** se; **i** nous

2 **a** Nous ne nous réveillons pas avant dix heures; **b** Tu te lèves tôt aujourd'hui!; **c** Vous ne vous habillez pas?; **d** Elles se promènent dans le jardin; **e** Elle ne se douche pas tous les matins; **f** Je vais me réveiller tôt demain.

3 **a** La deuxième maison est plus agréable que la première maison; **b** La cuisine dans la première maison est moins spacieuse que dans la deuxième maison; **c** La salle de bain est aussi moderne dans la première maison que dans la deuxième maison; **d** Le jardin est plus pratique dans la première maison; **e** La deuxième maison est moins tranquille; **f** Les chambres sont plus grandes dans la deuxième maison.

4 **a** une; **b** de; **c** une; **d** de; **e** de; **f** une.

UNIT 7

1 **a** je pourrais parler à …/pourrais-je parler à …; **b** il n'est pas là; **c** je voudrais parler à …; **d** ne quittez pas; **e** je vous la passe;

f je vais rappeler plus tard; **g** vous voulez lui laisser un message?; **h** il pourrait me rappeler? **i** oui, c'est moi, **j** le lui dire.

2 **1 a** pourrais lui parler; **b** peux lui laisser **2 a** pourrais-je; **b** n'est pas là; **c** pourrait me; **d** le lui

3 **a** going out at the weekend; **b** to go dancing – to go to a restaurant and then to a night club; **c** She is going to telephone them this evening; **d** Saturday evening at 8 p.m. in front of the railway station

4 **a** Raphaël – very tall, slim, short brown hair and green eyes; **b** Pierre, shorter than Raphaël, blond hair and blue eyes, beard and glasses

5 **a** veux; **b** cours; **c** quart; **d** a; **e** connais; **f** comment; **g** grand; **h** cheveux; **i** courts **j** barbe; **k** yeux

7 **a** Man: Starter: mixed salad; Main course: vegetarian dish; Dessert: cheese; Drink with meal: beer and bottle of red wine; Woman: Starter: snails; Main course: steak (medium done) with pepper sauce (dish of the day); Dessert: ice cream, two scoops of vanilla and one scoop of chocolate; Drink with meal: kir and bottle of mineral water; **b** plat du jour

8 Meat: steak with pepper sauce; Fish: trout with almonds; Vegetarian: mixed salad, vegetarian dish; onion soup

9 **a** T; **b** F; **c** F; **d** F; **e** T; **f** T

10 je voudrais commander; je prends la salade verte; je vais prendre le steak-frites; bien cuit; la tarte aux pommes; vin rouge; après mon dessert

11 **a** 3; **b** 5; **c** 4; **d** 1; **e** 7; **f** 8; **g** 6; **h** 2

Extra

1 **a** Etienne for Solange; **b** 7 p.m. on Thursday, café du commerce, opposite the cinema; **c** have a drink and then go to see a film

2 **a** She has a new boyfriend; **b** 1m 80 tall, curly black hair and blue eyes; **c** two weeks; **d** south-west France; **e** Jacques: windsurfing; Stéphanie: sunbathing

Exercices de grammaire

1 **a** Je voudrais …; **b** On pourrait …; **c** Elle voudrait …; **d** Il pourrait …; **e** Je pourrais ….

2 **a** Tu vas lui téléphoner; **b** Ils vont leur parler; **c** Elle va lui dire quelque chose; **d** Vous lui donnez de l'argent?; **e** Elles vont leur donner des bonbons?

3 on aime sortir; on va au restaurant; on adore; on va au cinéma; on rentre; on fait; on joue.

4 **a** Oui, j'en prends; **b** Non, ils n'en ont pas; **c** Oui, elle en a; **d** Non, je n'en veux pas; **e** Oui, il en mange; **f** Non, il n'y en a pas.

UNIT 8

1 ai vu; a mangé; a dansé; ai dormi; ai pris; ai lu; as fait; ai fait; ai perdu; ai dû; ont retrouvé; ai passé; ont acheté; avez fait; ont préféré; avons regardé

2 voir; manger; danser; dormir; prendre; lire; faire; faire; perdre; devoir; retrouver; passer; acheter; faire; préférer; regarder

3 a **1** with her English friend; **2** They visited museums, saw a play and a film; **3** He finished an essay; **4** He ate and drank a lot on Saturday evening.

3 b **a** ai fait; **b** a visité; **c** a vu; **d** ai fini; **e** ai invité; **f** a fait; **g** a bu; **h** a dormi

4 Elise a fait plein de choses avec sa copine anglaise; elles ont visité des musées, elles ont vu une pièce de théâtre et un film. Jean-Marc a fini sa dissertation samedi. Le soir, il a invité des amis à dîner. Sa copine Isabelle a fait un plat indien très épicé. Il a bu plein de bière et il a dormi toute la journée dimanche.

6 **1** d; **2** a; **3** e; **4** c; **5** b

7 c; i; d; b; h; e; a; g; j; f

8 had to work for his father; telephone not working; no time to go out and telephone

9 **a** Je n'ai pas pu venir à la soirée; **b** parce que j'ai rencontré un vieux copain dans la rue; **c** il a proposé d'aller dans un bar; **d** on a beaucoup bu; **e** je n'ai pas vu l'heure; **f** j'ai raté le dernier bus

10 **a** F; **b** T; **c** F; **d** F; **e** F.

12 **a** vacances; **b** suis; **c** Où; **d** combien; **e** semaine; **f** promenades; **g** allé; **h** fait; **i** Quand; **j** trois

13 **a** Normandy; two weeks; bad weather; read and slept; **b** Corsica; one week; good weather; went to the beach and did water-skiing

15 **a** il y a du soleil; **b** il y a des nuages; **c** il pleut; **d** il neige; **e** il y a du vent; **f** il y a du brouillard; **g** il y a de l'orage

16 **a** il fait très froid et il neige beaucoup; **b** il pleut souvent; **c** il fait très chaud et très humide; **d** il fait beau et il y a de belles couleurs

Extra!

1 Possible answers
Muriel: spent weekend with parents/Saturday went shopping/went to the restaurant/Sunday worked at the bakers/had lunch with Jean in the village restaurant/watched TV in the afternoon
Stéphane: had a good weekend/Saturday did some DIY/Sunday invited neighbours around for a drink
Loulou: went rock climbing with friends/camped outside/problem with mosquito bites and heavy rucksacks/backache but happy
Bernard: Saturday played the guitar with his band/evening concert in a bar/celebrated their success till late/slept late on Sunday/did not work

2 **a** to the Alps for three weeks; **b** went on cycle trips – hard but they saw wonderful countryside; **c** they followed its route; **d** fine, but not too hot and with some clouds; **e** good, traditional and not expensive; **f** fit; **g** He is working in his father's office because he has no money left.

Exercices de grammaire

1 **a** avons; **b** suis; **c** est; **d** ont; **e** sont; **f** as

2 **a** J'ai fait de la planche à voile; **b** Vous avez aimé ce film?; **c** Elles n'ont pas pris l'avion; **d** Mes amis sont restés ici pendant une semaine; **e** Tu es allée en vacances?;
f On a dû partir à dix heures; **g** Nous sommes rentrés le 20 juillet; **h** Elle n'est pas partie aux Etats-Unis.

3 **a** ai parlé; **b** a passé; **c** est allée; **d** sont restés; **e** ont loué; **f** ont fait; **g** ont vu; **h** ont adoré; **i** ont décidé

4 **a** pendant; **b** il y a; **c** pendant; **d** pendant; **e** il y a; **f** Il y a

UNIT 9

1 1980>1990; trois>quatre; mois>ans; 1998>1999; j'habite>je travaille

2 **a** pendant; **b** depuis; **c** pendant; **d** depuis

3 Past:
Il est né en 1975. Il a habité en Tunisie pendant 3 ans avec ses parents. Il a déménagé en France en 1978. Ses parents ont travaillé à Marseille pendant 10 ans.
Present:
Son père est à la retraite. Sa famille habite à Toulouse depuis 4 ans. Mustapha et son frère étudient l'anglais depuis 3 ans. Son frère travaille depuis 6 mois dans une entreprise en informatique.

5 **a** two weeks; **b** As soon as she arrived she felt happy/at ease; **c** English and Japanese; **d** yesterday morning

6 **a** s'inscrire, remplir, se renseigner, s'installer; **b i** Humanities Degree – English literature, **ii** Journalism

7 **a** depuis; **b** sens; **c** installée; **d** m'; **e** suis; **f** inscrite; **g** me

8 a i Florence: one month, Hugo: two weeks, Beate: one year; **ii** Florence: in a flat with a Spanish student and a German student, Hugo: in a hotel, Beate: in a flat near Victoria with her English boyfriend; **iii** Florence has made lots of friends, Hugo: nice, Beate: not as nice and funny as the French; **iv** Florence: lots to do, Hugo: too busy, dirty and polluted, Beate: lots to do

b a Elle s'appelle Florence, elle est italienne. Elle est en Angleterre depuis un mois et elle se sent déjà bien à l'aise. Elle a trouvé un appartement où elle habite avec d'autres étudiantes, une espagnole et une allemande. Elles sont obligées de parler anglais, et Florence a l'impression que son anglais s'est beaucoup amélioré. Elle s'est déjà fait beaucoup d'amis et elle s'amuse bien, elle ne s'ennuie pas une minute.
b Il s'appelle Hugo, c'est un étudiant français. Il est en Angleterre depuis deux semaines et il va y rester pendant trois mois. Il est venu pour travailler et apprendre l'anglais. Il n'a pas rencontré beaucoup de gens et son anglais ne s'est pas beaucoup amélioré. En ce moment, il loge à l'hôtel mais il espère trouver bientôt un appartement avec des étudiants anglais. Il croit que les Anglais sont sympas mais il n'a pas vraiment eu l'occasion de leur parler! Il n'aime pas trop Londres parce qu'il trouve qu'il y a trop de monde et que la ville est très sale et polluée.
c Elle s'appelle Beate, elle vient d'Allemagne. Elle est à Londres depuis un an. Elle travaille au bureau de tourisme à la gare de Victoria. Elle rencontre beaucoup de touristes et elle a l'occasion de pratiquer son anglais et son français. Beate habite avec son copain anglais dans un appartement, pas loin de Victoria. Ils y sont depuis six mois. Beate aime bien Londres, parce qu'elle trouve qu'il y a beaucoup de choses à faire mais elle croit qu'elle va préférer la France: elle pense que les Français sont plus sympas et plus marrants, et que leur cuisine est meilleure!

10 **a** F; **b** F; **c** F; **d** T; **e** F

11 **a** nom; **b** lieu de naissance; **c** Baccalauréat; **d** licence; **e** maîtrise; **f** mention; **g** connaissances en informatique; **h** employée de bureau; **i** bilingue; **j** un stage; **k** date de naissance, **l** société

12 c; e; i; b; a; g; f; h; d; k; j

13 **1** Julia est de Birmingham. Elle a une licence en littérature. En 1997 elle s'est inscrite pour faire une formation d'enseignante. Elle l'a réussie avec mention. Elle a déménagé à Londres il y a six mois et elle enseigne depuis deux mois.
2 John est né à Manchester. Il a une licence en littérature anglaise et il a passé cinq ans en Europe. Il a travaillé comme serveur et professeur d'anglais. Il travaille à Londres comme professeur depuis deux ans.
3 Carmen est bilingue espagnol-anglais. Elle a fait une maîtrise et elle s'est inscrite pour faire une formation d'enseignante l'année dernière. Elle l'a réussie avec mention. Elle n'a pas d'expérience de l'enseignement.

14 **a** 4; **b** 1; **c** 2; **d** 3

15 **a** reçu; **b** passer; **c** travaillé; **d** depuis; **e** stage; **f** obtenu; **g** fini; **h** encore; **i** économie; **j** maîtrise, **k** bonne

Extra!

1 **a** marketing manager; **b** degree in business studies with distinction; marketing diploma; **c** marketing studies; **d** six months with Nestlé at Vevey in Switzerland; **e** did a one-year intensive course in French and speaks it fluently.

2

	Qualifications	Work experience	Knowledge of languages	IT skills
Man	Degree in business studies	1 year in French company in London	English – fluent	not mentioned
Woman	MA in business studies	6 months in present job	Italian – fluent Russian – a bit	3 months training

Exercices de grammaire

1 **a** J'ai habité en Australie pendant trois ans; **b** Ils travaillent en Angleterre depuis deux mois; **c** Elle a étudié l'anglais à l'école pendant cinq ans; **d** Ils apprennent le français depuis trois mois; **e** Vous y avez habité pendant combien de temps?

2 **a** Claudia s'est inscrite à l'université en 1998; **b** Aziz s'est renseigné pour entrer dans l'école de commerce; **c** Ils se sont beaucoup amusés à Paris; **d** Claudia s'est mise à apprendre l'espagnol; **e** Aziz s'est mis à faire de la natation; **f** Claudia et Aziz se sont installés dans un appartement près de la Sorbonne.

3 **a** Non, je ne me suis pas inscrit(e) à l'université; **b** Non, elle ne s'est pas renseignée pour les cours de japonais; **c** Non, nous ne sommes pas installés dans notre nouvelle maison; **d** Non, elles ne se sont pas ennuyées; **e** Non, il ne s'est pas amusé; **f** Non, elles ne se sont pas senties à l'aise en France.

4 **a** Oui, je l'ai passé; **b** Oui, je l'ai envoyé; **c** Oui, elle l'a obtenu; **d** Oui, il les a réussis; **e** Oui, elles l'ont contactée; **f** Oui, je l'ai rencontrée.

UNIT 10

1 **a i** C'est quoi ton boulot? **ii** Tu vas bosser où? **iii** Je me casse; **iv** Veinarde! **v** On m'a refilé; **vi** C'est super; **vii** C'est l'enfer! **viii** Les mômes

2 **a** 3; **b** 4; **c** 2; **d** 6; **e** 1; **f** 5.

3 **a** bar/dogs not allowed; **b** restaurant/smoking not allowed; **c** swimming pool/running not allowed; **d** house/not open to public; **e** hotel/parking not allowed in front of the door; **f** restaurant/eating a picnic not allowed

4 **a** moi; **b** desolé; **c** interdit; **d** Pourriez; **e** peux; **f** défendu; **g** accès

6 **a** other cars cannot gain access; **b** to the car park; **c** There are no spaces left; **d** next to the tennis court

7 Pourriez-vous déplacer votre voiture parce que je ne peux pas sortir. Mettez-la à côté de votre caravane ou dans le parking (*or* au parking), s'il vous plaît. Merci.

8 **a** F; **b** T; **c** T; **d** T; **e** F; **f** T

9 **1** d; a; c; b; **2** b; c; d; a

11 terrible>génial; pas mal>bien; chantent>jouent; sympa>bonne; trouvez>pensez; beaucoup>vraiment; nuls>mauvais; super>fantastiques; intime>sympa; musicien>groupe

13 **a** F; **b** F; **c** T; **d** T; **e** F; **f** F

Extra!

1 **Babette:** since the weekend/works in the bar/comes from near Nice/economics – third year
Richard: two weeks/works at the swimming pool/comes from Lille/business studies
Stéphanie: two weeks/works in the crèche/comes from Paris/accounting and languages
Jean-Marc: two weeks/waiter lunchtime and barman evening/comes from Nantes/Engineering school

2 **a** for minor problems; **b** in the local newspaper or in the window of pharmacies; **c** They have the reputations of being able to solve all domestic problems; **d** In the case of a medical emergency or a serious accident; **e Police** are in towns, **gendarmes** are in the country.

Exercices de grammaire

1 **a** Oui, appelez-les. / Non, ne les appelez pas; **b** Oui, ferme-la. / Non, ne la ferme pas; **c** Oui, monte-la là bas. / Non, ne la monte pas là-bas; **d** Oui, emmenez-les à la piscine. / Non, ne les emmenez pas à la piscine; **e** Oui, laisse-le dans la voiture. / Non, ne le laissez pas dans la voiture; **f** Oui, finissez-le. / Non, ne le finissez pas.

2 **a** Ne pas passer; **b** Ne pas stationner; **c** Ne pas ouvrir la fenêtre; **d** Ne pas jouer à la balle; **e** Ne pas nourrir les animaux; **f** Ne pas marcher sur la pelouse.

3 **a** que; **b** qui; **c** qui; **d** qu'; **e** qui; **f** qu'

4 **a** lui; **b** eux; **c** toi; **d** Moi; **e** elle; **f** moi; **g** toi

SUPPLEMENTARY EXERCISES

Unit 1

1 **a** 6; **b** 4; **c** 1; **d** 2; **e** 3

2 d; g; e; b; h; c; a; f

3 **a** Bonjour! Ça va? **b** Au revoir, monsieur; **c** Je suis allemande; **d** Vous êtes américain? **e** Tu es étudiante? **f** J'habite à Londres mais je suis de Glasgow.

4 **a** Elle s'appelle Natasha. Elle est américaine. Elle habite à New York mais elle est de Chicago. Elle est étudiante en histoire de l'art; **b** Il s'appelle Bob. Il est irlandais. Il habite à Belfast mais il est de Dublin. Il est technicien; **c** Elle s'appelle Malika. Elle est marocaine. Elle habite à Lille mais elle est de Paris. Elle est serveuse; **d** Il s'appelle Luca. Il est italien. Il est de Milan mais il habite à Rome. Il est acteur.

6 **a** 20; **b** philosophy; **c** Naples; **d** because he likes French people, French food, literature, cinema and philosophy; **e** when he was 11; **f** because she is from Zurich; **g** because they are very interesting; **h** He is a waiter in an Italian restaurant.

Unit 2

1 1e; **2**a; **3**b; **4**c; **5**d; **6**g; **7**f

2 **a** habites; **b** étudiant; **c** j'ai; **d** son; **e** est

3 **b** Sa grand-mère a 75 ans; **c** Il a une nièce; **d** Son grand-père s'appelle Robert; **f** La copine de son cousin a 21 ans; **g** Le frère de Luc s'appelle Michel; **j** Sa tante a 44 ans.

4 **a** Il a 19 ans; **b** Ils ont quel âge?; **c** (Est-ce que) tu as des frères et des sœurs?; **d** Nous habitons avec notre frère; **e** Ils ont un fils et une fille; **f** Sa fille a six ans; **g** Mon copain travaille avec son père; **h** (Est-ce que) tu habites avec tes parents?

8 **a** Vous voulez un sandwich?; **b** Tu veux quelque chose à boire?; **c** Non, pas pour moi merci; **d** Tu veux un café?; **e** Un chocolat chaud pour moi.

Unit 3

1 **a** Paris, 12.30 p.m., having lunch; **b** Brussels, 12.30 p.m., eating a sandwich in the office; **c** Quebec, 7.30 a.m., having breakfast after having been jogging; **d** Kinshasa, 1.30 p.m., university law lecture; **e** Beirut, 2.30 p.m., swimming pool with her brother and her cousin; **f** Tahiti, 11.30 p.m., night club with friends.

2 **a** suis; **b** commence; **c** termine/finis; **d** mon/le; **e** des; **f** après; **g** les/mes;

h prenons; **i** fais; **j** vais; **k** arrive

3 a 1 3rd speaker; **2** 5th speaker; **3** 1st speaker; **4** 4th speaker; **5** 2nd speaker

3 b i 3; **ii** 4; **iii** 1; **iv** 5; **v** 2

4 **a** j'aime; **b** tu n'aimes pas; **c** elle aime bien; **d** vous aimez beaucoup; **e** nous n'aimons pas; **f** ils détestent…

5 **1** d; **2** a; **3** f; **4** e; **5** c; **6** b

Unit 4

1 d; f; j; e; a; h; g; b; i; c

2 **a** garage; **b** lire; **c** bibliothèque; **d** puis

3 **a** Pardon, vous savez où est l'Office de Tourisme? **b** Est-ce qu'il y a une poste près d'ici? **c** Est-ce que la bibliothèque est à côté de la gare? **d** C'est loin? **e** Merci beaucoup.

5 **a** aider; **b** voudrais; **c** le; **d** couleur; **e** l'; **f** le; **g** à; **h** prends

6 **a** Oui, je l'aime; **b** Non, je ne l'aime pas; **c** Non, elle ne l'aime pas; **d** Oui, ils l'aiment; **e** Oui, il l'aime; **f** Oui, je les aime.

7 **a** La jupe? Non, je ne l'aime pas; **b** Cette robe? Oui, je la préfère; **c** Tu l'aimes? **d** Oui, je l'aime; **e** Tu aimes ce pantalon? **f** Elle aime la chemise jaune, et moi aussi, je l'aime.

8 **a** J'aime le pantalon noir; **b** Je préfère ce pull gris; **c** Tu aimes ces chaussures jaunes; **d** Je ne les aime pas; **e** Vous préférez cette jupe rose? **f** Il n'aime pas cette veste verte.

Unit 5

1 **a** 4; **b** 8; **c** 3; **d** 7; **e** 6; **f** 2; **g** 1; **h** 5

2 b; i; d; c; h; a; j; e; k; f; g

4 b; d; a; c

5 **a** aller; **b** y; **c** en; **d** grève; **e** faut; **f** nous; **g** en; **h** à; **i** faut; **j** ma; **k** en; **l** là

Unit 6

1 **a** voudrais; **b** quel; **c** nom; **d** combien; **e** personnes; **f** lits; **g** plaît; **h** fait; **i** fait; **j** prenez

2 **a** (Est-ce qu') il y a un parking privé dans l'hôtel?; **b** Où est l'ascenseur s'il vous plaît?; **c** A quelle heure est-ce que vous servez le petit déjeuner?; **d** J'ai un problème dans / avec ma chambre; **e** Il n'y a pas de serviettes dans la salle de bains; **f** L'ascenseur au troisième étage ne marche pas.

3 **a** barbecue; **b** piscine; **c** printemps; **d** se lever; **e** réservation

4 **a** Constantopoulou; **b** Tamelikecht; **c** Wolfreys; **d** Lavillatte

Unit 7

1 **a** Allô; Pourrais-je parler à Helen, s'il vous plaît?; Ne quittez pas, je vous la passe; Merci. **b** Allô; Janet est là?, Désolé, elle n'est pas ici. Est-ce que je peux laisser un message? **c** Allô; Allô, je voudrais parler à Bruce, s'il vous plaît; Désolé, il n'est pas là; Il pourrait me rappeler?; D'accord, je vais le lui dire. **d** Allô; Je pourrais parler à Emer, s'il vous plaît; C'est moi; Allô, c'est Carol.

2 **a** c'est; **b** Qu'est-ce que; **c** dit/dirait; **d** va; **e** se voit/retrouve

4 **a** Isabelle est française et elle a vingt-cinq ans. Elle est petite et elle a des cheveux blonds et longs et des yeux bleus. **b** Alain est anglais et il a trente-trois ans. Il est grand et mince et il des cheveux bruns. Il a des yeux verts, une moustache et une barbe. **c** Joshua est américain et il a cinquante ans. Il est très grand et gros. Il a des cheveux noirs et courts et des yeux bleus. Il porte des lunettes. **d** Juliette est irlandaise et elle a dix-sept ans. Elle est grande et mince et elle a des cheveux roux. Elle a des yeux verts et des taches de rousseur.

5 **1** g; **2** f; **3** e; **4** a; **5** b; **6** c; **7** d

6 **a** steak; **b** truite; **c** pomme; **d** addition

7 k; c; f; g; b; a; i; d; e; h; j

Unit 8

1 **a** Nous avons passé un weekend excellent; **b** Qu'est-ce que tu as fait samedi soir? **c** Je n'ai pas pu venir parce que j'ai dû travailler; **d** Ils ont eu un problème avec leur voiture; **e** Lucie a adoré Paris, elle a visité tous les musées; **f** Je n'ai pas vu le film, mais j'ai lu le livre.

3 **a** Ils ont raté le dernier métro; **b** J'ai mangé dans un bon restaurant; **c** Qu'est-ce que tu as fait? **d** Nous avons passé un très bon week-end; **e** Il a eu un problème avec sa voiture; **f** Elle n'a pas pu venir avec nous.

4 **a** mon; **b** allé; **c** sale; **d** vu/visité; **e** pris; **f** a; **g** fait; **h** passé; **i** mangé; **j** est; **k** beaucoup; **l** l'; **m** décidé; **n** as

5 Chère Carole,

Merci pour ta lettre. Tu as de la chance d'avoir passé les vacances d'été en Inde. Veinarde! Il y a deux ans je suis allée en Inde aussi et j'ai beaucoup aimé. Vraiment, je trouve ce pays superbe.

Malheureusement, cet été je n'ai pas pu partir en vacances et j'ai dû rester à Lille pour travailler. C'est la vie! En juillet, j'ai trouvé un travail dans un restaurant qui n'est pas loin de chez moi. J'y ai travaillé pendant un mois. Pendant le mois d'août, j'ai dû étudier pour préparer mes examens et je vais les passer la semaine prochaine. Heureusement, j'ai aussi eu un peu de temps pour me relaxer. En juillet une vieille amie est venue me voir à Lille et on a fait plein de choses ensemble.

A bientôt j'espère.

Sylvie

Unit 9

2 **a** Ils travaillent à Brighton depuis six mois; **b** J'ai habité à Londres pendant six ans; **c** J'ai commencé mes études en 1996; **d** Je les ai terminées l'année dernière; **e** Je les ai trouvées très intéressantes; **f** Je me suis inscrite en cours de langues; **g** Je me suis bien installé en France.

3 **a** **Nadine**: English degree from Manchester University; graduated in 1995. Went to India in 1996 and worked in a primary school for a year. Currently working in a secondary school in Dakar. Been in post for two years. Next year she is going to return to England to do a Master's degree in education; **b** **Kofi**: Has a Master's degree in computing. Finished in 1995. From 1996 to 1998 worked for a bank in Lille. Has been working for an Internet company for two years and is starting to get bored and would like to find a different job, **c** **Elizabeth**: Has a degree in maths. When she finished her degree she decided to go travelling. She went to New York and spent nine months there. She has worked as a waitress in a bar, as a receptionist in a hotel and even done some babysitting. She would like to find a permanent job in London and would like to do a Master's degree in statistics.

4 **a** fini; **b** licence; **c** fait; **d** depuis; **e** connaissance; **f** me; **g** inscrite; **h** réussi; **i** me

183

Unit 10

1   **a** les mômes; **b** refilé; **c** me casse;
    d bosse; **e** quatre; **f** boulot; **g** plus;
    h l'enfer

3   **a** in the car park; **b** They are not allowed
    in the bar or the restaurant; **c** midnight;
    d Children must be accompanied by an
    adult; **e** no music after 10 p.m.

4   **a** Il est interdit de fumer ici; **b** Mettez-la
    derrière les autres voitures; **c** Ce n'est pas
    indiqué; **d** C'est sympa de travailler avec
    des mômes; **e** Désolé monsieur, vous
    bloquez l'accès au camping; **f** Il est
    défendu de jouer de la musique; **g** Ne la
    mettez pas là.

5   **a** The exams are starting soon and he has
    to finish two essays and hand in his
    dissertation; **b** in two months' time; **c** He
    thinks that they last too long; **d** He hopes
    to find work in another town, but before
    that he intends to go on a long holiday;
    e It's too big, there are too many people,
    too much pollution and everything is
    expensive; **f** work to earn enough to travel
    somewhere exotic

INDEX

OVERVIEW

	Communication skills	Vocabulary	Grammar
1	• greetings • introducing yourself • asking/answering personal questions	• greetings • nationalities • occupations/studies • workplaces	• masculine/feminine • verbs: *être*, *faire*; verbs ending in *-er* (singular forms); negatives • asking questions
2	• giving/understanding information about friends and family • ordering snacks and drinks	• family • numbers • snacks and drinks	• verbs: *avoir*; verbs ending in *-er* (plural forms) • articles • possessive adjectives
3	• talking about everyday activities • asking for/giving the time • explaining what you like/dislike/have to do	• days of the week • expressions of time • meals • leisure activities	• prepositions *à* and *de* followed by *le* or *les* • verbs: *aller*; verbs ending in *-ir* and *-re*; verbs followed by the infinitive
4	• understanding street signs • asking for/giving directions • shopping for clothes • expressing preferences	• directions and locations • buildings and shops • clothes • colours	• verbs: imperative • prepositions of location • pronouns *le, la, les* • demonstrative adjectives • descriptive adjectives
5	• locating places on a map • explaining what you are going to do • requesting/giving travel information • understanding timetables	• countries and regions • trains: travel, tickets, etc. • other means of transport	• prepositions before towns and countries • verbs: *aller* + infinitive; *pouvoir*, *devoir* and *il faut* • pronoun *y*
6	• making a hotel booking • making complaints • understanding holiday brochures • describing accommodation	• months and seasons • hotel facilities • home: rooms and furniture	• verbs: reflexives • comparisons (with adjectives) • *pas de*

	Communication skills	Vocabulary	Grammar
7	• making a telephone call • arranging to meet someone • describing physical appearances • ordering a meal in a restaurant	• expressions used on the telephone • expressions used to make suggestions • physical appearance • restaurant dishes	• verbs: introduction to conditional • pronoun *on* • pronouns *lui* and *leur* • pronoun *en*
8	• talking about what you did last weekend • explaining why you are late • talking about your last holiday • describing places and the weather	• types of holidays • holiday activities • vocabulary used to describe places • weather	• verbs: perfect tense • *pendant* and *il y a*
9	• talking about your background • describing your education • describing your work experience	• studies • exams and qualifications • vocabulary used to write a CV	• *pendant* and *depuis* • verbs: reflexives in the perfect tense; agreement of the past participle
10	• socialising and using colloquial language • asking for/giving help • asking permission/giving instructions • giving your opinion • describing your intentions	• expressions used when saying goodbye • some common colloquial expressions • accidents and emergencies	• object pronouns and the imperative • *ne … pas* + infinitive • *qui* and *que* • *moi, toi, lui, …*

From the publishers of *Breakthrough*

Foundations Languages

Meeting the language teaching needs of today

- Classroom courses

- Specifically designed for IWLPs and similar provision

- Tailored to the needs of a 20-24 week teaching year

- Focused on the needs of HE non-specialist language students including the growing number of international students

- A core classroom section is supported by ample self-study supplements to cater for all student abilities and timetabling provision

The price of cassettes includes a free site licence. Full set of tapescripts available on request, or downloadable from our website.

All course books are available on inspection to teaching staff where an adoption would result in the sale of at least 12 copies. Please email lecturerservices@palgrave.com

Contact:
Lecturer Services
Palgrave Macmillan, Houndmills, Basingstoke,
Hampshire RG21 6XS

tel : +44 (0) 1256 302866
fax : + 44 (0) 1256 330688
lecturerservices@palgrave.com

German 1
Tom Carty
Formerly Staffordshire University

Ilse Wührer
Keele University

French 1
Dounia Bissar
Cécile Tschirhart
London Metropolitan University

Helen Phillips
Bristol University

French 2
Kate Beeching
University of the West of England

Series Editor TOM CARTY
Formerly IWLP Programme Leader at Staffordshire University and the University of Wolverhampton

Italian 1
Mara Benetti
*Imperial College and
Goldsmiths College, London*

Carmela Murtas
Project Coordinator:
Robert di Napoli
University of Westminster

Caterina Varchetta
London Metropolitan University

Spanish 1
Cathy Holden
Edinburgh University

www.palgrave.com/modernlanguages

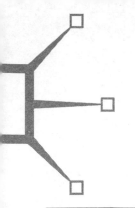

Breakthrough Languages

Ideal for self-study • Practise and develop your skills • Learn a new language

Level 1 beginner's courses

Easy-to-use book and cassette or CD* courses.

Available in French, Spanish, German, Italian, Greek and Chinese.

* CDs for French and Spanish only.

What is Breakthrough?

Breakthrough courses are aimed at the self-study learner. Each course offers:

* authentic, lively, conversational language
* a coherent and carefully structured approach
* an easy-to-follow sequence
* attractive photographs and Illustrations
* cultural information
* between 3 and 4 hours of audio material

Taking it further

Level 2 in Spanish, French and German
Level 3 in French

Increase your vocabulary, fluency and confidence with these higher level book and cassette courses.

Available from all good bookshops, or direct from Palgrave Macmillan.
Please call Macmillan Direct on 01256 302866
All course books are available on inspection to teaching staff where an adoption would result in the sale of 12 or more copies. Please email lecturerservices@palgrave.com
For further information log on to www.palgrave.com/breakthrough

Extra practice

Activity Books with imaginative and varied exercises

Available for Level 1 French, Spanish and German